World War II
FIGHTER-BOMBER PILOT

Valiant Multi-Mission Air War
What It Was Like

—Third Edition—

Colonel William B. Colgan, USAF (Ret.)

HERITAGE BOOKS
2019

HERITAGE BOOKS
AN IMPRINT OF HERITAGE BOOKS, INC.

Books, CDs, and more—Worldwide

For our listing of thousands of titles see our website
at
www.HeritageBooks.com

Published 2019 by
HERITAGE BOOKS, INC.
Publishing Division
5810 Ruatan Street
Berwyn Heights, Md. 20740

Copyright © 1988, 2008 William B. Colgan

COVER ILLUSTRATIONS: Left: P-47 fighter-bombers, 86th Ftr Gp, Europe, WWII (Painting by Larry Selman)

Right: This photograph was a news release from the European Theater in WWII and was published in many homefront newspapers in April 1945. The original caption in part:

USAAF FIGHTER-BOMBER BASE, France – Uncle Sam holds a hand of six aces that are hard to beat – a sextet of P-47 fighter pilots whose combat missions total exactly 1,000. Left to right, standing: Major William B. Colgan, Waycross, Ga., 195 missions; Lt Col George T. Lee, Norwood, Mass. 245 missions; Captain Walter C. Taylor, Newark, N.J., 119 missions; Seated left to right: Captain Jesse R. Core, Little Rock, Ark., 126 missions; Captain Bushnell N. Welch, Wellesley, Mass., 189 missions. Not in the photo: Major John R. Dolny, Minneapolis, Minn. 126 missions. Add them up. Total 1,000.

These pilots held top command and operational positions in the 86th Fighter Group. They continued to fly combat missions until the war's end, with final totals such as Lee well over 250 and Colgan 208, however Captain Walter Taylor was killed in action on his 126th mission. They are all among the fighter-bomber pilot legends this book is about. (Photo: U.S. Air Force)

All rights reserved. No part of this book may be reproduced or transmitted in any form or by any means, electronic or mechanical, including photocopying, recording or by any information storage and retrieval system without written permission from the author, except for the inclusion of brief quotations in a review.

International Standard Book Number: 978-0-7884-4531-6

Foreword
To This Third Edition

When I started writing the original manuscript for this book in the 1980s, I was not sure I was fortunate to be in a position to write firsthand on a subject widely recognized as seriously lacking in formal histories, personal accounts and news coverage. Fighter-bomber flying and fighting was just that. In fact, it was often said that fighter-bomber pilots (and their multi-mission, deadly, low-altitude operations) are best known for being unknown. Certainly in World War II they and their missions were less acclaimed than the pilots/crews and missions of the great strategic bombing effort and the fighter air battles – even though the fighter-bomber war was also of major and telling impact and fiercely fought. Still, with a subject so unsung and unknown, an author might fear his work would end up the same.

Now, some two decades later, regardless of initial worries and to what extent they may in fact have come to be, I feel extremely fortunate to have been in position to write on the subject and to have it published in two editions and three printings prior to this edition. And I'm deeply grateful and honored for universal reader acceptance and praise of it.

This has come from professionals in the fields of history, education, writing, and the military, as well as from the general public. It has been cited as a vital contribution to history, for accuracy of combat operations and tactics, as a much needed and long-overdue book, and for a very readable and exciting story. It has been used as a textbook at the U.S. Air Force Academy. Of utmost delight to me was full acceptance as definitive, "our story," by a very special group of readers – the large number of officers and men, both pilots and ground personnel, who served in "fighter-bomber" units in World War II. Surely an author could never wish for a more authoritative endorsement than this – one by those whom the book is about.

Today in 2008 the U.S. Air Force and Navy/Marine combat aircraft inventories, operational and programmed, consist overwhelmingly of multi-mission/multi-role fighters. These include the F-15E, F-16, F/A-18, F-22, and F-35. The American people will see these multi-purpose fighters as their primary combat air power for generations to come, and every time the USAF Thunderbirds and Navy Blue Angels fly too.

The original preface to this book is retained as fully valid. It cited a primary goal of portraying the war of World War II fighter-bomber pilots/crews and their units. Evidence is strong that was done. It now seems in order to highlight the direct tie in heritage of those forerunning fighter-bomber pilots/crews and units to today's and future U.S. military multi-mission pilots/crews and units – and emphasize that this book is prime historical roots, legacy and legends for this modern air power – an especially fitting and timely book today.

Contents

Acknowledgments		v
Preface		vi
Introduction		viii
Chapter 1	Pearl Harbor	1
Chapter 2	Early Service and Training	8
Chapter 3	Fighter Pilot and Off to War	19
Chapter 4	Southern Italy	32
Chapter 5	Winter Lines of 1943-44	51
Chapter 6	Anzio—Cassino, Too	63
Chapter 7	Break from War	81
Chapter 8	Southern France	88
Chapter 9	The Rhone River Valley	106
Chapter 10	Po River Valley	118

Chapter 11	Winter Lines of 1944-45	133
Chapter 12	Forward Air Controller	145
Chapter 13	Special Missions	158
Chapter 14	Push on Germany	166
Chapter 15	Across the Rhine	180
Chapter 16	Final Days	190
Index		208

Acknowledgments

I am deeply grateful to many agencies and people for their assistance and encouragement while writing this book. My appreciation for such help is extended to the U.S. Air Force Historical Foundation, to the U.S. Air Force, Office of History, for assistance with research, and to the U.S. Air Force, Office of Public Affairs, for a review of a synopsis of the proposed book.

Regarding photography, I would like to give a special thanks for assistance in research and acquisition of photos to the National Air and Space Museum, the National Archives, and to the World War II pilots of the 525th FS, 86th Fighter Group, for combat gun camera film. I am also appreciative to L. D. (Dagwood) Damewood and Ron Langley for their expert advice and assistance.

I would like to extend a thanks to Karen H. Sluman for her maps and diagram of formations.

A main source of encouragement came from many friends and individuals in expressions of interest and belief in a need for this book. I'm extremely grateful to all, including the following, who played special parts in spurring me on: Bette G. Wahlfeldt (author), Calvin K. Ellis (World War II fighter-bomber pilot), and George Pyle of England (World War II RAF fighter pilot).

I'm sure my deepest personal appreciation has to go to the two ladies who assisted with the manuscript. Thanks ever so much to Marcy Acton for her expertise and the typing. And thanks and love to my wife, Anita, both for her forbearance as I abandoned all semblance of a normal life in working on the book, and as my main co-worker throughout preparation of the manuscript.

Bill Colgan

Preface

This book was written with the objective of providing a general interest story of World War II—history, too—that would make a contribution as a further source for knowledge and remembrance of that massive bloody struggle. Especially, it is material that can add to the public awareness, combat history, heritage, and lore of the fighter-bomber pilots who fought in a pioneer multi-mission role in World War II and support of ground forces during World War II.

A book this size could never tell a full story of the various units, types of airplanes, time frames of the war, and the ground personnel who made the flying possible. I believe it will show, through its primary content of combat, action and unit operations, the kind of war that was fought and experienced by all fighter bomber pilots and the other officers and men in their outfits.

While a personal story, based on my service in World War II, it is meant as a testimony to the dedication, valor, and sacrifices by the personnel of fighter bomber type units in that war.

The author at the War Zone in Europe.

Introduction

I am extremely pleased and thankful to be able to use a few quotes from very prestigious and authoritative sources as the basis from which to introduce the subject of the "fighter-bomber" and the air war it involved for the pilots.

The following words are found in the coverage of World War II in *The American Heritage History of Flight:*

> —as throughout the Battle of France—the American tactical air forces were writing a new page in the history of warfare through the intimate powerful, almost omnipresent air support given the armies. Between these air forces and the ground forces they worked with, it was, as Patton said, a case of "love at first sight."

©1962 American Heritage Publishing Co., Inc. Reprinted by permission from the *AMERICAN HERITAGE HISTORY OF FLIGHT.*

Fighter-bombers, as a key element of the tactical air forces, played a very major part in the making of that history.

These words are found in the December 1944 issue of U.S. Army Air Forces' (Intelligence) wartime magazine, *Impact*, which was distributed to squadrons in the field to supply information on combat operations worldwide and developments in new equipments back home:

> Fighter-bombing is highly dangerous due to the accuracy and concentration of German automatic weapons and small arms fire. Losses are not light. Therefore the achievement of pilots who must pound in there at low level day after day, certain they will be shot at, is a truly heroic one.

Note: The contents of *Impact* were confidential and not released to the public until over 30 years after the war. They have now been published under sponsorship of the U.S. Air Force Historical Foundation by James Parton and Co., New York.

This quote gives considerable insight into the nature of the fighter-bomber air war and how the pilots fought it.

Based on my experience in combat while flying fighter-bomber operations, I would describe "fighter-bomber" in the USAAF as the term commonly and widely used in World War II, officially and otherwise, in reference to the employment of fighter units, fighter airplanes, and fighter pilots (plus the total resources of the tactical air forces—other fighters, night fighters, attack planes or light bombers, medium bombers, reconnaissance, troop carrier, etc.) in the tactical role of providing air support to ground forces. That role for the fighter-bombers was multi-mission, using first-line fighters such as the P-47 to do both air-to-air and air-to-ground combat in performance of three major tasks: (1) To gain and maintain air superiority over the battle zones; (2) To interdict enemy lines of supply and communication, and isolate the battlefields; (3) To provide direct close support to friendly forces engaged in battle.

Once the enemy air threat was reasonably under control in a theater or situation, we as fighter-bomber pilots spent the majority of our combat time on air-to-ground missions of interdiction and close support, operating against an extremely wide range of targets, using a variety of high explosive and incendiary bombs, rockets, and the aircraft guns in attacks of dive-bombing, low-level bombing, and strafing. We fought mainly at low altitudes, working from the front lines to several hundred miles deep into enemy territory—airspace in which we encountered almost the full spectrum of enemy air and antiaircraft defenses from airplanes and heavy flak on down to the deadly light stuff.

We attacked many pre-assigned targets, but also roamed the skies over enemy territory to search out and hit targets of opportunity—or did both on the same mission. We often received new close support or other

P-47, fighter-bomber mission takeoff. (Courtesy U.S. Air Force)

"hot" or lucrative targets while in the air from both ground agencies and other airborne pilots, and we flew various special missions. Our mission leaders operated under some of the very strictest of ironclad command and control procedures when assigned a specific objective and when providing close support to friendly ground forces, yet operated with an almost complete freedom of decision when performing armed reconnaissance or just "out hunting" deep in enemy territory.

At the same time, we also escorted bombers, flew air patrols over beachheads, attacked enemy airfields, and got jumped by enemy fighters when on air-ground missions.

In that overall role and environment, fighter-bomber pilots flew more different kinds of missions, performed more varied tasks, and faced a wider range of combat situations than most other pilots in the war.

In pilot's terms, it might be said we fought a war that kept us quite flexible, but that almost always came back to the business of slugging it out from the air at close quarters with the enemy on the ground, while still protecting ourselves and friendly ground forces (although often with other friendly fighters involved, too) by shooting it out with enemy fighters when necessary or the opportunity presented itself.

While fighter-bombers were part of the tactical air forces in Europe, the fighters of the strategic air forces did much air-to-ground work, too, particularly in the latter part of the war. All fighters could be and were used air-to-air or air-to-ground as needed in the total employment of air power, as were other airplanes used in dual roles. For example, even the heavy bombers at times flew missions in support of ground forces.

In the earlier phases of the war against the Axis powers (mainly in North Africa, Sicily, and southern Italy) the USAAF airplanes most widely recognized as fighter-bombers were the P-40 and the A-36. In the later stages of the war against Germany (in both Europe and the Mediterranean) the P-47 simply became almost synonymous with "fighter-bomber." Yet it was also one of the three main fighters (P-47, P-51, P-38) of the strategic forces in the main air battles over Europe, those connected with escort and

A-36 over Vesuvius, Italy (courtesy of U.S. Air Force).

screen of the heavy bombers, and P-51s and P-38s were found in the tactical forces too.

Both the Allies and Axis used large numbers of fighters as fighter-bombers in the war.

There is certainly no intent to imply that fighter-bombers were unique as history-makers in World War II. New and history-making capabilities and methods of warfare were unfolded by all services. Among these, fighter-bombers did bring a new and particular kind of scourge from the skies upon the enemy forces on the ground. While, as happens in most combat, a grim price was paid in losses, American and Allied fighter-bomber pilots inflicted a huge amount of destruction and damage on an amazing variety of targets, and killed and wounded an unknown but certainly a very large number of the enemy in the war. They were undeniably a major factor in World War II.

Also, there is no intent to imply that fighter-bombers fought a rougher air war than anyone else. Naturally, any kind of fighting in a war can be highly dangerous, and is always with its own full share of heroics—whether in the air, on the ground, or on or under the sea.

Thus, regarding the air war in general, The September 1944 issue of *Impact* is quoted from, one which contains a few words about the flak situation for everybody:

> The Lufwaffe, with its back to the wall, is fighting the world's greatest concentration of air power with the world's greatest concentration of flak.

Fighter-bomber pilots were well aware of the pounding taken by bombers from flak, and of their losses to both flak and enemy fighters. I would never have wanted to trade places with any of the bomber crews. And, while talking about German flak here, it is fully realized that the war against Japan had its share of antiaircraft fire, too.

Still, the intensity of German flak and other gunfire (in both tracking and barrage fire), and combinations thereof gave the low-altitude combat skies of World War II a very violent and deadly reputation. Those particular skies were the normal domain of fighter-bomber pilots on the great majority of their missions.

A few words are probably in order about the term fighter-bomber and its limited use as an official designation or title in World War II. For example, if an inspection was made of most units involved in fighter-bomber operations, there would be no obvious evidence of those units being "fighter-bomber"—in fact, the evidence would be to the contrary. Signs at the headquarters or orderly room, Operations, and other sections of the units read "Fighter Squadron." Manning documents and rosters listed the pilots as "1055, Fighter Pilot, Single Engine." Technical Orders, the bibles on airplanes, specified the unit airplanes to be fighters, such as the "P-47D Fighter Airplane." From such official records, neither the units, pilots, nor airplanes were "fighter-bomber."

German automatic-weapon flak guns, the deadly threat at low altitude. (Courtesy U.S. Air Force)

That didn't, however, stop those units, pilots, and airplanes (as well as their type of combat operations, their bases, and almost anything else about them) from being called "fighter-bomber" on an international basis during the war.

Perhaps an excellent example of the widely accepted and common usage of the term fighter-bomber in official channels in World War II is found in the following words from a General Order awarding a unit citation to a fighter group:

> ... were it not for the unceasing, resolute attacks made by the 79th Fighter Group, which, as the sole American fighter-bomber Group operating in this area ...

Similar widespread usage of the term fighter-bomber during World War II in connection with certain fighter units is found in news releases, orders awarding medals, unit histories, service histories, and many other records. Also, in those uses a tendency is noted to always keep the hyphen in the term, whether referring to a fighter-bomber or a fighter-bomber pilot or unit.

In all probability, some exceptions and variations can be found in almost any attempt at a general or catch-all statement about units, airplanes and flying in the vast, far-flung forces, and varied, global operations of the USAAF in World War II. Some exceptions can be found in this matter of fighter units accomplishing the fighter-bomber work.

A few organizations did hold official designations as fighter-bomber units during World War II. A specific example is the 86th Group. While

One of the many varied scenes of fighter-bomber destruction left along the entire route of the war against the Axis. (Courtesy U.S. Air Force)

equipped with a A-36, a dive-bomb or attack version of the P-51, that outfit was officially the 86th Fighter-Bomber Group and likewise were its squadrons. Yet well before the war's end, the A-36s were replaced with P-47s and the organization was redesignated the 86th Fighter Group as were the squadrons—while they kept right on doing fighter-bomber work. Several other groups were also officially "fighter-bomber" at various times.

"Fighter-bomber" has been used in the title and throughout this book on the basis of its overall usage and recognition rather than as a specific offical designation, and the story encompasses the kind of war fought by all pilots who participated in fighter-bomber type operations, whether they served in a fighter unit or one of the few that was a fighter-bomber unit.

In a story dealing mainly with my experience and the units I served with, it is realized that flying tactics and policies in World War II could and did vary between theaters, air forces, groups and even squadrons within groups. Many such variations and differences are discussed throughout the text. However, the tactics used, and decisions made, on the specific missions covered herein are strictly "as it was" on those missions, whether for better or worse. They are not meant to reflect any service or headquarters endorsement thereof as "the way" all missions of that type should have been flown.

The story also involves my life as well as combat experiences. Certainly, not all pilots had the same background, lived the same lives, or thought the same things anymore than they all flew the very same missions in the same time periods and locations in the war, or had the same experiences. Yet a story of war that does not involve some of the personal lives of those in it can hardly tell a story of what it was like for them—and this book is mainly about what it was like to be a fighter-bomber pilot in World War II.

Chapter 1

Pearl Harbor

It was often said during World War II that the young Americans growing up in the face of that war had lived in a very special time in the history of our nation. Of course, World War II was not a one-generation war. The growing-up years of all who fought in that enormous global struggle would encompass birth dates going back to the turn of the century or beyond and coming on up to the mid-1920s or later.

The older servicemen of World War II would have remembered the years spanning World War I, the previous ungodly bloodletting, which was supposed to put an end to war, and which itself had ended less than 21 years before the next and bigger one got underway. Many of the older servicemen in World War II could have been directly connected with some of the trademarks of the "Roaring '20s"—flappers, speakeasies, bathtub gin, rumble seats, flagpole sitting, silent movie stars and generally high spirits and wild times.

Still, it was a younger crop of "growing ups" who would go into the bloodbath of World War II in the greatest numbers. They (except possibly the very youngest) would have been in on some of the "golden age of sports." The names of Ruth, Dempsey, Jones, and many others, as well as the nicknames of "Galloping Ghost" and "Four Horsemen," were a big part in the lives of even the very young. So were some in aviation, including Lindbergh and his *Spirit of St. Louis*. Most all would have remembered well the news of the stock market crash of 1929, even if many of us didn't understand what it meant.

All of the servicemen-to-be and servicewomen-to-be, however, were there going into the 1930s and the Great Depression. As the economy ground to a near-complete halt, and the doors of factories and businesses all across the land were closed, as were those of banks, there was no doubt what depression meant. Incomes stopped or dropped and in many cases what little may have been saved before was now gone as well. For a long time the scene across the country was one of smokeless smokestacks, soup kitchens, bread lines, and hobos. It was also a picture of families listening to the radio or merely sitting on the front porch—which a lot of people did anyway, but now was about the only kind of recreation most of them could afford. Before it was over, perhaps the saddest scene of all was that of the U.S. Army routing the down-and-out veterans from their shanty camp in the nation's Capitol.

Still, throughout the ordeal, there remained an unwavering spirit and belief in the country and the future. Above all, families seemed to unite and pull together, both for survival and to provide the best they could, under the circumstances, for those growing up.

While basically broke too, the government launched into the New Deal, a series of programs aimed at both helping the people in need of jobs and sparking improvement in the economy. In the process, various sets of initials became part of the language and lives of all. Of the many programs, the CCC and WPA were probably best known to the average citizen.

In time, as someone back then said, either because of the New Deal or in spite of it, the country passed the crisis and began to recover. Along came an end to Prohibition and a new program called Social Security.

By the time many of the younger servicemen-to-be were entering high school, the outlook overall was probably for the better. There were new names and faces in the news, among them Louis, Owens, DiMaggio, and Williams in sports, Earhart in aviation, and the stars of movies—now with sound and in color—such as *Gone with the Wind*. There were also some names and faces in a different light, including Dillinger and Pretty Boy.

Airships were majestic in the skies, but our Navy had their losses in storms—and one of the saddest scenes of those days was found in newsreels of Germany's *Hindenburg* collapsing in a giant ball of fire in New Jersey.

Probably the most distinctive symbol of the era to the young was dance band music, keyed by that of Goodman and in turn by Miller, James, and others. Jitterbugging swept the land, as did some near-lunacy called marathon dancing.

News from around the world was not good. Mussolini and Hitler were in power, and war had already come in parts of Asia, China, and Africa. Yet far more ominous was its coming in Europe in the fall of 1939 as Germany invaded Poland, and much more bad news followed from across the Atlantic in the ensuing months.

The late 1930s and the start of the 1940s, for the young of America, were not without scars and lingering effects of the Depression. Some young people still had to help families by combining work with school or even giving up the latter, as so many had been forced to do earlier. Many dreams and goals of careers in various professions had gone down the drain, or would now require a miracle of some sort to fulfill.

At the same time, if some opportunities and niceties of life were missed by many of those growing up, perhaps something was gained inside from it all that otherwise might not have been.

As the 1940s arrived, there were no "ifs" or "mights" about many things. These were days of renewed hope. They were certainly days of fun and filled with a zest for living. More than ever, they were days of a strong and proud love of family and of country. These were very special days, but they did not last very long.

I was born into that era in December, 1920, in the small town of Quitman, Georgia. My early years centered around a close-knit family. In time there were four of us kids, three boys and a girl, each two years apart in age with my sister the youngest and me second-oldest. We had a wonderful, caring mother and a proud, strong-willed and hot-tempered father, but also a totally devoted husband and father. The story of that family, as a whole, through the 1920s, 1930s, and early 1940s is a story in itself of much love, honor, and determination—as was the case for so many families in those days.

The sudden death of our father in 1931 sent us and our mother to live with her widowed mother. There we moved into a very large white frame house. Actually, we crowded into it since it was already pretty well occupied. Several of our mother's brothers and sisters were unmarried and still lived at home. As compared to my previous family of just parents and kids, I was now part of a family more than twice that size, which spanned three generations under one roof. I was 10 and the Great Depression had just hit with its full impact.

The town was Waycross, Georgia, with a population of close to 20,000. Waycross was a major railroad center and the location of huge shops for repair and overhaul of locomotives and rolling stock, plus some fabrication, too.

Six main rail lines converged on the town like the spokes of a wheel. Trains, freight and passenger, came and went around the clock. Tracks not only split the near center of the town, they cut through almost every section of it as well as surrounded various parts of it. Seeing trains, hearing trains, and waiting at crossings for trains were all part of life in Waycross. Also, if your family head didn't work for the railroad, you were probably well outnumbered by kids whose fathers did work there.

Our new family was a railroad family. The grandmother's husband, W. W. Phillips, an engineer, had been killed in one of the more famous train wrecks of the railroad for which he worked. Two of his sons now worked for that same railroad.

While the people of Waycross felt the Depression like all others in the country, the railroads did keep going and perhaps Waycross fared better than some other towns. Surely it did better than farming communities hit by the extensive drought and dustbowl days of the mid-1930s, and better than many factory towns where the main industry folded completely.

I mention the railroads of Waycross because I, too, would someday go on to work on the railroads—half a world away and in a way I couldn't have imagined as a boy.

My high school days, as for many in the 1930s, were a mixture of school and work with some limited sports squeezed in. I kept near straight-A grades throughout and took courses such as Latin and all the math and science available, with an eye on college possibilities. I went out for football at the earliest opportunity; making the squad as an undersized sub back was about all that came of it. We didn't have varsity baseball, but we had an unofficial team that played various town teams. Along about this time I made my biggest mark on the baseball scene, one that would be talked about for long to come in those parts. I hit a curve ball, by a very fine pitcher, over the schoolhouse in Gilchrist Park. Nobody could remember a ball going completely over it before.

During school years I worked for a sign painter for awhile, then ushered and took tickets in a theater. A great deal of work went into a somewhat amazing variety of family undertakings to make extra money—we worked on an uncle's farm, made beehives, strung tennis rackets, raised chickens, grew flowers, and made floral arrangements. I also squeezed in some of the other normal extracurricular pursuits of high school days—girls, some social activities, automobiles (if only the loan of one from aunts and uncles), and school clubs such as the Hi-Y.

Upon graduation, I gave college no consideration at all, regardless of whether it could or couldn't have been afforded. Instead, the next couple of years I worked in a series of jobs—bookkeeper in a hardware store, scrap cutter in the railroad shop, and then a storekeeper there. These jobs were usually interrupted or given up each summer as I traveled around playing semi-pro baseball. I could make substantially more money doing that than on most jobs. Also, I sure preferred it to being an usher, a bookkeeper, or a storekeeper. I didn't mind cutting scrap with a torch, except when we cut up an old locomotive, which I had always viewed as being more alive than a hunk of steel and iron.

In the late summer of 1940, I signed a contract to play professional baseball. I was with Thomasville of the Georgia-Florida League, a team that needed replacements for key players sent up to higher leagues late in the season. They put me at third base as Thomasville fought a nip-and-tuck battle for the pennant in this league.

That fall and winter I spent helping take care of my now gravely ill mother. I stayed with her through each night, while other family members, who did so in the day, slept. She passed away in early 1941.

I played pro baseball again in 1941, this time as a 5-foot, 11-inch, 170-pound outfielder, right at home with the Waycross Bears, an affiliate of the Atlanta Crackers. In the fall I went into training as a locomotive fireman with the Atlantic Coast Line Railroad. If the baseball went no further in the future—as it probably would not—I could look forward to a career that would lead to being a locomotive engineer. When I got into firing, I loved it. The very largest steam locomotives in our division were mechanical stoker-fed coal jobs, but some of the largest hand-fired coal locomotives ever used were on the same runs. I liked being on either, but when on the hand-fired engines. I guess there was more of the real feel and tradition of firing.

In the fall of 1941, that's where I stood in my life.

Of course, there had been war clouds hanging over the country for a couple of years—since September of 1939, as Poland fell, and terms such as *blitzkrieg* and *Stuka* spread around the world. The Germans had taken Norway, overrun the Low Countries and France, invaded Yugoslavia and Greece, and had gone roaring deep into Russia with what had to be the most powerful military force ever assembled anywhere. If there had been any ray of hope, it was in the skies of the Battle of Britain, but the indiscriminate bombing in cities of England—and in turn, of Germany—had put a new and horrifying light on the fighting. Certainly, it was a different image than we had held in mind while playing "war" as kids, where only the brave in uniform were out in the action.

There had been many changes in the American scene since the war started in Europe. Uniforms were one of them—many more Americans were seen in them. The National Guard and Reserves had started to be called into service back in 1940. The Selective Service System, or draft, started that same year. While in past years the odds of knowing someone in the regular services were pretty slim, now many friends were in the service, as well as in services of combatant nations such as the RCAF (Royal Canadian Air Force). Some new terms of war were heard too: Bundles for Britain, Lend-Lease, Eagle Squadron.

On Sunday, December 7, 1941, I went to church, then had dinner with the family. Afterward, two friends and I drove along Highway 84 to Valdosta to see three girls in college there on a triple date—if one can consider an afternoon visit as dating (the girls had a Sunday curfew of 6:00 P.M., at the all-girl school). We were approaching the Alapaha River when the music on the radio was interrupted to announce the Japanese attack on Pearl Harbor and other military installations on Oahu in Hawaii.

I guess the three of us concluded one thing from the very first words in the announcement: The United States was now going to war. That in itself wouldn't have been a real surprise in view of events in Europe, but perhaps it was more of one that it would be against Japan, even though there had been much news of problems between the two countries.

We went on and met the girls on schedule. Even though it was a sort of windy and chilly day, we walked around the campus for awhile—talking some about the Jap attacks, but more about the things we usually talked about.

I had first met this girl, Anita Lamae Allen, back when she was about 13 years old and I was about 16. She and I were never very far apart thereafter—at least not in spirit and heart. If there had been no torrid display of a great new romance bursting upon the local scene, and we both dated others at times, it was a foregone conclusion all along that we were a pair. In the years since I first met her, she had grown into a slim but very shapely and extremely attractive young lady.

On this Sunday in December 1941, we finally gave up on sitting on the campus in the chilly weather. The six of us rode around and stopped by a drive-in. Not much was said about war, even as more reports came over the radio interrupting the big-band music.

As I said goodbye, she asked if I would be over to take her home for the upcoming holidays. I only said, "Don't count on it; better have your father come."

On the way home, I again weighed a dilemma that I had been through before regarding the railroad job and the military draft. I had not yet registered for the draft but would have to on the next registration. Once I did, as a railroad fireman, there would surely be a total deferment or exemption from military service—little, if anything, was more essential to a war effort than the railroads. While that would increase my older brother's vulnerability in the draft, when we were not at war the railroad job had been considered important enough to go ahead and do it. Now that we were going to war, the picture was a bit different. Also, I had always assumed that I, like most all others of fighting age, would go if we got into the war. As things stood now, I would never go to war and if I didn't want that to stay the case, then something would have to be done about it very soon. In fact, I wondered if there might even be a freeze put on essential jobs to keep one from leaving.

I stayed off call that night and instead of working on Monday, I listened to the radio much of the day. There was coverage of the president's "a date that will live in infamy" speech and the quick declaration of war by Congress. There was further news on the extent of the damage and terrible loss of lives at Pearl Harbor, and a highlighting of the vulnerability of American forces in the Phillipines and throughout the Pacific.

By Monday night I had decided. Tuesday morning I checked out with the railroad, then went with a few friends to the Navy recruiting office. As a kid, I had never dreamed of being a pilot. I wanted to be a surgeon. However, several local high school graduates were now pilots in the RCAF and that had sparked considerable intereet among others about the possibilities of doing so in the U.S. services. The prospects of that could have been considered as poor-to-nil, but that's what I went to talk about anyway.

The Navy recruiter was out of the office. The Army recruiter next door advised me that the Navy man had gone to the head and/or for coffee, so I started with the Army instead. The Navy man came back in a few minutes and I talked to him, too.

By Tuesday, I, like many others, was mixed up in a trend sweeping the town—and, I guess, the entire country. If any one person mentioned enlisting, a few more on the spot probably decided to go, too, making many small groups or packages of volunteers.

In such a group with me were a pair of brothers, David and William Kennedy, long-time close friends and neighbors, one a top tennis player in the area. The other member, Wayland Hiers, also a good friend, was a well-known athlete, an outstanding football lineman and a state-level Golden Gloves heavyweight boxing champ.

While we had made no blood oath or pact to stay together "till death do us part," we did agree on going into the Army. There, assignment to the Army Air Corps could be guaranteed, and a program did exist to apply for pilot training. From my standpoint, that was the deciding factor. However, if that did not work, there seemed more chances in the Army Air Forces for other aircrew member positions than in the Navy, and all of our group was interested in that possibility.

Both recruiters did indicate things might change any minute in pilot training, and while they did not recommend anything other than immediate enlistment, the hint was there that waiting might be the best bet. Maybe I should have waited, but I didn't; I enlisted in the U.S. Army, just like thousands and thousands of others were enlisting in all services all across the country in the days immediately following Pearl Harbor.

Chapter 2

Early Service and Training

On the morning of December 12, David, William, Wayland and I boarded a train for Jacksonville, Florida, where we took the oath and then went on to Camp Blanding or something similar in name. There, in a tent city surrounding a few warehouses and a railroad spur, we took the initial steps of being soldiers. On the surface it looked like mass disorganization, but it worked. They kept us in lines all the time. In a line it's hard to get lost or foul up too badly.

After about five days we boarded a train for Keesler at Biloxi, Mississippi, for basic training. I guess it was actually Keesler Field; if so, it made no difference. What we did there had nothing to do with an airfield, only a drill field, and the place always stayed just Keesler to me. At Keesler, the four of us were still together—in fact, we were double-decked in the same bay of one of the two-story wooden barracks that would become the standard of living for so many servicemen during the war while in the U.S.A.

In somewhat over a month—or perhaps two—of doing certain things over and over, basic training was completed. I'm sure every recruit realized the purpose and need for basic training, and the challenge to Keesler and other installations that were swamped with incoming enlistees and draftees. But, as one recruit said, that didn't mean you had to like it. Another said basic was like flu—you suffer through it and once it's over you try to forget all about it.

As basic neared an end, the recruiter's promises continued to hold true for us, but I would not have bet money on any of them as we left home. We were in the Army Air Forces and we were now given a chance to state a preference of a technical school. We all selected armament and all got it.

We boarded a train for Lowry Field, Denver, Colorado. As I rode and looked out the window at what was strange countryside to me—particularly so across the treeless expanses of western Kansas and eastern Colorado—I made a determined resolution. The daily association with close friends from home—and, I guess, just young human nature—had kept my hometown and past life in the forefront. What we were doing here in these uniforms came through as only a deviation or diversion from a main interest and base back there.

If it was humanly possible, I was going to reverse that situation. If I ever got back there to stay, I'd pick that up again as my main interest, life, and home. In the meantime, wearing this uniform and wherever I was would be my interest, life, and home. As the train rolled on westward, I wasn't leaving my world, I was going to it.

Certainly, that was not a vow to forget or sever ties with family and the other loved ones back there. We were just apart. Love, dreams, and prayers would have to be handled from apart rather than me trying to live a daily life in two places.

On arrival at Lowry, we were again bunked together in a bay of the same kind of barracks located out on a far perimeter of the base. If coming to a school, we had not come to a campus environment. It was strictly military—in many ways stricter than Keesler. However, there was no doubt that school and education was what we were there for. It was a professional operation in all respects—staff, teachers, instructors, and facilities—as we undertook to learn armament from handguns to machine guns, from bombs to all their fuses, and from fighters to heavy bomber airplane systems—plus, of course, all official nomenclature thereof. I plunged in as if I loved it.

Near the end of the course, and with summer approaching, our hometown foursome parted ways. Some bomb groups being formed needed armorers immediately and volunteers for those units would have a known next assignment. This was a potential opportunity to become aerial gunners. Everybody was for it except one—they went; I stayed. I never did see any of them again during the war. Wayland Hires became a crewmember on B-24s and died in action in the Mediterranean area. After the war a VFW post was named in his honor. The Kennedy brothers stayed together and served as ground crewmen in a B-17 unit in England. The eldest was seriously injured in a ground accident and spent many months in hospitals during and after the war.

On graduating, I became an instructor in the school at Lowry, moving to the Headquarters and Headquarters Squadron of the school. I worked on the flight line teaching the machine gun synchronization system on a P-37 fighter. The P-37, a forerunner to the P-40, never went into full production. It was somewhat unusual in that the cockpit was back almost to the tail of the airplane. So were the .30-caliber guns that were synchronized to fire between the propeller blades. That was done with a system of cams and rollers at the engine with piano wire running back to actuate the firing system of the guns at the correct time. However, with the P-37 the rounds had so far to travel from the gun barrel to the prop that the guns were set to

P-37. (Courtesy National Archives)

fire some four inches in front of the individual blade that the round would pass behind.

We operated under the premise that every time we rigged the system, the plane could be taken out and the guns fired. An old soldier in our barracks had told of pilots who had spent the rest of their careers having money withheld from their pay to go towards paying for an airplane they had wrecked. I often wondered if they took this airplane out and shot the prop full of holes, how long it would take me to pay for it on $21.00 a month.

If my service career at this point seemed oriented more away from combat than toward it, there was another part to the story. From the beginning I had pursued the submission of an application for pilot training. It had been a nightmare.

At Keesler the policy was that basic trainees couldn't submit anything. I did get a clerk to let me read the applicable regulation. Once all the supporting documents were gathered—birth certificate (which many people didn't even have in 1941), transcript of grades, letters of reference, etc.—I was well along in armament school. Then, in my school squadron, I had some trouble just getting a clerk to make out an application form. Once he did, the first sergeant and then the adjutant chewed out both him and me for wasting time and effort. I understood why when I got in to see the CO. He advised me that I was needed as—and would *be*—an armorer; somebody else could fly. He handed the application back.

In a day or so I was back in the orderly room. This time the business was another program cited in a notice on the bulletin board. It advised that anyone could apply for paratrooper training—just as the regulation on pilot training said that anyone could apply for that. Naturally, the clerks were leery of me and another application. I had to risk speaking with the first sergeant. In the process of his kicking me out, I did determine that this outfit didn't approve of any students applying for either paratroop or pilot training—or anything else. To me, it looked like a case of the Army Air

Forces having one policy and this squadron overruling it in favor of their own.

What to do about that or how to do it, I had no idea. I was aware that jumping over the head of a CO could be very risky—in fact, fatal. Still, I had seen a sign in front of base headquarters indicating an Aviation Cadet Application or Recruiting Office located there.

My first chance to go there was the next Sunday morning. However illogical it was to go when no one would normally be there, desperation sent me on the long trek in heavy snow. Once there, I'm not sure I ever contacted anyone from that office. The office door was open, but there was no one in sight. I was nervously standing in a waiting area when a most impressive officer, with the leaves of a major on his shoulders and the wings of an experienced pilot on his chest, walked through the door and said "Good morning."

He listened to my story, reviewed the application, and talked at some length with me, ending with, "Let me look into this." He did, and without any repercussions in the squadron, I was back over at that building in a few days to take the required written exam.

I took the test, sweated out the result, and then received word that I had passed it. The official orders of appointment in the Aviation Cadet Program specified I could not be reassigned from Lowry while awaiting entry into the program. This accounts for my separation from my hometown foursome and my staying at Lowry for the short period of instructing.

That summer I boarded another train, this one to San Antonio, Texas, and Kelly Field. As a cadet, I would be in the AAF Gulf Coast Training Center. I had been away now for over six months and was facing close to a year more in some other part of the country without a chance for a leave, yet, I was perfectly happy headed for Texas. In fact, San Antonio, with Randolph Field on one side and Kelly Field on the other, had always been shown in the movies and newsreels as the hub of Army pilot training.

This train full of cadets-to-be included a smattering of college graduates and students but the large majority were high school graduates. Most were in their very early twenties, with a few ranging on up to 26 or so.

Upon arrival at Kelly, we stayed there no longer than it took to double-time up a hill to a big tent city called the "Cadet Center," where we were assigned tents on the double too. From then on things never slowed as we were processed in as aviation cadets. The physical came first.

In addition to a most thorough examination, there were tests of mental and muscular coordination—which somebody said were psychomotor tests—used to select those for pilot training vs. those for navigator or bombardier training. I got through it all and came out in pilot training.

Quite a few others didn't fare well at all. Some simply didn't pass the physical. Others were pulled out for special exams and some were not passed. One tragic tale floated around about a tall young fellow who wanted to be a fighter pilot. He had heard pilots over six feet tall were not put in fighters, so he sort of slouched down when his height was measured. In that unusual position, a doctor spotted a problem with the guy's back and disqualifed him.

Perhaps above all in impact on a new cadet's mind was yet another hard truth about the program. It was foreknown that there would be a high failure or washout rate. Of all who were here now for pilot training, it was probably reasonable to say that not over 50 percent would ever put on pilot's wings. Some rumors told of a much higher washout rate than that. From the very start, any area of the program could wash a cadet out. Even afternoon retreats and Saturday morning parades were problems for some. In the full heat of summer, numerous cadets keeled over in the ranks. On repeat cases, a special medical evaluation could mean washout.

As the start of flying training approached, our class designation of 43-C meant that those who finished would do so in March of 1943. The training was in three phases: Primary, Basic and Advanced. The first step, Primary, was conducted by civilian schools under contract to the AAF. Of some dozen or more such schools in the Gulf Coast Center, spread through Texas and a few surrounding states, cadets were given a chance to request the location of their choice. I asked for Pine Bluff, Arkansas. I got Coleman, Texas. I and some others going to Coleman had to get a map to find it—a small town located between Ft. Worth and San Angelo. I doubt if many cadets ever requested Coleman, yet all who went there were probably glad they did.

There was supposed to be no hazing in the program. When we pulled into Coleman, we found out our upper class didn't know that. Also, if one had dreamed the beginning of flying would lessen the physical training or ground school load, he was wrong there, too. PT would go on forever, and the study of airplanes, theory of flight, navigation, meteorology, and other subjects would go on and on, too.

I had thought of military pilots learning to fly in biplanes with radial engines—the type always seen in movies. The airplanes here were slick-looking low-winged jobs with an inline engine—PT-19s.

To an aviation cadet, the most important person in all the program is probably his first flying instructor. I was extremely fortunate in having an excellent instructor who was quite self-controlled and civil. Rumors had indicated that few of the civilian instructors in Primary were of such a calm and collected nature, and that *none* of the military check pilots would be.

As I had heard, the sensation on my first takeoff was one of the ground dropping away rather than the plane going up. After that first flight I came down quite confident about this business of learning to fly. Also, I didn't get sick—which I wasn't sure about, as I had been awfully seasick once on a bottom-fishing boat in the Atlantic. Some cadets did get sick. Most got over doing so; others never did and they were gone from the program.

The airspeed indicators in the front cockpit, where cadets flew, were painted over. S-turns, stalls, chandelles, spins, regular landings, forced landings, spot landings, etc. went on and on—all done without airspeed indicators. Yet in the back seats, where the instructors sat, the paint had

PT-19, this one probably a test vehicle rather than a regular trainer. (Courtesy National Archives)

been scraped off most of the airspeed indicators.

I soloed about on schedule, and once in the air by myself, probably began my earliest visions of "hotness." Usually, however, the next time up with an instructor or the first check ride (in-flight test of flying progress) would bring me back to the real world and to my senses.

Of course, the milestone of the solo was never reached by many cadets and out they went. The dreaded "pink slips" (failure reports) and always-sweated check rides got many more. Better than 25 percent probably washed out in the early stages, just trying to learn to fly, but that flying was graded against a rather high standard.

Overall, I pretty well breezed through Primary. I'm sure that was largely due to my instructor, who had every one of his students complete the course. I was somewhat amazed that there were enough well-qualified civilian pilots in the U.S. to do the initial flying instruction for the thousands of military pilots trained in World War II. There must have been, because that's who did it.

While it was essential to move on in order to complete the program, leaving any Primary flying school was seldom looked upon with joy. That's because the next step is Basic flying training. We were only going a short distance—to Goodfellow Field in San Angelo, Texas. On this trip no rumors were needed; we knew what was in store for us. Coleman was a dry town—in a dry county, I guess. To get a beer, cadets caught the bus to San Angelo on Saturday nights. There, in a big nightspot on the edge of town, members of our class had talked to many cadets already in basic at Goodfellow. They told of bad things to come. One said, "Enjoy Primary while you can—when you leave you'll be in hell or some other basic flying school." During primary, I had switched from drinking Cokes in the local drugstore to getting on the bus and going for a beer. A little later I'd be puffing on Chesterfields, too.

Basic flying training meant going back completely to the military, with the possible exception of some ground school teachers and instructors. Goodfellow was a large, crowded installation and cadets could be seen everywhere in formation, moving to and from classrooms and the flight line.

BT-13. (Courtesy U.S. Air Force)

The sight of it was a bit depressing. The ramp was covered with BT-13s instead of the little plywood-winged PTs of 175 hp we had been flying; these were larger, heavier airplanes with a 450-hp radial engine. They were called Vultee Vibrators—whether affectionately or not might be debated. One key difference in the airplanes to cadets was that the BT-13s had an enclosed cockpit and a radio interphone system between cockpits. Everything said by an instructor about a cadet's flying could be clearly heard. In the PTs, sometimes the Gosport tube system of communication and open cockpits mercifully garbled some such comments from instructors.

Over and above the grind of essential flying requirements—all to be done in a precisely military manner—Basic brought on experiences in several new areas of flying that most cadets would hardly forget. There was instrument flying and an insidious drill of "center the needle, center the ball, check the airspeed." Then came checking the clock for timed turns and navigation, and the altimeter and anything else available—but you had to be back to needle, ball, and airspeed quick and often. Luckily, this all started on the ground, including classes, practice at Morse code, and hours in the Link trainer. The Link was a ground training device for practicing instrument flying procedures under a hood with only cockpit instruments for reference. I guess it served its purpose well; there certainly was a knack to be learned and developed if one was ever to fly instruments by needle, ball, and airspeed. I probably hated a period in the thing as much as any cadet ever did, but when I had a spare hour in the day's flight line schedule or on a weekend, I'd go ask for extra time in the Link.

Then there was night flying. Just getting up and down in the dark had its thrills. Keeping the stars and other airplane lights "up" and those of and autos "down" could be a problem at times. Some pilots got disoriented or had vertigo. While the instruments provided a solution, needle, ball, and airspeed didn't always provide a real *quick* one.

However, the greatest thrill of night flying came in blackout landings. Many long and cold nights, including some Saturdays, were spent on auxiliary grass fields rotating flights among cadets to make landings with no lights. While accidents could occur in any flying, now the program was moving into a good likelihood of that and of people getting killed. Some did. Even so, night flying became a prime source of jest and jokes among cadets. In Basic, certain terms had become a part of cadet language. Among them was "head up." That could mean to be alert, but it didn't. It was short for "head up and locked," or, on occasion, put another way, "It must be awfully dark up there, Mister"—which had nothing to do with the night, either. "Knucklehead" was so well known as a term applied to cadets that our class book included a sketch of him among the photos of the class membership.

Cross-country flying was a big part of Basic. Whether using dead-reckoning navigation and pilotage, or abandoning that in favor of following highways and railroads, some cadets did get lost. That in turn could result in them flying low enough to try to read town names on railroad stations. A number of BT-13s terminated their flights at some strange and out-of-the-way places.

Cadets continued to wash out in Basic. Perhaps it was rougher to see a friend go out there than in the earlier phases of flying. With the completion of Basic, a major milestone in flying training was faced. Some cadets would go to single-engine Advanced training and the others to twin-engine. The former—in theory at least—were headed toward fighters, and the latter to multi-engine airplanes of various kinds. We had received some information on the types of airplanes used in Advanced training; I hadn't paid much attention to the twin-engine jobs, except to note that one of them was reported to take off, cruise, and land all at the same airspeed. My name had come out on the list for single-engine Advanced and the AT-6 used there had been my only interest.

AT-6. (Courtesy U.S. Air Force)

My next destination was Eagle Pass, Texas, located almost straight south on the Rio Grande and Mexican border. Suspicion of real hellhole possibilities flashed in the minds of the unknowing.

On arrival, Eagle Pass Army Field was seen as a very tidy, small installation. Sparkling new AT-6s and a few P-36s occupied the ramp. During our stay there, Eagle Pass and its across-the-river neighbor, Piedras Negras, would become quite dear in our hearts for their hospitality and friendliness. The area would be long remembered as a great place to serve. In that regard, it has been said that Eagle Pass was one of the best kept secrets of World War II.

We were in a new atmosphere. Ground school went on for the first half of the course, but now emphasized combat-related subjects such as gunnery, aircraft recognition, etc. In flying there seemed less of an emphasis on check rides and more toward combat skills. It was still the military for sure, and everything operated that way, yet it was different to have Royal Air Force (RAF) pilots among the instructors, and both American officer student pilots and Peruvian officers flying with us.

I lucked out with a fine and most conscientious instructor, even though he was fairly new at it. In the AT-6 we had moved up to some 600 horsepower. It was an excellent flying airplane with performance closer to that of fighters. For a cadet, certain things about it had to be kept in mind, too.

It had retractable landing gear. Forgetting to raise the gear after takeoff could be embarrassing, particularly if one proceeded on to do acrobatics with the wheels still down. Forgetting to put the gear down on approach for landing could cause a flurry of activity in radio calls, red lights, and flares being fired about. It could also cause a cadet to wear a mock set of wheels around his neck everywhere he went for a week or two.

Then too, AT-6s were known to ground-loop. If a cadet got through advanced training without some degree of a ground-loop occurring, he could be proud. I managed to avoid ground-looping and kept from wearing wheels around my neck, but I *did* find out an AT-6 does a rather sloppy loop with the wheels down.

Formation flying and acrobatics received a lot of attention. For most cadets, formation flying went back to the very first time they were allowed to solo, even though they were not supposed to fly formation until later in the program. Acrobatics in various forms had been involved from the very start and certain cadets had included a few attempts along the way at self-invented "new" maneuvers. I had scared myself badly enough in Primary to thereafter leave the development of "new" maneuvers to others.

We went to Matagorda Island for gunnery. They deliberately turned us loose unsupervised to ferry the airplanes. I guess we did just what we were expected to do in that situation, and if anybody went other than "buzzing" all the way, I never heard about it. I guess some of us were getting pretty "hot" in our own minds, if not in those of anyone else.

The first gunnery missions quickly took a lot of that "hotness" out.

Some pilots found out that hitting a ground target panel with a .30-caliber machine gun was not necessarily as simple as it might seem. Some who did hit found out that hits didn't count when one was disqualified for firing inside the foul line and/or nearly flying into the target. Then, in air-to-air gunnery, many heretofore "warm" pilots came down to learn they had put a total of zero holes in a towed banner target.

I was sweating gunnery. We had shot skeet all along, which was supposed to relate with aerial gunnery, but I was rather a poor shot there. Yet when flying, once I got the patterns working right and could concentrate fully on the sight bead and target, the holes came along fine. Before it was over, I put some pretty fancy scores in targets. Most everybody else was hitting, too.

My instructor asked each of his cadets about personal desires of flying fighters versus bombers, or perhaps instructing. I had in turn asked him if it would be a good idea to fly four-engined airplanes so one might use the experience after the war. He didn't even answer—just glared at me. I assumed something about that wasn't a good idea, so I quit fooling with ideas and said I wanted to fly fighters.

The days just before graduation were eventful ones. For one thing, I got to fly the P-36. They were assigned for that purpose, but spare parts were a problem and only a very few cadets in our class ever flew one.

Once ready to go on a first flight in a single-seat fighter, the thing I sweated most was starting it. The normal starting system on this P-36 could not be used. Instead, it had to be started with a bungee. That was a long elastic line with a "boot" on one end and a "Y" in the line on the other end. The boot was placed on a prop blade in an overcenter position as one man held the prop there. Several men on each side of the Y ran down the ramp stretching the bungee. Once fully stretched, the man on the prop flipped it beyond center and jumped back; the bungee spun the engine and the boot flew off the prop and went whistling down the ramp between the men on both sides of the Y.

If the engine doesn't start, it all has to be done again. What I was

P-36. (Courtesy National Archives)

worried about was that it might not start because the cadet in the cockpit goofed the start some way—and what kind of looks that cadet would get from the men who had to begin the operation all over again.

However, the engine started on the first try. On takeoff, the plane leaped off the ground and in a very few minutes I was entirely thrilled with its pep, performance, and flying qualities. A few minutes later, everything went wrong. The prop ran away, the engine overheated, and smoke filled the cockpit. My first flight in a fighter ended in my first real emergency landing. I managed to get it back on the runway at Eagle Pass AAF.

Most of Class 43-C would be commissioned second lieutenants in the Army Air Corps Reserve. The remainder—and many in following classes—would be commissioned the same rank in the Army of the United States, which would be in effect "for the duration plus six months." Many aviation cadets also graduated as flight officers rather than second lieutenants as World War II progressed.

The first assignment after graduation was of extreme interest. Rumors were rampant that most would go to a central instructors school for future duty at basic and advanced flying schools. The rumors turned out to be true and a majority of the class was so assigned, as essential in the rapidly expanding flying training program. There was a considerable list going to bombers, where apparently there was an immediate need for pilots and copilots as well. Relatively few were on orders for fighter training. It was with great relief that I managed to edge my way through the crowd to the bulletin board and see my name on that little list going to fighters, with an assignment to Dale Mabry Field at Tallahassee, Florida.

On graduation day we flew all the airplanes in a mass fly-by, were discharged from the U.S. Army and commissioned right back into it, and at a formal parade and ceremony became officers and pilots. It was a very proud and thankful day—perhaps especially so at the moment the silver wings of a pilot were pinned on me.

Chapter 3

Fighter Pilot and Off to War

Before departing Eagle Pass there were a few milestones experienced in the life of a new officer: One, paying a dollar to the first enlisted man who saluted you. Two, "signing out," while listing a new serial number prefixed by an "O." Three, traveling on your own to the next duty station, instead of on a troop train.

My older brother, who had come out for graduation, and I caught a ride with a couple of officers who were headed east. Once underway, I doubted the wisdom of the decision. With ten days leave enroute, they didn't want to waste any of it on the road. They drove at breakneck speeds day and night, and trips like this—rushing home on leave—may have been among the more hazardous events in stateside military service. Yet we made it, and any time saved to spend at home was indeed very dear.

My family was a bit apprehensive about this flying business. My grandmother asked if I had a good copilot and crew. When I said there wasn't any, I don't think she believed it then—or, in fact, ever did.

The hometown had changed dramatically. There were more trains than ever and more people in town, but a lot fewer boyhood pals among them. The town now had an Army Air Field, still partly under construction, I guess, but it apparently didn't take very long to build a field of soil-cement runways and frame buildings. I'd heard Eagle Pass AAF was built in 120 days.

What hadn't changed at all was the long-standing relationship between Anita and me. My much-too-short leave was spent mainly with her. With a duty station as close as Tallahassee, there might be chances for more visits home in the near future.

On signing in at Tallahassee, it was learned that most of us would not stay there. We would go to one of a number of Replacement Training Units

(RTUs) in the Southeast. While many units had been formed and trained together before going overseas, and more would be, the odds now were in favor of us going overseas as replacement pilots to units already there.

Dale Mabry did have an RTU, one flying P-47s—a big, new high-altitude fighter. This type airplane, it was heard, was going to England for escort of bombers. Surely, there was no better assignment a fighter pilot could have in combat. Because of that, and the closeness of Tallahassee to my home, I ventured a query: If it made no difference otherwise, could one ask to stay at the RTU in Tallahassee? I was ushered in before a somewhat pompous captain who merely advised me that I would go where I was told.

When told a few days later, the orders were to go to Sarasota, Florida, for RTU in P-40s. I didn't know much about Sarasota, except that it was the winter quarters for the Ringling Brothers and Barnum & Bailey Circus, and of course was located on the Gulf coast in south Florida. All of that was great and Sarasota just sounded like a good place to be stationed as compared to many others. (In time, I rated it the world's greatest.)

The base was little more than a set of runways, taxiways and ramps, with only the minimum of buildings for flying and support activities. The 337th Fighter Group's headquarters and two of its squadrons were located there, with the group's other two squadrons on a separate field in the Tampa-St. Petersburg area. RTUs were not schools in the sense of separate faculty and student organizations. All pilots were assigned or attached to regular fighter squadrons, where the experienced pilots made fighter pilots out of those just out of flying school. (Later in the war, many such combat-type groups in the U.S. were disbanded in favor of base or other training organizations.)

Our first day of duty was quite revealing. When welcomed by our Commanding Officer, or Squadron CO, there was no doubt thereafter that we were here to learn to fly fighters. Once assigned to a Flight within the 98th Squadron, we received the word on *how* we were to fly them.

The Flight Commander was a veteran of combat with the RAF. His assistant, who was my instructor, had completed a combat tour in Alaska. From conversations with pilots in the nightclubs, we had learned these two officers had well-known reputations as outstanding and hard-flying pilots, and that if we newcomers were assigned to their flight, we were in for some tough flying. Of the four Flights (A, B, C, and D) in each of the two squadrons at Sarasota, that's just the flight to which I had been assigned.

First came a stated philosophy of training by our flight commander, Capt. Chester VanEtten—if a pilot couldn't learn to fly a fighter right, it was better for him to be killed here than to get to combat and have the enemy do it while perhaps jeopardizing other American pilots in the process. I never remembered any mention of the possibility of washing out or being sent elsewhere if we didn't fly right. The *only* alternative to doing it right seemed to be getting killed. (Afterwards, one friend asked if I believed all this. I did—and once the flying started, a *lot* of people believed it.)

That flying started right away for me. We had something of a minimum

P-40s, with practice bombs, on the runway at Sarasota, 1943.

but adequate briefing on local procedures and the P-40, which in this unit were P-40Ks. I was settling down to really study the Tech Order when my instructor came by and said, "Let's go—the airplanes are sitting on the ground."

He would fly "chase" behind me on the checkout flight in a standard, single-cockpit P-40. There were no two-place or two-cockpit versions of fighter airplanes for that purpose or other training, either in the RTUs or combat units in the USAAF (except for a few rare cases of special-use or homemade jobs.)

As we walked out onto the ramp, a flight of four P-40s came in on initial approach for their break into the overhead landing pattern. On the break, two of them "pulled streamers"—condensation trails—off the wingtips. The instructor sort of exploded into a loud berating of the other two pilots (and some of their ancestors) for not "pulling streamers." I gathered that in this flight, one should "pull streamers."

After starting the Allison V-1710 in-line, liquid-cooled engine, I planned to taxi out pretty slow for a couple of reasons. First, the pilot can't see anything straight ahead in a P-40 on the ground, so he has to weave or "S" along the taxiway to see where he's going. A pilot in that airplane for the first time gets the feeling he's completely blind to the world up ahead, which is where he has to go. Then too, I figured by creeping along I could recheck the cockpit and maybe even study where things were a bit more.

However, right after the engine roared to life, I looked over at the instructor to see him motioning to move on out. Out we went and I never looked inside the cockpit again until checking the mags at the end of the runway. Looking over again at the instructor, I got the feeling I was taking too long for that, so got tower clearance and smartly moved out and took off.

There was a saying around that one could tell a P-40 pilot because his right leg was larger and more muscular than his left. To say that a determined and forceful amount of right leg is needed to counteract engine torque on takeoff in a P-40 is certainly no understatement.

Where, in the P-36, I had been impressed and comfortable on takeoff, in the P-40 I was somewhat disappointed in performance, but that may have been because I wasn't sure if I was flying it or it was just taking me along for the ride. However, in a few minutes things looked a bit better about who was going to win out between me and it.

Among other things I learned on that first flight was that on high-speed dives, the pilot needs trim and/or a good strong left leg for control. Thus, pilots who dive-bomb in the P-40 should have *two* well-developed legs. I also made it a point to learn how to pull streamers—just make a tight, high-G turn and pull or yank back till you get them, if you don't stall and snap first. I pulled a good set of them on the break for landing.

Each flight in the airplane added more confidence as a variety of air work and acrobatics were accomplished. To me at this stage the P-40 seemed to be an airplane that was not an easy one to fly—at least not precisely. The pilot had to work at it, more so than in the trainers. It didn't nicely land itself in RTU just because you put it somewhere over the runway.

RTU was the time to work a hat into shape and condition worthy of fighter pilot status. Of course, the grommet was removed immediately upon purchase, which allowed the material to flop somewhat. Some pilots settled for that and let normal wear break them in. Others tried expediting the process through various treatments of crushing, soaking, and shaping.

As we progressed on through RTU, some changing of the times was evident. At the start, mock dogfighting with any other fighters found in the skies was a regular part of flying. There was one strong exception—the airplanes on gunnery missions. There was no playing war with hot guns, even though pilots at times in the club would challenge each other to duels over the field in the morning with them.

In unscheduled dogfights, at least one P-39 from a nearby base had spun in and crashed in a fight with P-40s. As a result, fighting the P-39s was prohibited. Fights in the traffic pattern were stopped, too. Things moved ever closer to allowing only scheduled and pre-briefed dogfighting. Where before all pilots had been forced to be keenly alert and looking at all times (or to keep their heads on swivels) for other airplanes anywhere around the clock—especially behind you—now there was little need to look for any "enemies" in day-to-day flying, only for "friendlies" that you might otherwise crash into.

Obviously we had gotten in on the very end of a program that strived for combat realism even if at the expense of some safety. At the same time, from what was known and heard, the losses in all training across the country must have mounted up to some staggering figures. In any event, safety was now getting considerably more attention by the command levels above this flight. I guess that was the safest and best way for commanders of RTUs and even students while there, but I wondered if it was either safest or best for these pilots and their commanders when overseas in combat.

One place I didn't feel like risking anything unnecessarily was in the traffic pattern. Even at this stage of great vulnerability to "hot-pilot" tendencies, I was not among the fliers of extremely tight landing patterns, nor had we been pushed to do that by our instructors or unit. Pulling streamers was fine, and then flying a good, compact pattern, but no record-setting stuff was called for. The theory behind the 360° overhead patterns for fighters was to have airplanes in combat zones come in low and get on the ground quickly to minimize vulnerability in the pattern to enemy fighters (or, in some cases, to antiaircraft fire).

Getting down quickly was involved, but things got carried far beyond that among many pilots. It became a contest to see who could get down from break to touchdown in the fewest seconds. Arguments among claimants often mentioned times such as 17 seconds, whereupon the next to speak might make it 14 seconds. Some pilots flew ungodly tight patterns; maybe they did meet or even beat those times. Yet one deadly fact about tight pattern contests was that the *real* record-holders were never there to state their times. They set the records by spinning in from somewhere in the pattern.

Tight pattern contests and buzzing hometowns or other inviting spots, such as the undersides of bridges, were prime sources of some tragic loss of lives during World War II.

Of course, gunnery was a major part of RTU. The P-40 had three .50-caliber guns in each wing (some models, two per wing), but only one gun on each side was normally used in training. Once again, some otherwise hot pilots were cooled off a bit until they could get some rounds into a target.

To me, as a student, gunnery in a P-40 was a case of trying to make the airplane cooperate, which I wasn't sure it wanted to do. That took use of the trim system, concentration, and flying to settle it down at the right place and time. Then, for ground gunnery, firing in range, pushing the foul line a bit, and trusting the sight pipper instead of looking out to see where the bullets were going pumped .50-caliber rounds into the target just fine. On my first air-to-air firing pass, I shot the towed banner target off almost in my face. Shooting a target off was not desirable because there could be no scores recorded and the mission had to be flown again. (It was liked even less by the tow pilot if the cable was cut closer to the tow airplane than to the target). Since the amount of lead on the target had to be eyeballed by the pilot for deflection shooting in a P-40, I just cut the lead back a bit on the next mission and got some holes in the target. From then on, as long as I concentrated and flew the airplane in the proper groove, me and aerial gunnery got along just fine.

There were no big graduation ceremonies for RTU, but there were plenty of sincere handshakes and thanks for the instructors and supervisors in the unit. I for one was extremely glad I had come to this unit and this flight—and to Sarasota, too. Looking back, I guess I was glad of their policy "Better to kill off students here than send out weak ones." Surprisingly to some—but I don't think to this unit—not one student pilot had been killed during our stay. That was certainly not always the case in RTU classes. RTU wasn't a long course—only some two months and about 60 to 80 hours of flying time in the P-40. That time, plus our 225 hours in flying school, was what these fighter pilots at this stage of the war had flown as they went overseas. Their orders were back to Tallahassee.

I did not have those orders. Mine were to stay at Sarasota as a fighter instructor in the same flight with which I had trained. I griped. They inferred that was okay, go ahead and gripe, but it had to be this way. At least one more instructor was essential in this unit until more combat returnees came in.

They gave me a few days off, so I went home. The police had a 1941 Ford convertible for sale, acquired in a high-speed chase; it was a real beauty except for a couple of bullet holes in it. I bid on it and got it. As always, my time at home was spent with Anita. The war hadn't killed or dulled anything at all between us, but at the same time it wasn't leading us on the path we had always figured we would be taking together about this point in life—that of going the rest of the way as husband and wife. I thought quite a bit about that on the way back to Sarasota and in the following days.

Back at Sarasota I was fully welcomed and accepted as a member of the unit by the Group CO and commanders on down, and was fully included in social events and activities, even though I was really a neophyte among the much more experienced and combat-tested pilots and officers.

However, I wasn't given students to train in flying the P-40. I was scheduled to tow targets and lead flights of students on gunnery missions, while also doing some instructing in gunnery.

We had one P-47C in the squadron as a tow airplane. P-40s were also used for that purpose when required. The P-47 sitting among the P-40s looked like a monster—big, fat, and heavy, and some said ugly, too. However, it had a big Pratt & Whitney R-2800 radial engine of 2000 horsepower and huge four-blade prop to move the rest of it around.

On my checkout in the P-47, the big roomy cockpit was different and the nose blocking the forward view was just bigger and wider than the P-40's. The mag check was quite smooth—on some mag checks in the P-40, I had been tempted to look around on the taxiway to see if anything shook off the airplane during the less-than-mild disturbance.

On this first flight in a P-47, I taxied up the runway and stood by as a target tow cable was attached, then took off with a target in tow. In the air the big fighter was extremely smooth and quiet and any feelings of "big and bulky" disappeared.

After the tow mission, I dropped target in a clear area on the far side of the field, then took the P-47 up to altitude as a part of the checkout. I went a bit over 40,000 feet—more than twice as high as one would normally try to take a P-40. Later, some people would say you shouldn't be up there as a single airplane in an unpressurized cockpit depending solely on the oxygen mask. I'm sure that most pilots who flew in P-47s went up to some very high altitudes at one time or another, a lot of them higher than this.

From that altitude I rolled over and came down in a vertical dive to see how fast it could be made to go—as I had done in P-40s from lower altitudes. It went fast, but I have no idea *how* fast because the altimeter, unwinding like a spinning top, became of greater interest once I realized I was no longer in control. The stick would not come back. Finally it moved a bit and the nose came up a fraction. Immediately thereafter things were normal again and the airplane came out of the dive. The rest of the time I towed targets in the P-47 I never went back up to high altitude to try a repeat of that operation. Later I would learn that what I had done was restricted in P-47 training and something never to be done just for the heck of it ... and also that I had been very lucky to get out of compressability without knowing what it was or anything about coping with it.

Naturally, I liked leading gunnery missions much more than towing targets. Fortunately, I got more and more gunnery work as time went by. For aerial gunnery, the nose of the ammo was painted. Each pilot got a load of ammo of a different color. With fresh and soft paint on the ammo, it came off and marked quite well on the target cloth and accurately gave the hits of each of the four pilots firing on that towed target.

Some rumors may have been heard that certain RTUs were suspected of meeting training quotas through special means of qualifying students pilots who had trouble hitting the target on their own. These might include loading all the guns in a flight with ammo on which the paint was so old and hard that none of it would mark on the target, plus loading all six guns in the instructor's airplane. Then, when the flight returned without any colors showing, the total hits would be spread around among all the pilots. A more straightforward approach to quickly qualify a weak shooter would be to give a good shooter the same color ammo as the weak one, then give the weak one credit for all hits of that color.

If such shenanigans went on anywhere—which I strongly doubt—it wasn't where I was. We held over weak gunnery pilots and kept going out on missions until they could either hit or the unit gave up on them.

Most RTUs reportedly gave only a limited air-to-ground training, mainly just the required ground gunnery and bombing with "Blue Bird" or "Blue Boy" sand-filled practice bombs.

The Group CO naturally had a personal P-40. It was painted with the famous sharkmouth design on the nose and multiple colored bands around the fuselage. It was a beautiful airplane and a very good one, too. One of my extra duties was to fly it when it needed to be flown, such as when the unit needed it and the Group CO or my flight leader were not available. We three were the only pilots who flew it.

Overall, I couldn't complain about anything in what I was doing or where, and I guess I should have been quite pleased. However, I did have a restless and discontented feeling that just wouldn't go away—that is, until one Sunday in mid-July when I guess I got too realistic in an unscheduled dogfight with the Group CO. Anyway, the event triggered a release from the RTU if I chose that. I did, and with a set of orders to Tallahassee, I wasn't restless anymore. I was wondering what lay ahead now.

I was leaving with over twice the normal RTU flying time in P-40s, which had added to my confidence in flying it. But most of all I was glad to have both trained under and been selected to work for the very strong and combat orientated Flight Commander in that squadron, Captain VanEtten.

I had time for a couple of days at home before reporting to Tallahassee. Gasoline ration coupons for such a side trip were no problem; there were always enough "B" or even "C" coupons to be found among officers for a little extra driving. On the drive home, I thought a lot about Anita and marriage. On arrival, I told her of my sure and immediate overseas duty. Officially, my orders specified nothing except to go to Tallahassee, but any pilot knew what that meant when coming *from* an RTU instead of going *to* one.

Then I asked her to marry me, and she said yes. We expedited a few arrangements and were married—now might be the only chance there would ever be, even though we would be together only as long as I was in Tallahassee. We didn't know if that would be a day, a few days, a week, or what.

We checked into one of the two main hotels in Tallahassee and were treated almost royally. They put us in an extremely nice room, which, if it wasn't the bridal suite before, they now called it one. There were a number of other married and overseas-headed pilots staying there with their wives. Some were veterans of married life, others were fairly short-timers at it, and a few were last-minute types like ourselves. Almost instantly we all were friends and bound together in common lot of this place and time being the last chance of mates being together before combat duty.

Perhaps it wasn't the traditional honeymoon of newlyweds slipping away to seek seclusion from families and friends. In fact, it wasn't that way at all. When the men went to the field each day, the women joined together for shopping, lunch, etc. At night certain couples might slip off in seclusion, but usually all joined for dinner and even some night life at a place that might have been called the Cotton Club.

Of course, those going overseas were not supposed to know when they would actually leave, but on a Friday most of us knew it would not be before the next Tuesday. Thus, Anita and I took a trip home to finalize plans for her to stay with an aunt and uncle while I was away. Some friends, a married couple, accompanied us back to Tallahassee and would drive home with Anita on Tuesday. We also made arrangements to sell the car there.

The very last day, Anita and same friends came out to the base and, with a few duties meshed in, I spent most of it with them at the officers' club. We even went to a movie. That night we were back at the hotel.

In the morning at the train station, I said goodbye as we stood by the car. Our time together had been much longer than I had expected—close to two weeks. The wartime honeymoon had been great, but most of all, as we parted, the main message between us was that regardless of what happened from here on, we were both thankful and glad we had done it. My last look and remembrance was of my tall, lovely wife waving a tearful goodbye.

Overseas orders were "restricted" and lengthy, with movement numbers and many instructions of various kinds, but they never said where you were going. Our first means of finding out if we were to fight the Japanese or the Germans was to watch which direction the train took when it left

Tallahassee. If it went west, it was almost certain to be the Japanese; if it went east, it was almost certain to be the Germans. The train went to the east, and south, too, and Miami could be guessed as the initial destination. It was.

One night in very early August of 1943, we boarded a DC-4, which departed the U.S. on a southerly heading. This was the first time I had ever been in a passenger-type airplane, and by going south it could be assumed we would be flying across the Atlantic on the southern route from South America to Africa.

In that summer of 1943, the news from the war was much better than it had been in early days. The American and Allied forces in combat during those grave days had done their job. The enemy expansion had been held in most of the world and now was starting to be pushed back. In the Pacific, the Battles of the Coral Sea, Guadalcanal, and Midway had been turning points. The island of Attu in the Aleutians had been retaken from Japan. The Germans and Italians had been kicked out of Africa and our forces were now fighting in Sicily. In Russia, each German summer thrust had been held, and a major victory won at Stalingrad. Apparently a tremendous battle was being waged this summer at a place called Kursk in Russia.

Yet in 1943 the Japanese still held most of their far-flung gains and the Germans a major share of theirs. It would take a long war yet to get either one back where they came from—if it could be done at all.

On the flight overseas I didn't really keep up with just when and where we landed along the way. Georgetown in British Guiana and Belem, Brazil, were mentioned. I remember one airfield was cut out of a jungle of huge, magnificent trees. But most of all I remembered the awe-inspiring sight as we flew across the mouth and delta of the mighty Amazon River on a bright, clear day. Our final landing was at Natal, Brazil, a jumping-off point in South America for Africa.

There, a transport version of the B-24 bomber sat on the ramp to take us across the Atlantic. Somebody said it was designated a C-87, called the Liberator Express. It didn't strike me as being of great beauty. This one was painted a dull black, about the color of a mudfish. It was also missing one of its four engines.

We waited five days for a replacement engine. Then finally we boarded the converted bomber about three A.M. on a dark, rainy morning. Rumors were that the airplane would be so heavy it could only get off at that time of day.

When the last of us stepped on board in the rear of the plane, the tail fell down on the ramp, and I assume the nosewheel came up off it. We got off and tried loading again, and the same thing happened. This time we were told to stand up and crowd forward. We did and the tail came up. We huddled that way in the pitch dark while the pilot taxied out.

In takeoff position, we sat down. The tail went down again. Holding brakes, the engines were run up to power. As they roared and strained, and the airplane vibrated and creaked, the tail came up and the takeoff roll was started. In the pitch dark it was hard to tell, but the impression was that the roaring, groaning, and shaking continued with not much else happening. Then—*slowly*—the thing got underway. After an ungodly long roll, it lumbered off and out over the ocean.

Ever since enlisting and all along the way up to now, I had known that each of those steps were all leading to one thing—combat in a war. Yet, there had been no real impact of it. Sure, leaving the family and my wife had the shadow that I would not see them again before that combat came, but any real impact of facing war itself hadn't come until sitting there in the total dark in an airplane headed for that war.

I said a prayer. It probably wasn't much of a prayer, but it's the same one I would say each time before I flew in combat. It did not ask for mission success or for safe return of me or others. I simply gave thanks for all blessings received, asked for forgiveness of sins and for mercy upon a soul, and requested divine guidance, spirit, and comfort for loved ones at home.

We landed at Dakar, French West Africa. I didn't say a prayer of thanks on arrival. I would not ever say one of thanks on arrival back from combat missions, either. I had thought about it, and decided not to ask God for help in fighting and not to thank Him for anything about it, either.

At Dakar, it was recommended—but not ordered—that we not go into town. The reasons were spies, incurable strains of VD, and some reports of shanghaiing. With that picture presented, most everybody went—taking the precaution to stay in groups. I am pleased to report that nothing seriously exciting happened.

One thing we did in Dakar was get a start on assembling our "Short Snorters." These were collections of foreign paper monies glued or taped together into long strips or rolls—reported to be an act of fellowship among those who had flown across the ocean. One officer got off to a tremendous start on "Short Snorter" material when a rather pretty French prostitute in a cafe agreed to exchange various foreign bills from her sizable collection of them. However, that was the *only* transaction risked between any of our group and that young lady.

Of course, American servicemen overseas did not have U.S. money. We had "script" or "funny money" as it was often called. It was fairly small printed slips of paper, with no coins at all. Some people never did get the feeling they were spending money when using the stuff.

The next morning we departed again, this time in a C-54, a military DC-4. It stopped for fuel out in the desert somewhere in Morocco. Fuel was pumped from drums into the plane. There was one old hangar with junk in it going back to French World War I airplane parts. It was hot, and instead of the breeze blowing off the desert cooling you off, it made you hotter yet. When people mention hellholes again in the future, a mental picture of this airport will probably pop into my mind.

Then we went on to Oran—at least I guess it was Oran. A well-known movie star was seen dashing about, apparently serving as officer-in-charge (OIC) of the passenger operation. We moved on again, this time in an RAF C-47. For the first time since we left Tallahassee, our destination was

A World War II "Short Snorter."

known: Tripoli, Libya. On approaching the field there we saw the first live signs of war. From several ships among the many in the harbor and offshore, tall columns of smoke rose as they still burned from a recent enemy air attack.

On the ground, we reported to the U.S. Ninth Air Force. We were expected, and were welcomed and briefed by a full colonel of A-3 or Operations. Each of our assignments and orders to units were already made. Most were to P-40 outfits, but some went to a P-38 Group.

I was assigned to the 79th Fighter Group, a P-40 group located in Sicily. However, one of my gunnery students from Sarasota, who was going to send me to P-38's. I believe the 1st Fighter Group was mentioned, but I wouldn't have bet on it. That change could make a tremendous difference to a pilot.

The P-38s could be expected to fly mostly escort or screen for bombers and be engaged mainly in air-to-air combat, even though they would do considerable strafing and bombing, too. A pilot there would stay a fighter pilot. The P-40 units, on the other hand, were mainly used in the tactical roles of providing air support to ground forces. The pilots assigned there would become fighter-bomber pilots—and, in most cases, that is the only way fighter-bomber pilots ever came to be.

The first time I heard the term "fighter-bomber" used in an offical nature as a category of pilot was here, during the colonel's talks with us. I had heard it used a few times by combat returnees, but had viewed it as more or less a nickname for those doing air-to-ground work. Now it appeared most of these arrivals were going to become one of this new breed called "fighter-bomber pilots," even though our training and thinking had really been as fighter pilots.

The P-38 assignment died for me when left to a "wherever you want me" basis. That was the particular P-40 unit I was slated for. From that moment on, I was destined to be a fighter-bomber pilot.

While plenty of aftermath signs of war had been seen since arrival in North Africa, on leaving the headquarters we got a first feel of it when buffeted pretty good by the explosion of one of the burning ships outside the harbor. We accepted an invitation of welcome to the British Officers' Club and Mess, located on the harbor in what had been described as Mussolini's past vacation palace in this part of the world. For many of us, this was the beginning of a close association with British and Commonwealth forces. It also offered an introduction to British "issue rum"—a heavy, potent grog that apparently came with the rations.

The next morning, the other P-40 bound pilots left for Cape Bon. I went into a field hospital. It wasn't the rum, unless a very little of it could generate sudden, very high fever. Two days later I woke up and during the next three days gained my initial appreciation and respect of the medics, in particular the U.S. Army nurses. To this time I had not been on sick call once since entering the service, and never did know what caused this bout—perhaps it was a delayed reaction to the dozen or so shots taken all at once before leaving, including those for yellow fever and plague.

Once released from the neat little tent-city hospital, I checked in with headquarters again. There I was greeted with the words, "You are just the guy we are looking for." They needed a pilot to ferry a P-40 to Cape Bon. Off I went in a desert-camouflaged P-40F, often known as the "desert" or "Africa P-40."

The P-40F had a Rolls-Royce designed Merlin V-1650 engine, built in the U.S. by Packard. One could quickly spot a P-40 equipped with that engine because there was no carburetor airscoop on top of the nose. The F was also heavier than some other P-40s, and its performance was a bit disappointing on takeoff.

I flew along the coast looking over countryside below, which had been the scene of fighting between the German forces, including the Afrika Korps, and the British Eighth Army in the latter's push from the east; particularly noting the location of the Mareth Line. Off to the left at a distance I could see the mountain terrain that held Kasserine Pass and the overall scene of the American and Allied forces' advance into Tunisia from the West.

My destination airfield on the Cape Bon peninsula, nearest point to Sicily, was a huge grass area with airplanes and tents spread here and there around the edges. It was almost dark when I arrived and the whole place seemed buttoned up for the night. Finally spotting some activity of a few men and a truck, probably guards, I set down nearby.

This was the base of a P-40 combat outfit, veterans of some past scenes of action I had just flown over. We were to fly a few missions with them before proceeding to our units. I flew four quick missions with the 316th Fighter squadron, 324th Fighter Group—mostly formation flying with

P-38. (Courtesy of U.S. Air Force.)

combat intervals and simulated attacks on ground targets. One mission was live firing of all the guns at leftover German vehicles and tanks out in the desert. I noticed that these combat pilots didn't seem interested in pulling streamers on the break. Even though I had a perfect record of streamers at Sarasota, I didn't try here and don't think I ever deliberately tried to pull them again in a pattern—but there would be plenty of streamers pulled in other ways.

Tunisia offered an excellent first look at who and what we would fight. Besides German POW compounds in the area, there was destroyed and abandoned equipment of all kinds, ground and air, strewn throughout much of the countryside. It was a welcome sight overall as representing a tremendous loss to the enemy, but not necessarily a reassuring sight because what was left here surely didn't come from some second-rate military force.

In a few days we went off in little groups in various kinds of airplanes to our units. A few others and I crawled into a strange-looking little RAF transport—riding on top of a load of equipment and gear. It apparently took off, cruised and landed at the same speed, and didn't—or couldn't—get very high, either. At Malta some of its load was taken off, but it flew the same on the next leg—probably still way overloaded, but just not as much so as before. One could gather that in this type of theater transportation, the loading procedures had more to do with what could be crammed in rather than any weight-and-balance considerations.

The little plane crossed the coast of Sicily in a valley and then struggled on up higher ground in the general direction of Mount Etna. Soon it plopped down on a dusty strip, which the pilot identified as Palagonia LG (Landing Ground). The trip to war was over. This was the current base of the 79th Fighter Group, to which I and the others on board were assigned for combat flying.

Chapter 4

Southern Italy

We were welcomed by the Group CO, Col. Earl E. Bates, a professional career officer, who had commanded this organization for several months in combat. The 79th flew and fought under control of the British Desert Air Force rather than a U.S. numbered air force, and primarily provided tactical air support to the British Eighth Army. It and its personnel were veterans of the Western Desert side of the African campaign (as the British Eighth Army pushed the German forces back across the desert), and of the fighting in Tunisia and Sicily. Of the several U.S. Groups with the British in Africa, the 79th could not lay claim to being the first to enter the fray from Egypt. A companion P-40 outfit, the 57th FG, held the valid claims as "first" from that direction. The 79th came along a bit later, and somewhat in the nature of a fighter outfit chose to be identified as "Not the first, but the best."

The 79th had been on tactical air-to-ground operations most of the time and still were, yet there had also been a lot of air fighting. These pilots had seemed to have a knack for either having just been relieved on patrol or tangling with the fighter escorts, while others, such as the companion P-40 group pilots of the 57th, had some tremendous field days in shooting down transports ranging from trimotor Ju 52s to huge six-engine Me 323s and gliders as the Germans were trapped in North Africa. The 79th did have an impressive record of air kills from escort and patrol activities against fighters; for example, one squadron shot down 15 Me 109s over Pantelleria in 15 minutes without loss to themselves. They also had various ships and boats, including a couple of destroyers, among their claims.

However, it was the key support given to the ground forces at places such as Mareth, El Hamma, and Wadi Akarit that set the pattern for what we would be doing in combat—bombing and strafing enemy ground forces and their support facilities.

Back at Denver, while awaiting entry into cadets, I had spent much time in libraries studying military and aviation subjects, but I had run across very little on the subject of tactical air support of ground forces. The act of dropping bombs on enemy forces by various nations went well back into history—by balloon as early as 1849 and by airplane around 1913. One source did mention "tactical" in connection with World War I, when some 1000 or more Allied airplanes of various types were used against German forces in the St. Mihiel sector in September 1918. Of course, ground forces had been bombed and strafed in the Spanish Civil War and the Japan-China conflict of the 1930s and early 1940s, but what had developed in World War II made all previous efforts only first steps. While the Stuka had gained fame for ground attack in the early days of the war (and continued to do so on various fronts), fighters had been pumped into that role in large numbers by all combatants. North Africa had been the largest effort and proving ground to date for American, British and Commonwealth fighters in tactical air operations. It had been mentioned as a classic situation and example, and much had been learned and developed. Thus, if we were to be fighter-bomber pilots, we had come to a proper place to learn the trade.

Our visit to Group headquarters was brief, and other than seeing some of the personnel from there now and then in the future, few of us pilots would need to visit that headquarters again. In fact, unless one wanted to talk to the chaplain or see the dentist, there was no need to ever go there. Everything else needed to fight and live was found in each of the three squadrons under the Group, where the pilots were assigned.

On the way to my squadron, the 87th FS, in a jeep, the escorting pilot at the wheel provided a sightseeing trip through the airfield. It was British-constructed, which is why it was a landing ground, or LG, instead of an airfield. It had a single runway of some 3500 to 4000 feet of scraped bare ground. My escort mentioned crosswind takeoffs and landings as a normal part of flying. The olive drab P-40s spread around the strip had no fancy or distinctive paint jobs, but they looked sharp and clean, if on a dust bowl airfield. Of special note was another special little force of airplanes with the squadron P-40's—a few German fighters, Me 109s and FW109s. They had been collected along the way as spoils of war and some were kept flyable for use by squadron pilots.

The Squadron CO, Maj. Benjamin F. Uhrich, was pretty close to bald. However, he wasn't an old man at all. I wondered on-the-spot if that's what combat flying did to you, but in only a few minutes with the man I got the strong impression that I was fortunate indeed to be in this unit with a true gentleman for a CO. That impression never changed; it only gained strength in future days.

Major Uhrich made a specific point of talking about the squadron and its personnel in addition to the main subject of flying and fighting. Squadrons were self-sustaining; they were the only units under the Group. If necessary, each one could go separate ways and keep up full operations. In the 79th FG, even though together on a field, the squadrons still lived and

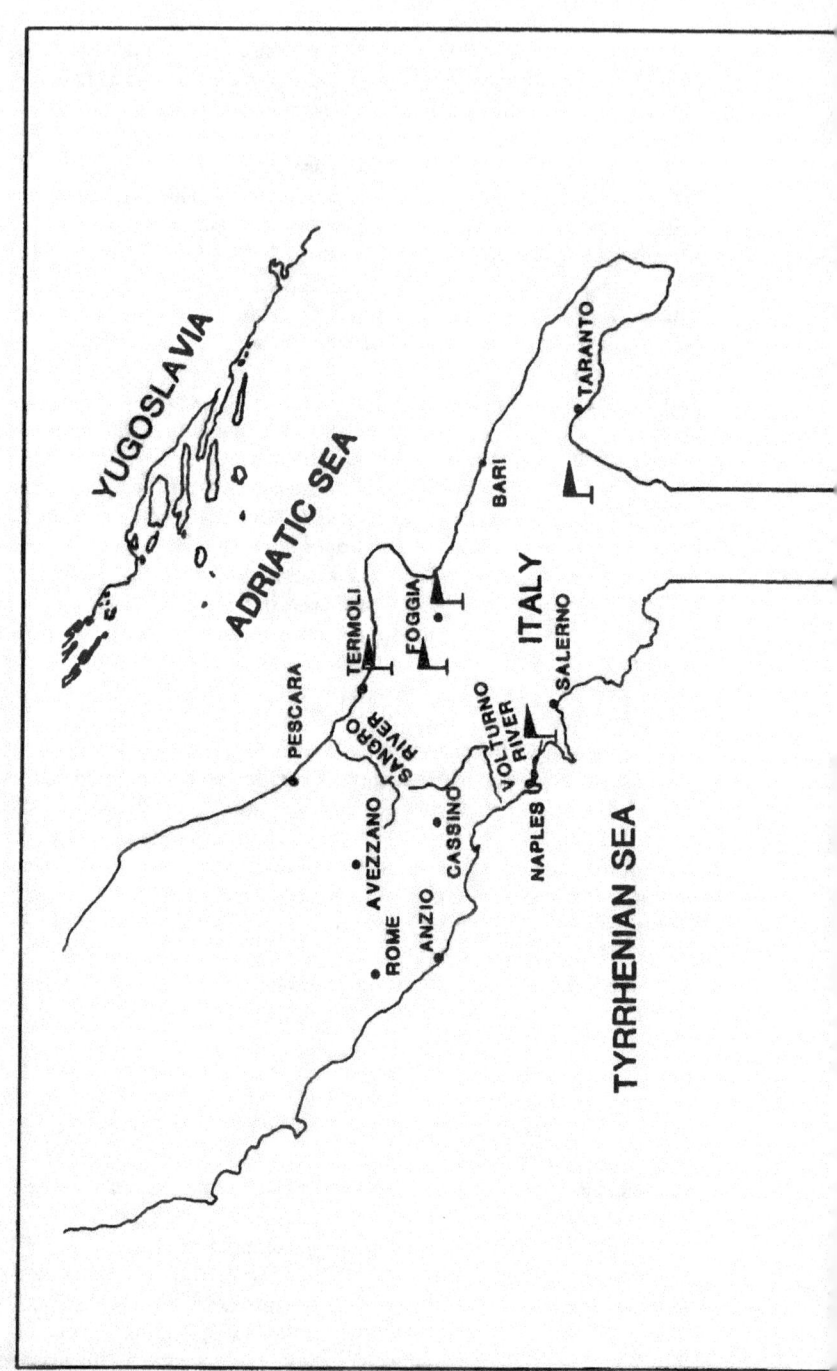

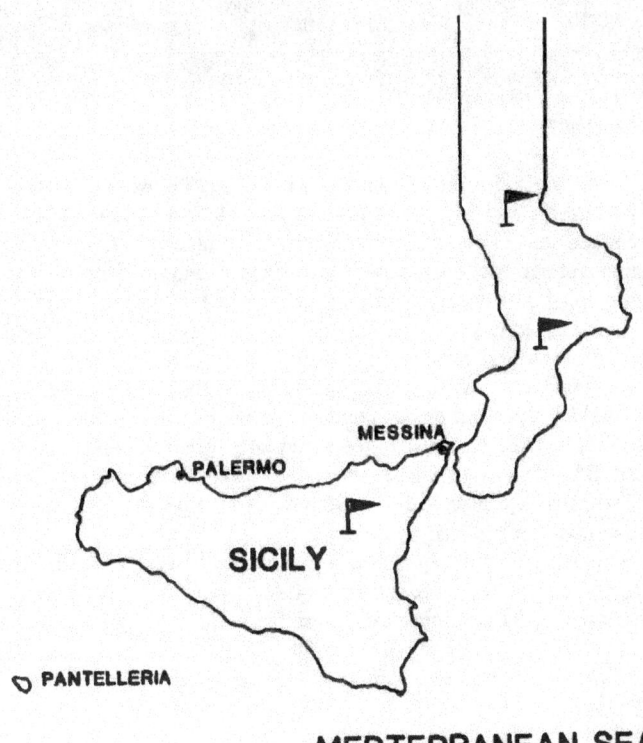

ea of combat actions covered in Chapters 4, 5, and 6. The flags mark the locations of airfields flown from

One of the German airplanes in my new squadron, a FW 190.

worked separately. Each squadron ran and manned its own functions and facilities: administration, pay, intelligence and operations, briefing, maintenance and supply, communications, ordnance and armament, parachute and personal equipment, flight surgeon and medicine, vehicles and motor pool, kitchen and mess, and officers' club.

Fighter squadrons were authorized 25 airplanes, plus five more for wartime. Most units always had 30 airplanes. Manning figures, particularly on pilots, varied at times and places. An example of the actual figures of one specific fighter squadron at one point in the conflict might be generally representative: authorized, 57 officers and 245 NCOs and enlisted men; assigned, 53 officers (included 9 non-flying) and 242 NCOs and enlisted men. That same squadron had over 60 officers at times and was down to about one pilot per airplane once, too.

No pilot in a combat squadron, regardless of its type and size, ever failed to realize two things about his unit: One, that it was his home and life in war. Two, that without total devotion and attention to duty in every part

"Without which there could be no flying."

of that squadron, the flying and fighting could not be done.

In the 87th there were now almost two full sets of pilots. There were the original pilots, or "old heads," those who came overseas with the unit; then there were the replacements, or "new sprogs," like me. Some of the original pilots had already gone home; the rest were very close to having flown the 80 missions that would qualify them for rotation back to the U.S. While not every one of those pilots planned to go home then (the CO and a few others would stay longer), there was still going to be a mass turnover in pilots right away.

Although we newcomers had reached our combat outfit, we would not reach combat immediately. There was yet more training. For one thing, we learned that the P-40s in this group were not P-40Fs as we had flown in Africa. They were P-40Ls, which used the same Merlin engine but were lighter airplanes and had somewhat better performance. That was welcome news, but someone went on to say one of the reasons they were lighter was that most of the armor plate had been removed.

There was no standard "book" to be pulled out and studied here on air-to-ground missions—the procedures, tactics, and techniques—any more than there had been such a "book" on air-ground operations back in training in the States. We were told how it would be done here in accordance with the orders of higher headquarters and or Squadron Commander. We learned that the tactics and techniques—weapon deliveries, formations, etc.—was largely left up to the squadron COs, and that the 87th FS and its two sister units in the Group, the 85th and 86th Fighter Squadrons, differed substantially in various tactics and techniques.

For example, the 87th flew in a formation none of us had ever flown before, and which neither of the sister squadrons flew—"straight line a-breast." While possibly harder to fly and overall less flexible than the basic combat formation flown in RTU, straight line abreast provided better visible coverage and protection against enemy fighters and may have helped eliminate accidental flak hits enroute and returning from targets (such as an 8mm fired at a leader only to hit the wingman behind him or vice versa). Straight line abreast was used primarily for "going" and "coming," and not always for weapon delivery, armed recce, and the like.

This formation had a few new wrinkles. If the wingman, or the element, was turned into by the leader, whoever was turned into went up instead of down during the crossover. The leader, remaining underneath, was responsible for preventing collisions. Also, on a break into enemy fighters, each pilot broke "in place" and the wingman on the outside nearest the enemy became the leader during the engagement, while the previous leader flew as wingman. Reportedly both procedures came from the RAF. Flying this formation was a bit strange initially, but once proficient in it, most pilots liked it.

On Cape Bon we had lived on the field in tents, ate from mess kits, and became familiar with straddle trenches. Here with our combat unit, our mess, club, and quarters were in a large villa and surrounding structures well

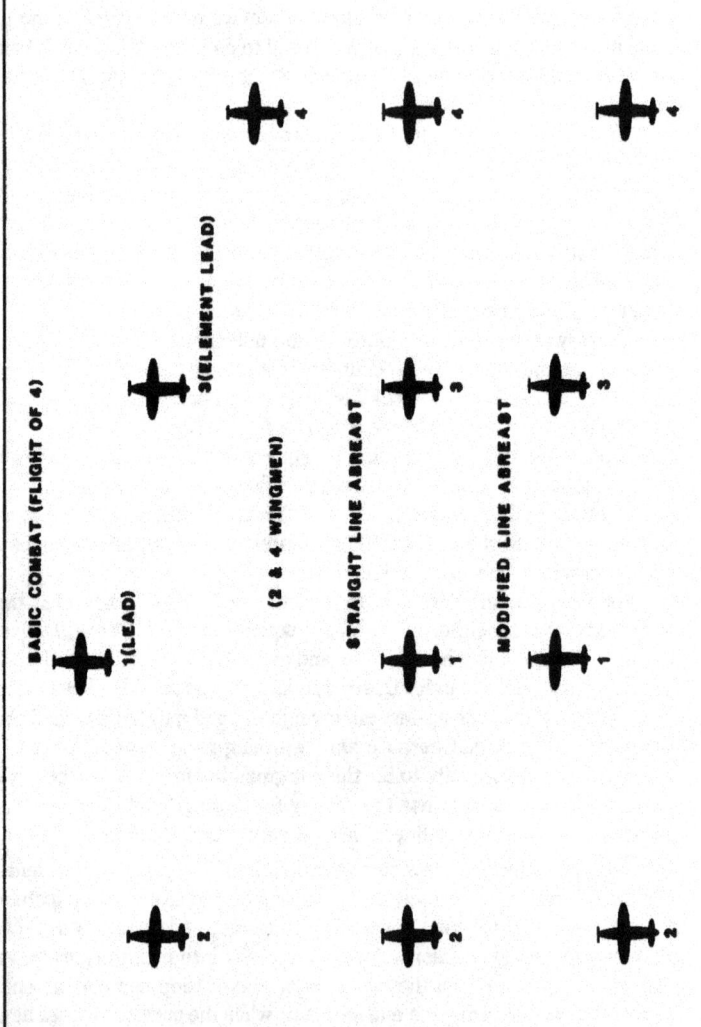

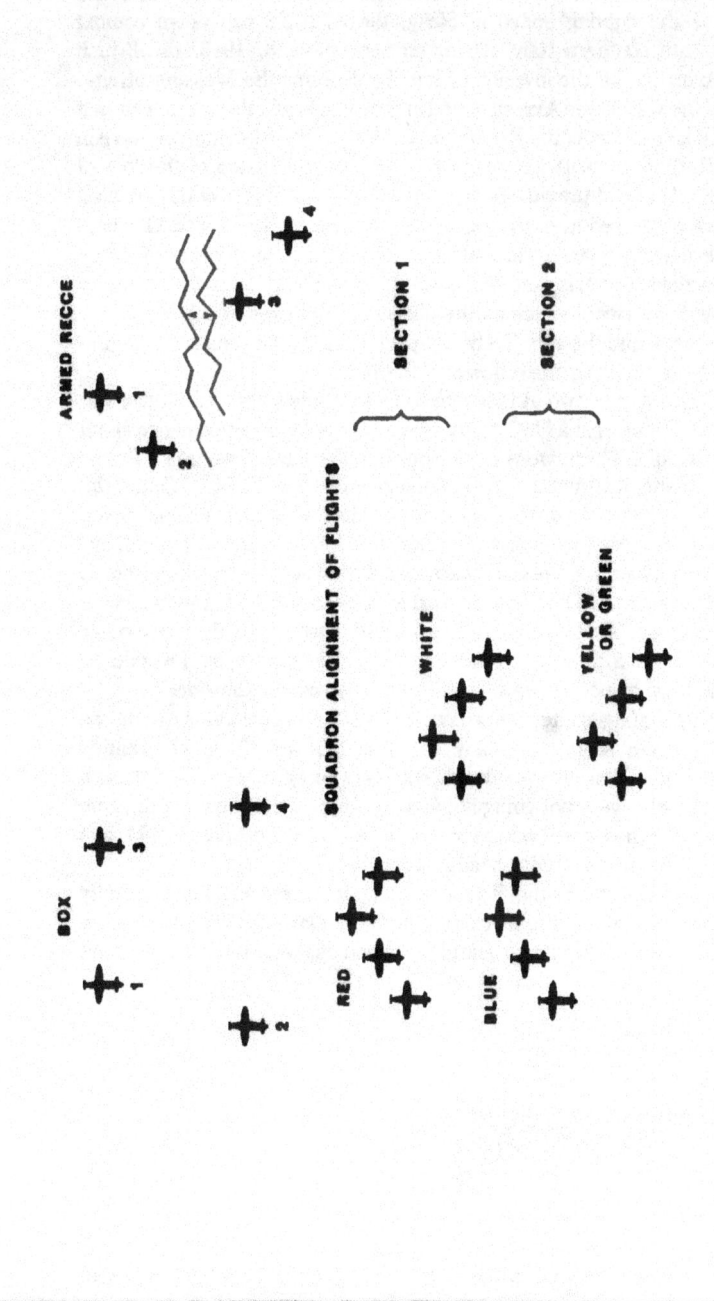

Representative formations used by fighter-bomber squadrons.

removed from the field. While maybe a bit crowded, quarters-wise, the fact that the plumbing worked was considered a near-miracle for a war zone.

Since the fighting ended in Sicily, the 87th FS had flown combat missions into southern Italy. Then, on September 3, 1943, the British Eighth Army led off the invasion of Italy by crossing the Messing Straits. Italy quit the war on the Axis side, and in time would join the Allies. Our unit continued its support of the British, now in Italy. By mid-month we were in Italy with them at Isola LG near Crotone, near the instep of the foot of Italy. This field had previously been an enemy base. Most of our enlisted men were quartered in barracks, while we went back to tents. Our captured German warplanes were left behind. One had been wrecked, some were salvaged for parts, and there was the complication of flying any of them this far forward—such as the chance of Spitfires or other fighters firing on them, and the very likely prospect of British Gurkha ack-ack gunners on Isola shooting them down in the pattern.

The first day or two at Isola offered a few sidelights to the main war effort. Jack Benny and a USO show arrived there for a performance about the time we did. There were a few spoils of war here. One was a flyable Italian airplane, a trimotor job, perhaps an SM-79 or SM-81. One of the Group staff organized a crew to fly it. When they took off, the plane nosed straight up. Somehow they sort of walked it back down to the ground, but missed the runway, and the gear was sheared off when they ran into a bomb crater. It was surmised by onlookers that they took off with the elevator trim full nose-up. There were some six men on board. I could see one other pilot and perhaps a crew chief being led into such a venture, but I wondered about the kind of people who would go along just for the ride.

A couple of days after our arrival at Isola, my name came out on the combat mission schedule. Many of us had flown 10 or 11 training missions—enough to start wondering what was going on. However, the few "old heads" who were not going home were flying with us quite a bit. One could conclude they were taking a pretty close look at what they would have here when all the other "old heads" went home.

For days I had been studying the current situation maps. I had carefully prepared my set of maps to be carried in the airplane and religiously kept them up to date, memorizing features, headings, reported flak, etc., but

An Italian trimotor plane such as this made a last flight. (Courtesy U.S. Air Force)

above all keeping track of the Bomb Line, the inviolate safety line that was projected out in front of friendly ground troops. Beyond it, mission leaders were free to attack enemy targets on their own. On it, or anywhere short of it, they were prohibited from any attack unless specifically directed and/or controlled. The Bomb Line, plotted up-to-the-minute, was the paramount consideration and feature on all briefing and personal maps used in air-ground support and fighter-bomber operations.

At the early morning briefing for my first mission, the attention was not on the Bomb Line in front of the British Eighth Army, as had been expected. Instead, it was on the one in front of the Salerno beachhead well to the north. The invasion there, which started a few days before we moved into Italy, had come under heavy enemy pressure. In fact, the American and British forces on the beachhead were in danger of being cut into and thrown back into the sea. The British Eighth Army had undertaken a thrust in that direction.

Some of our unit missions were supporting that advance, but my mission was among those being diverted to Salerno to provide direct support for the beachhead forces—about maximum range for our P-40s. The target was specified in coordinates of the map grid system and re-checked by physical features on both aerial and ground charts. Once we were in the target area, the mission leader, a captain and veteran flight leader, would have the task of finding it, as well as double-checking it against the Bomb Line. The flak was not going to be meager or sparse. My first thought was that the unit would pull me off this mission and put an experienced pilot in. They didn't.

I was scheduled as Red Two, on the leader's wing, where most pilots fly their first mission. This was an eight-ship effort, each P-40 loaded with a 500-pound general purpose (GP) or high explosive (HE) bomb and 20-pound fragmentation bombs (or "frags") on the wings. There was no special briefing for me, just a check to see if I had questions, which I didn't.

In the air, it was an extremely hazy day, with very poor visibility. Between that and the natural tendency of a first-timer to fly too close to his leader, I had to fight myself a bit to stay out where I should be. I'd always assumed there would be some dramatic impact when one first flew over enemy territory, but as we crossed the Bomb Line I was still working away at staying in proper position and looking around for enemy fighters. Thus, I just made a mental note that "you are now over enemy territory."

My first view of flak came before reaching the target area. A few 88mm rounds burst up ahead and slightly high on my side of the formation. Even in the haze, the bright red-orange fireballs and black, greasy-looking smoke could be clearly seen. As we neared the next Bomb Line, that around the beachhead—and we were approaching it from enemy territory—up came more 88s, this time much closer. These could be seen *exceptionally* well. I had always assumed that any flak nearby would have a distinct impact of some kind on one. It didn't, really, other than recognition that the expected experience of being shot at was, in fact, happening.

Between the haze and smoke from the beachhead area, visibility was very poor. The leader did an excellent job of swinging wide over some prominent coastal checkpoints and then finding and conforming the target. In the process, some tracers and whitish-grey puffs of light flak or automatic weapons came into play. These are attention-getters.

Then, on the dive bomb run, which was not started very high due to the poor visibility, one other truth of fighter-bomber work entered the picture: You must remember that if you drop GP bombs (with instantaneous or short delay fuses, as these were) too low, your own bomb blast and shrapnel will blow you out of the air—while the enemy probably watches in awe.

The bomb release was fine, but on pullout I lost the leader in the haze and smoke—a bad feeling on one's first mission. Luckily, I found him again right away. The same thing happened after the next pass of releasing the other ordnance and strafing the target area. As we circled above, the second flight went in.

We went home in pairs. My fuel was considerably lower than that of the leader, and while he had checked me for damage with none showing, it became a sweat near the end. With a good and accurate navigation job by the leader, Capt. William B. Rogers, on the break for landing I could read five gallons—if you consider trying to read a fuel gauge to that level as having any meaning at all.

On the mission there had been no navigation aids of any kind (transmitter, beacon, DF, etc.) available in either the beachhead area or at our field. That would be the normal case for fighter-bombers throughout the war. The mission leaders had to do their own in-cockpit navigation under all circumstances. It could be assumed that no one was going to be foolish enough to set up navigation aids for our use on forward fields or areas, which in turn the Germans could use to find targets—or vice versa, either.

I had a few inner feelings after that initial mission. Most of them were fairly vague, but there was one rather firm feeling: *79 more of these was going to be a lot.*

My next mission was very similar, another one back to the Salerno beachhead area. This time, from briefing on, I may have taken a bit more note of various things around me, both in the air and in preparation for the mission. In the latter regard, we had no chapel tent or facility on the flight line, so there were no last-minute services or prayer sessions—everybody was on their own for direct contact. I said my short prayer only after climbing into the airplane.

Perhaps the toughest moment prior to a mission was the ritual of taking your billfold and other personal items from your pockets, and maybe a class ring off a finger, and placing them in a box before going to the airplanes. The reason for doing that could hardly be overlooked or ignored.

Otherwise, most pilots just went from the briefing and picked up their equipment of helmet, goggles, mask, and parachute, and threw the latter across the hood of a jeep or in a weapons carrier for a ride to the airplane. There wasn't really any "suiting up" done, since most pilots flew in khaki uniforms and combat boots, even though some British mosquito boots, expensive Egyptian jobs, and U.S. cowboy boots might be seen, too. (However, pilots who wore fancy slip-on boots in airplanes ran the risk in a bailout of being seen hanging in a parachute with no boots on at all.) One did not need to check out a gun and survival knife before flying. We wore .45-cal automatics and probably a knife all the time, the latter usually a bayonet sharpened to a razor's edge. A yellow inflatable Mae West was worn on most missions, and maybe a canteen. Limited medical and survival items were carried, usually in a couple of small kits stuffed into pockets. Typically, one might contain, among other items, some compresses, bandages, packets of sulfa powder (probably sulfanilamide) and ampules of morphine. Each pilot also had a very neat little map of the area he would fly over and possibly a few other materials. Many pilots, like myself, used any remaining space for cigarettes and waterproof matches.

My second mission was flown on a clear day with good visibility. I saw much more in all respects—the invasion fleet and support forces offshore, signs of battle, the target and enemy positions, our results, and flak. This time the rapid rate of fire and intensity of the automatic-weapon flak left no doubt as to how it earned its deadly reputation. Of course, one doesn't see the small-arms fire, but it was there because two airplanes had holes from it. This mission, as the first one, was rated a very successful and effective mission, among the many flown by various units in support of Salerno.

Then the ground war situation changed sharply. Salerno was no longer in jeopardy, but rather a general push northward was underway from there and from all across Italy as the Germans fell back. This generated a classic situation for tactical air. We went on a strong effort against the retreating enemy in the open, while still pumping support in at any main points of resistance. We also went into a series of rapid moves to forward bases, keeping pace with the advancing friendly forces.

I flew 15 straight strafing missions, and many other pilots did the same. On some we carried bombs for initial use on certain targets; on others only the guns were available. Either way, repeated strafing passes on each and every mission usually expended all the ammo on board. There were no great columns of massed vehicles. The Germans were not in a rout or panic retreat, but rather just steadily moving back. That put many vehicle targets of all kinds on the roads in small convoys and in singles, pairs, etc. The weather was excellent and each mission went searching the roads to locate and strafe them—or on armed-reconnaissance or armed-recce missions.

Strafing was an emotional subject among pilots—and reasonably so, since it was a very likely way for a fighter-bomber pilot to be killed. But strafing was a key part of the fighter-bomber pilot's war, and their commanders normally had policies and tactics governing risks vs. gains on various targets, situations, etc., for armed-recce efforts.

On some missions we got by with little or no flak. On others, we recced our way right into it, with no prior indication or knowledge it was there—yet that would hardly ever change, especially for the highly mobile light flak automatic weapons. I had my first good taste of the 88mm heavy flak at very low altitude (technically 88s may have been classed as medium flak, but to fighter-bomber pilots they were heavy flak). Some past advice in stateside training had been that the big flak guns couldn't touch you at low altitude. I sure wish the originator of *that* theory had been with me on one particular mission. The trees in the area were not much to speak of in height, but while cutting close beside a little stand of them on a ridge and turning back into a strafing run in the valley below, a salvo of 88s blew the tops out of the trees. That might be an interesting sight to see from afar, but it is not exactly a lovely scene when it happens right off your wingtip. The next time around on another pass, with me trying to stay lower, they shot lower and got some of the ridge.

Most missions consisted of eight airplanes, two flights of four. While one flight recced and strafed the other covered—and vice versa, except then the cover was usually good only for warning since they had no ammo left. Vehicles of all types were found—mostly trucks, some tanks, command vehicles, staff cars, and motorcycles. Many pulled over when attacked; others kept going full-speed—especially motorcycles. Some of them as well as other vehicles were blasted off the roads by our guns. Others went over cliffs while trying to speed on down the road.

Of course, the main object was to get "flamers," to set vehicles on fire. Those—and ones going over cliffs—were the only claims made of "destroyed" vehicles. All others strafed were listed as "damaged." The surest way to get flamers on these individual targets, as well as blow vehicles off the road (plus save ammo for the next target), was to hit them solid and simultaneously with rounds from all six guns, and do it in very short bursts. When possible, a pilot would want to hit a tank with all the firepower he had—and all together.

The guns in each wing were harmonized or boresighted for the rounds to converge at a point out in front of the airplane—both with each other and with the pilot's line of sight through the gunsight. That convergence point, also set for a particular airspeed, had apparently always been based on air-to-air considerations and in most fighters was only some 750 feet or slightly better out in front of the airplane. The pilot had to get reasonably near that range to hit a small target with all his guns.

That is *close* for an airplane hurtling right at a ground target and any obstructions around it. These strafing passes (plus many less close-in types) bring out three critical factors in a fighter-bomber pilot's war—factors the pilots have to live with from the very start and on throughout their tours. *One*, any misjudgment, target fixation, or too-late attempts at aiming corrections will send the airplane into the target, ground, or nearby trees or other obstructions. *Two*, if the target is a load of ammunition or other explosives, it can—and very likely *will*—explode right in the pilot's face, sending up a fireball, truck parts, slabs of highway, still-to-explode ammo, and other debris right into the path of the airplane. *Three*, if a pilot is seriously hit by flak in this or any other low-altitude attack, his chances of ever reaching enough altitude to allow a bailout are slim indeed—as are any other chances of survival in most terrain and situations. Thus, on strafing attacks, these factors and considerations go along with a pilot on every pass, as well as the knowledge that he is flying into the most effective ranges of enemy automatic-weapon flak and small-arms fire.

From the first day, a pilot knows he must never lose concentration against that first factor (flying into the ground), even if he is being hosed and barraged with a solid sky of flak. From the beginning, he knows there is not a great deal he can do about factors two and three—they are inherent risks in strafing. Factor two may have been the most insidious—the better the pass made and shooting done on an ammo vehicle, the better the chances were of it exploding in your face.

All strafing was not the same. In many cases, it would be neither necessary nor most effective to get into point-blank range. There would be area targets of troops, supplies, etc., when you would not want all rounds impacting together. Also, there would be columns and other targets when you would want to "walk" the rounds down or through the targets. But there would also be targets such as enemy airfields where you would not just *risk* encountering flak—it *surely* would be there and in great intensity.

Even though we had been baptized with a bunch of strafing early in the game, we knew that there would always be more as long as we were fighter-bomber pilots. That baptism for us was extensive. Plain arithmetic showed that a pilot with 15 missions, making up to eight and ten (in a few cases more) passes per mission, would have made well over a hundred strafing passes up to this point. Those passes provided extensive experience in low-altitude flying and shooting, plus some—if extremely limited—comfort from living proof that it is possible to fly through truck parts and pieces in the air and not hit them. But there was no proof you would miss them the next time.

In this situation we had not been operating in intense flak, only in and out of some on most missions. We shot many individual trucks, tanks, and small groups of vehicles (which might not always be profitable) but the totals on these missions mounted into substantial numbers of vehicles destroyed and damaged—perhaps to 20 or so of each category on some efforts. While we had battle-damaged P-40s, we had no losses.

I guess by now I had reached some kind of understanding in mind on how compatible combat and I were to be. I was concerned and worried about the prospects overall—in fact, probably downright scared. Frankly, I did not expect to get back home to the U.S. Yet any fears about immediate events, whether upcoming missions or those in progress, seemed overridden if not completely blanked out by concentration and the urge to perform properly and effectively. In other words, I was not afraid of what we were doing, or while doing it; I was just quite doubtful about the end outcome of it all for me.

On the ground the Group and Squadrons moved five times in three weeks, leapfrogging up southern Italy to keep up with the war. These

Battle-damaged P-40.

moves were accomplished without loss of a single mission or sortie.

The units were split into two parties, A and B. A would move out as an advanced ground party to set up at the new base, while B would continue to keep the unit flying at the old base. When A was ready at the new base, the airplanes went out on combat missions from the old base, then landed at the new one. A kept them flying there as B moved up to rejoin. Sometimes, a small C party was also used as a caretaker or guardian of supplies at the old base until another type of unit took over or it was abandoned. Obviously, during such moves there was an extra workload and burden on all ground personnel, but they never failed to handle it fully and completely.

Whether on a base or on the road in convoy, these units did not present a picture of a purely GI operation. For one thing, many of the tents were British, and some were German and Italian. There were extra vehicles— also British, German, and Italian—from lorries to trailers and motorcycles. There was an enormous supply of Jerrycans, and these most useful cans may have been among the greatest new developments of World War II. I wouldn't say that when we moved we looked more like a Gypsy caravan than a military convoy, but there was some resemblance to the former.

From Isola LG, A party moved to a field called Firmo LG. The airplanes followed in a day or two. B party came up but did not stop, bypassing this new LG and going on to set up as the advance party at Pisticci LG. Once reunited there, off went A to an airfield called Penny Post. There they only shook hands with B before moving out again to a field identified as Foggia #3. Of course, these moves took us up Italy behind the British Eighty Army on the eastern side of the peninsula to the area of Foggia, where the USAAF would establish a large complex of airfields for future operations—even surpassing that the enemy had at Foggia in the past.

Life on the ground along the way had been of classic proportions in fighter-bomber operations, too. When our squadron personnel arrived at Firmo LG the engineers were still blasting away olive trees to make a runway. At Penny Post they were still clearing mines and some troops had been killed in the process. This field contained many destroyed enemy airplanes, reportedly the result of P-38 strafing missions. At Firmo and Pisticci, we flew only two or three days before moving on. On the shorter stops, tents were not even unloaded; we slept on cots set up among the olive trees.

Everyone referred to our food as C-rations. They were non-perishable rations but apparently packaged for field kitchens instead of for individuals—someone said that made them B-rations. Anyway, we could look forward to a rotation of relatively few selections, such as canned "bully beef," chili, salmon, and luncheon meat as the main courses, the latter always called Spam whether it was or not. I got along fine on this, but I could see that powdered eggs and I were not going to make it together over any kind of long haul. There was plenty of orange marmalade—maybe the entire world's supply was in the military—and that on a piece of hardtack could fill in a bit. Then, as in all units, some extra food was scrounged. The pickings

Jerrycans and C-47 cargo planes. (Courtesy U.S. Air Force)

in southern Italy were not too good, but we found a few turkeys, and a goat or ram once in a while.

In the combat flying, the strafing never stopped. We did, however, begin to fly more bombing missions on interdiction targets and enemy positions as the Germans began to slow their withdrawal and put up stiffer resistance all across Italy. If strafing was about as close to a glamour mission as fighter-bomber pilots flew, dive-bombing was the bread-and-butter-work. There was no computing function of any type in the sight or bombing system in the P-40. The pilot had to eyeball the amount of depression used on each bomb release. In theory, if one was in a 90-degree straight-down dive, straight ahead would be the aimpoint, but otherwise some depression was needed in selecting an aimpoint, and the more shallow the dive, the greater the amount. On very shallow or near-level releases that aimpoint wasn't even in the sight picture but under the nose of the airplane.

We made vertical or near-vertical dives on point targets, such as enemy gun positions. Starting at around 6000 feet—sometimes considerably lower—we rolled inverted and pulled through into the dive. On targets such as rail lines, "shallower" dives were made to achieve the best deflection accuracy possible. I guess you could say that dive-bombing in World War II was more an art than a science—an art practiced under fire. You could also say that probably the most valuable single service fighter-bomber pilots could provide to their units was to work hard at it and consistently dive-bomb effectively.

On my 10th mission I started leading flights of four on the armed recce missions. When my 20th mission was put on the board, I was scheduled to lead the mission. The mass turnover of pilots was well underway and some of the newcomers had to be used as mission leaders. I was one of two selected to try it at this early stage in our combat flying.

That mission, flown from Foggia #3, was to be an eight-ship interdiction effort on a fairly small bridge. We were in the airplanes and approaching start-engine time when the Squadron CO, Operations Officer, and Intelligence Officer roared up in a jeep with a change in the mission. They handed me a map with a course laid out across the Adriatic Sea and an X marked just off the islands of the Yugoslavia coast below the city of Split. That was the reported location of three ships, enemy freighters. They were now the target.

I couldn't figure out why the CO or Ops Officer didn't tell me to get the hell out of there, and one of them take over the lead of this mission, but they didn't. As the other pilots were given word of the mission change, I studied the map, especially the islands and coastline. If I got over there and didn't spot the ships, I didn't want to be faced with the decision of which way to turn to look for them. Thus I planned to arrive at an island I could easily recognize and from which the ships should be slightly to the right. If they were not in sight, I'd go that direction in search of them.

When we arrived off the island, the three ships were clearly in sight just off to the right. They were frighters. One was of oceangoing size, the other two probably coastal types. I would have liked to have set up for a very low skip-bomb run and throw the bombs right into the hulls of the ships, but the bombs were fuzed at short delay—1/10 second. A pilot had better not ever forget and skip-bomb on the deck with such a fuze setting if he wanted to live any longer. The only choice with this ordnance was to dive-bomb.

We did, and we put eight pairs of bombs quite close to the hulls of the three maneuvering ships, but did not hit any one of them directly. Then we strafed and put every round of ammo from all eight airplanes into the ships—and I don't think we missed with any of those. There was some defensive fire from the ships when we attacked but there was none coming up when we left. The large ship and one of the others were dead in the water, and the third was limping in a circle. I sweated both enemy fighters and my navigation on the way back, but none of the former showed and the latter got us home.

At the debriefing, I was quite dejected at not having sunk some of them or leaving them engulfed in flames—but they *had* been putting off some smoke. All we could claim was the bomb misses close enough to probably do damage and three ships thoroughly strafed—in other words, three ships damaged to an unknown extent. I was in my tent about an hour later when the CO walked in and handed me a slip of paper on which was noted a reconnaissance report on the ships—all burning, and abandoned or beached. Higher headquarters changed the mission results accordingly.

On my next mission I flew again as mission leader. This time we went after a small bridge, hit it, and strafed a few vehicles, too. From Penny Post I had flown my first major enemy airfield attack—on Pascara airfield up the east coast. On that effort I flew wing on a pilot who had only two missions to go before returning home. He apparently was a bit concerned about those last two anyway, and he sure didn't like the idea of strafing an airfield on one of them. We ended up destroying 18 enemy airplanes and damaging

Attack on an enemy airfield. (Courtesy U.S. Air Force)

over 30 others. The fellow I flew with did finish his other mission and go home. When he left he was still grumbling about that airfield mission at the end. On that mission, I was fairly happy at the time to see us working on the fringes, where the enemy airplanes were dispersed, rather than flying out in the open center of the field, where the tracers seemed the thickest.

Then, just as we had gone to Salerno to help out in a threatening ground situation, we went on repeated missions to hit a strong German force that suddenly counterattacked on the British and kept at it for some 24 hours, threatening to cut off a sizable force of tanks and troops. For our efforts on bombing and strafing in a successful outcome on the ground, the British Commanding General personally telephoned his thanks.

Of all the varied missions fighter-bomber pilots flew, these plain old support missions of pounding enemy ground force positions in heavy battle situations may in the long run be the most gratifying of all—if not the most spectacular or glorified.

Chapter 5

Winter Lines of 1943-44

Foggia #3 was a large grass airfield with no buildings—an all-tent operation. As we settled in there in October, the American Fifth Army had taken Naples and moved on north on the west; the British Eighth was well north of Foggia. Our operations continued in support of the Eighth with across-the-board missions—and still much strafing—but a number of changes were starting to show in the war and our operations.

The weather was one change. It started to rain some and we encountered more and more weather on missions. The space for an attitude indicator in our airplane cockpits had been blank holes; now such instruments had been received and installed. We did not have much information on using them, and some pilots left them caged and ignored them. Others saw nothing but possible good there and we experimented with them until we thought we knew what they would and would not do.

P-40 units certainly didn't fly "all-weather" missions. Some units reportedly stayed out of clouds altogether. Ours did not. We penetrated weather on climbouts and letdowns when necessary (over friendly territory it was in close formation; over enemy territory it was in combat formation). We didn't plan to stay in clouds for extended periods, but even on a short penetration a flight indicator was a godsend over pure needle, ball, and airspeed.

Life on the ground changed some, too. Until now the only U.S. Post Exchange service we had was a few items on a table in the orderly room—cigarettes, shaving cream, etc. Now, U.S. Post Exchanges were being set up in the area. While at Foggia, the Group welcomed on board its first Red Cross girls—two ladies who would serve coffee and doughnuts to troops throughout the organization. They were quartered in a tent like the rest of us—but, of course, it was their own private tent. While pilots could rotate back to the states after a tour, ground officers and the men had no rotation system—they stayed overseas for the duration of the war. Apparently the Red Cross girls did too, since these two much-admired and appreciated ladies would be with the unit on and on.

At Foggia #3 we had a control tower, which we had not had at all on some of the LGs along the way in past weeks. When we had flown without control towers, the mission leaders and pilots looked around and cleared themselves for takeoff and landing. There was evidence now of the Americans moving into this area in force—I'm sure they were not planning to fly from fields so austere they had no control towers.

The Ninth Air Force dropped out of the African and Mediterranean picture to reestablish in England as the tactical air force in that theater, joining the strategic Eighth Air Force also based in the United Kingdom. The Fifteenth set up in the Foggia area as the strategic air force in Italy. The Twelfth Air Force, veterans of support to American (and Allied) armies in Africa and Sicily, was the U.S. tactical force in Italy. That overall alignment of U.S. numbered air forces would remain in effect on through the war against Germany, but we continued to operate under control of the British Desert Air Force for the time being.

A major organizational event occurred within the 79th FG while at Foggia. That was the addition of a fourth squadron—the 99th FS—an all-Negro P-40 unit. They were not new to combat, having been in considerable action already. They had been transferred from their past group to this one. As I knew the story, they were the first all-Negro unit formed (at Tuskegee, Alabama) and the first all-Negro unit into combat.

With much enemy equipment left around, the 86th FS put a German Ju 88 into flyable shape. I'm sure they had plans for the airplane to haul fresh eggs, fruit, etc. (and possibly some spirits) from less war-ravaged parts of the theater, but they were told it was to go back to the U.S. for examination and evaluation. The Squadron CO, due for rotation home, flew the Ju 88 from Foggia #3 to Wright Field at Dayton, Ohio. I never did hear what route

Ju 88 prior to its flight from Foggia, Italy, to Wright Field, Ohio.

Bridges of various kinds were key targets.

he took or of any experiences enroute, only that it arrived safe and sound.

Along about the time I was first being scheduled to lead missions, we were assigned to knock out a large bridge over the Sangro River, where the Eighth Army was encountering ever-stronger enemy resistance below it along the coast. There were stories from Africa about one unit bombing a bridge for days, only to later have their ground parties move forward and be somewhat embarrassed to drive right on across the much-bombed—but still intact—bridge. We cut the bridge over the Sangro and did it in one day. It was reported as unusable from then on.

At Foggia, we carried 1000-pound GP bombs on the P-40s. Apparently, the tech orders listed the capability of the bomb/station rack as a maximum of 500-pounds. Some units had long since ignored that limit and used 1000-pounders. I assume we were doing the same.

On most bases in Italy we were rarely without some RAF or Commonwealth squadrons on the LG. Often it was a Spitfire fighter outfit, or a "Spit bomber" unit. Also usually nearby were Allied fighter-bomber outfits flying Tomahawks or Kittyhawks, as their P-40s were called. In the USAAF the P-40 was a Warhawk, but few pilots seemed to call them by than name. Normally, they were referred to as just "40s."

In our squadrons, a pilot eventually had his own individual airplane assigned. That did not mean he was the only one who flew it, but it usually had his name on the side and he could name the airplane if desired, or perhaps even have some artwork painted on it. Most of all it meant the tie of a pilot and a crew chief and ground crew as a team with "their" airplane. I had an airplane assigned fairly early. Our squadron was assigned the highest-numbered airplanes in the Group, 70 through 99. Number 99 was available and I chose it, but not on the basis of the number itself. It was an excellent flying airplane and gunnery platform, with an outstanding ground crew to take care of it.

After some fairly heavy losses of pilots just before I joined the squadron, there had been a rather amazing streak of none in the past few weeks. Then, on recent missions, we had two pilots shot down. They were hit on dive-bomb runs; both bailed out and were hidden by Italian farm families until friendly ground forces advanced. Both returned to the unit. Flak was definitely more concentrated in many areas now.

Cloud cover in the target areas did provide some additional payoff on strafing missions. When we managed to get in under the weather, the Germans usually had taken to the road in greater numbers on the assumption that we would not be there in such weather. Under these conditions, we caught some pretty fair concentrations of targets on the roads.

At the same time, the weather had us completely grounded from flying on quite a few days. Most of us spent considerable time sitting in tents in the rain. I did some sitting and wrote letters, but usually on such non-flying days I was at S-2 (Intelligence) and Operations studying the war, or at times even in the orderly room reading regulations and manuals. If the weather was good I usually hung around the flight line.

I had started to receive some mail. My wife was patriotically using V-mail forms, and religiously writing a letter each day, which she would continue to do as long as I was away. Our mail going out was censored. Among other things, you could not tell anyone at home where you were (only the APO number) or what you were doing.

If the Foggia area was starting to get quite Americanized, where we moved in mid-November quickly took us away from that trend. We were back solely with the British—and almost under the nose of the enemy, too. That was to an LG called Madna, hard on the coast of the Adriatic Sea below the town of Temoli. It took more than one try to get there.

When the advanced parties arrived, they bogged down in the mud, and the move was held up momentarily. As they were finally getting unbogged and setting up, they were strafed by a Ju 88, fortunately without casualties.

When we took the airplanes in, it was obvious why the LG was right on the coast—that's the only place it could be squeezed in among hills, knobs and the mountains inland. Where it was was not really big enough. The airplanes of our four squadrons and one South African unit were crowded immediately around and almost on top of the runway. The tents for the line, mess, quarters, and everything else were almost on top of the airplanes.

The runway was the shortest we had used to date. It had a sharp slope downhill to the sea. It was slick, and the taxiways were slicker. Early in our operations from Madna it was necessary to use ground crewmen as wing riders to guide the pilots when taxiing. That was an extra workload and a dangerous task for them, but the taxiways were simply too narrow and slick to allow adequate weaving for the pilots to see ahead. Any airplane that left the runway or taxiway could settle up to the bombs or wings in the mud. Everywhere around the field vehicles and humans struggled and groped with the stuff. Landing approaches were quite slow and most touchdowns were three-point or even tailwheel-first.

Yet from that LG and under those conditions the Group launched into record-setting mission and sortie rates—and into a situation of heavy ground fighting, enemy defenses, bad weather, and urgent need for air support by friendly forces. These conditions sent pilot losses up to record levels for the Group.

The Germans were fighting fiercely in establishing defensive lines across Italy, generally from the area of the Sangro River on the east, through Cassino in the center, and on to the Volturno-Rapido River areas on the west. Our main line of interest was always the Bomb Line. Its name always stayed the same because no new or special identification was necessary for each campaign or battle location. However, the German defensive lines on the ground south of Rome were referred to by various names. Gustav and/or Winter were heard most often, with mention of others including Hitler, Dora, Barbara, and possibly others. It didn't mean very much to us what the lines or positions of the enemy below were called; what mattered was that whenever there was a serious or major fight on the ground, fighter-bomber pilots would be directly involved in a slugfest type of air war with the enemy ground forces—the pounding of enemy army positions and interdicting the battle area. We also knew the enemy would not be short of flak in such situations with which to slug back.

The weather imposed demanding challenges. Whether reaching the target by penetrating weather or going underneath, many bomb runs were started at very low altitudes—while very vulnerable to enemy fire, which was now concentrated and intense in our main interdiction and support areas. We also became ever more vulnerable to our own bomber blasts. Trying to bomb through breaks and holes among the clouds in hilly and mountainous terrain can be fatal, and it was to some.

The Luftwaffe came out to challenge us. Apparently the enemy fighter pilots were using the cloud cover as a screen for surprise attacks. Our squadron fought off several such attacks and scored a few victories in the process, though I was never on one of the various missions that the 109s and 190s engaged.

Operating under low overcasts, in and around clouds, or in other conditions that reduce the bright sunlight (early morning and late afternoon as well) produces a bit different pilot's-eye view of flak. More is seen. The 88 bursts are brighter and seem closer. The tracers whizzing by are more

German Me 109 fighter. (Courtesy National Archives)

brilliant and persistent streams of color. The twinkling sparkles across the sky, which generate the light flak puffs, become more a spread of blue-white fire. But the view is not the *real* bad part—when operating under these conditions more planes are hit and losses go up.

We attacked a number of flak positions head-to-head. That had never been widely recommended as either a profitable or healthy practice, but frequently the positions could be spotted from the low altitudes and numerous flak guns and their gunners appeared in our mission results along with the various other targets destroyed and damaged.

In combat flying, there was a swap of information between our squadron and the fourth squadron. I was one of a few pilots on detached service to fly several missions with them. On those missions, I found their airplanes to be in topnotch shape and so was their combat flying. I was quite proud to have served briefly in combat with them.

Shortly after our arrival at Madna the mass changeover in pilots in our squadron had been fully effected. For a while there we were surely the most under-ranked squadron in the war. The original CO had gone home with 100 missions. He was replaced by a most energetic and dynamic First Lieutenant, George T. Lee, who already had about that many missions. Lee also immediately proved himself to be an outstanding commander of a combat unit. With a First Lieutenant CO, there was a Flight Officer as Operations; another Flight Officer and a First Lieutenant held two of the Flight Leader (or Flight Commander) positions. I and a companion Sarasota product (one class ahead of me in RTU), as Second Lieutenants, filled the other two Flight Leader slots. The rest of the outfit was made up of a few First and a bunch of Second Lieutenants, plus one or two other Flight Officers.

The Flight Officers in key positions were experienced pilots, ex-enlisted pilots and combat veterans. We "new sprogs" of August and early September were not exactly that anymore. Many of us were reaching the halfway point in missions for a tour. Also, the rank structure didn't stay that low for very long. By mid-December the CO was a Captain, the senior Flight Officers were commissioned, and I along with some of the newcomers of my time were First Lieutenants.

A few other of the original pilots had stayed for a while to provide experience during the transition period. One of these, First Lieutenant Bruce L. Morrison, had flown 110 missions and played a very key part in working with new leaders.

The weather now kept us from flying for two or three days at a time off and on. We were really cooped up in wet tents, but there wasn't much to do. Minefields and mud held down any strolling around the countryside even on the better days. Once I walked over a hill behind the airfield and found some 22 U.S.-manufactured tanks spread out on the face of the hill. Each had been hit with an enemy round or projectile that apparently stopped and destroyed the tanks in place. It was hard and grim evidence of the nature of the ground war we were supporting.

Every squadron had a bar they were proud of. Most had been made

A squadron bar.

with loving care—some from wings of enemy airplanes, others from more conventional materials. Many times there was not much to drink in back of them—at least not much of anything good to drink, and no ice or mix either. There was no supply system of liquor in the AAF other than mission whiskey and perhaps some for medicinal purposes. A shot of mission whiskey was available to pilots after a combat sortie. It was usually 100-proof straight rye—excellent stuff, and based on the name of one famous brand, it was commonly called "Old Overshoes." A shot of that whiskey slugged down without mix or chaser would indeed take your mind off things for a minute or two.

There was nothing of such quality in our club. There, it was whatever could be found locally. At Madna that was some wine and cognac or brandy, some in bottles without names or labels. As far as vintage went, yesterday might be a good year. One custom—blamed on the New Zealanders or perhaps the South Africans—was to take several bottles of various bad spirits and mix them all together. Why that would improve anything was never made clear, but it was argued that the mixture always had more "body" to it. I guess from the given name of "Purple Passion" the mixture was supposed to turn purple. Sometimes it did; sometimes it didn't. When it didn't, it wasn't very pretty. Either way, some people drank the stuff.

Once, when weather had us on the ground, the dentist came by suggesting an off day like this was a good time for a checkup. I went over and sat in his chair, praying that I had no cavities—because a GI dental technician stood by if needed to power the drill with a foot pedal. The thought of that kind of drilling on a tooth scared me more than some of the things we were doing in the air.

On close support missions we started using direct radio contact with ground force units to receive targets. Airplane VHF radios were used, some apparently having been provided to the ground forces. It was rumored that we were working initially with Canadian forces, but I never really knew. Nor did I know the rank, position, or service of who we talked with on the ground.

The ground unit would give both six-digit coordinates and a description of the target. Artillery was also available to put smoke marker rounds on the target if needed. This, of course, could get a priority target hit quicker than if sent by land lines all the way to the unit before the airplanes took off, and reduced the time and effort needed to find and confirm the target. It also allowed a specific target to be given from the ground for our normally offered or volunteered follow-up strafing passes. For example, after a bomb drop, the ground units could relay information such as "There is a concentration of troops in the group of trees just east of the gun position you bombed." Strafing there instead of just shooting at the same general target area should kill more of the enemy. Most of all, the direct contact with ground forces could open the door for attacks on the enemy closer to our troops while still ensuring their safety. For example, when talking to the ground units, a "dry" pass could be made if necessary, and the ground personnel could confirm or deny that an attack there would be okay.

Attack on any target near our troops was on a "positive, 100 percent sure" basis. The mission leader had to know *for sure* he had the correct target, not just know beyond any reasonable doubt he had it. This was true even with the direct radio contact with ground troops. We had to know where our troops were and confirm the correct target in relation to them. We carried aerial charts, ground maps, photos, and other target materals if available. (I used a system of taping the key materials to both thighs. On a change or diversion, I did a quick-change act with maps and charts; I also wrote coordinates, headings, notes, etc., all over the canopy, cockpit, and my uniform.) Still, regardless of techniques used, no target was attacked until it was confirmed where our troops were and that the target was the correct one a safe distance away.

At Madna, the runway started to sink into the mud. It finally sank to the point where a new base and runway was laid right on top of the old one. This was done in an unbelievably short time—with the old runway down below, never to be seen again.

The potential for a major disaster at Madna was considerable. Airplanes, bombs, munitions, gasoline, and people were all but piled on top of each other. Just the gasoline alone throughout the area could have done the place in. In addition to that used for airplanes and vehicles, every tent had a gasoline-fed stove for heat (most of them were German equipment left in the Foggia area) with a trailer or two and many spare Jerrycans of gasoline around. The kitchen also used the stuff and it was said that if a kitchen crew hasn't blown up a field stove yet—they will. (Our kitchen crews never did, that I know of.) Gasoline was also used for filling cigarette lighters (usually sticking the lighter into a jeep gas tank) and cleaning clothes, but when cleaning ODs or other heavy clothing, one had to remember not to rub them together or even stir them very much with a stick. Apparently some poor souls somewhere had done such things and static electricity set off an inferno with them in it.

Christmas came and the troops in Italy were served turkey dinners. It was even a nice day at Madna with no rain—which also meant it was no day off.

I got to go to Capri on a break with the Ops officer and another pilot. It was a welcome rest. Rumors had it that neither the Allies or Axis ever bombed Capri because they both wanted and used it for a resort. Other than being overrun with supposedly resting troops, possibly some shortages, and no way to travel internationally, I'm not sure the permanent social set living on Capri ever paid any attention to the war around them.

We returned to the squadron in about a week to learn that while we were gone a storm had hit Madna and torn down almost every tent on the place. The already-overworked ground pesonnel had to rebuild the base while keeping the airplanes going in the clear weather that followed the storm. This was cold weather, which put some ice on top of the mud.

The good weather held in January and many of our missions now went on deeper interdiction efforts—up to the main communication routes in the valleys east of Rome, and along the coast from Pescara on north. Bridges, rail lines, major roads, and enemy communication and supply facilities were the main targets. Strafing targets were plentiful—vehicles of many types, supply dumps, and even the prized targets of locomotives and trains.

I had wondered if strafing a locomotive, an object of love to me, would leave me with some remorse as had happened in earlier years when I helped cut one up with a torch. It didn't. In fact, my mind throughout each attack was solely on boring in to minimum range and really blasting the boiler with simultaneous impact of all the guns. That really "blew" one—it might even knock it off the tracks. For that reason, all else being equal, I liked coming in 90 degrees from the side on a loco. Sometimes conditions sent us in from the front or rear, and in the latter case we tried to concentrate the rounds in the cab and rear of the boiler. Of course, that's where the engineer and

A prized strafing target. (Courtesy U.S. Air Force)

A few good reasons for stopping trains. (Courtesy U.S. Air Force)

fireman were. That didn't bother me at all, either. Trains and the people who operate them are tremendous supporters of wars. Destroying trains was an important part of fighter-bomber flying and fighting.

We also attacked marshalling yards and freight cars. When strafing freight cars, the technique was a bit different. You were usually shooting at a bunch of them, whether in a yard or on a train. Starting to shoot farther out and spreading rounds throughout the cars might find a type of cargo that would start some good fires. Some pilots were not against doing a bit of sampling fire on boxcars from a good distance out—when loads of ammo in freight cars and trains explode, it's usually a much bigger bang than from a truck, and all the sky in your face might be full of fireball and parts and pieces of freight cars.

Strafing, particularly in long bursts, could lead to a small sidelight hazard—"cookoffs." A round remaining in the chamber of the barrel could heat up enough to fire itself even though all gun switches were off. Flying along on the way home, when a round fired on its own it could be a little startling until the pilot realized what had happened. Cookoffs were another good reason not to fly airplanes in trail on the way home. A round could fire even after the airplanes were on the ground and parked. Our airplanes were tailwheel types and the guns pointed up while on the ground, so a cookoff would normally sail up over men and equipment elsewhere on the field, but the armament crews and others right at the airplane always risked a cookoff until the guns were cleared of rounds in the chambers.

That could not be done in the air in most fighters. When the ammo was loaded for a mission, the guns were charged by putting a round in each chamber. From then on they were hot and stayed that way unless all the ammo was fired. An airplane in a crash or fire on or around the field could have the guns fire as well as its ammo explode. That was an extra hazard to crash crews and other rescuers. Still, uncharged guns make a fighter airplane rather useless in a war, and I knew of no units who only charged them at the takeoff runway and then uncharged them there after landing. They stayed charged.

If I had told myself I wasn't scared on missions, there are certain things that come along at times that could belie such a belief—at least momentarily. On one mission we had bombed a bridge and strafed vehicles in one of the main valleys. We came out quite low towards the sea to get out of the more intense flak (and it was now intense on any of the major routes) before climbing to altitude. As we flew along on the deck I saw an explosion on the ground just up ahead, then more explosions near the first. It dawned in a flash that we were flying right into the impact area of bombs from a friendly bomber formation up above. There were going to be many, *many* of those explosions in a second or so, and we would be right in the middle of them. As hard as a P-40 could be pulled into going both up and out, thus did we do, and I was scared pretty well there for a few seconds as I flew up through a stream of bombs coming from above. Once clear, we spotted the bombers as RAF A-20s. Perhaps that is a rather rare occurrence, but it is one more deadly possibility in a fighter-bomber pilot's war—that of being bombed from above while on a low-altitude mission.

We had flown a few escort missions for the light bombers. They bombed from around 10,000 feet, possibly a bit higher at times. The German 88s could zero in on them in a bomb run until it looked more like a blob of thick black smoke moving across the sky than a formation of airplanes. I prayed for those guys.

On one mission we made an exciting find—a sizable column of armored vehicles on a side road in the mountains in deep snow, some 18 or so, mostly tanks. At least two of our squadrons were used to pound the armor with both bombs and strafing. Some vehicles were destroyed outright; fires were started in a good percentage of the rest and the road was blown away in several places as well. The strafing involved rather treacherous flying and we did not get away without some loss.

About January 13 we received orders to move again. There wasn't really anyplace to go further north, nor any need to move up anyway. The Germans were not too far removed in that direction, and every indication was that they didn't intend to go any farther away. This move would also be conducted a bit differently than normal. A ground party would move out in advance as usual, but then the airplanes would move over a period of several days instead of all at once.

The ground party pulled out on the 15th. In the following days, some missions would go out and recover at the new destination. Some of our squadron started flying from the new base on the 18th, but the Group still flew missions from Madna up through the afternoon of the 20th, when we gave the railroad station and oil storage facilities in Populi a working over.

I was among the last of the pilots in our squadron to leave Madna. We flew a close support mission, started to head back toward Madna, but then turned westward. When we checked in at the new destination, it was with a new and different call sign than our normal one, which had been used for takeoff and during the mission. We landed on Capadichino Airdrome in Naples.

The 79th FG was involved in more than just a move; it had been transferred from control of the British Desert Air Force and out of the British Eighth Army area to assignment under the U.S. Twelfth Air Force and in the U.S. Fifth Army area. On January 21 our squadron was set, with all airplanes on Capadichino—or "Capo," as it was commonly called.

Officers were quartered in houses near the field, the men in apartments nearby. Naples had a large post exchange, theaters, and various clubs including a large and plush officers' club on a hill overlooking the town. There were also hoards of MPs directing traffic and roaming the streets checking troops for dogtags and that ties were worn properly. Naples was filthy. It was also completely overrun with GI vehicles and troops. Capo was a large grass field with high stone walls off each end and was crowded with units and airplanes.

In Naples, the Group had been descended upon by U.S. news correspondents covering this new unit in the area. In fact, they and photographers were all over the place. There may have been some special attraction to a strange outfit from the wilds of the unknown side of Italy, particularly to one that had an all-Negro squadron in its midst and three others that showed up with a little Gypsy tint in their convoys.

One of our pilots said maybe these correspondents knew more about us and our past record than we thought they did. Another said that maybe they knew why we were here in Naples on this 21st day of January, 1944—which most of us didn't.

A fighter-bomber field, east side of Italy, fall-winter, 1943-44.

Chapter 6

Anzio—Cassino, Too

That night we knew that tomorrow's efforts were not going to be normal eight-ship fighter-bomber missions. The schedule showed we would be flying in full squadron efforts of 16 ships during the day, and the airplanes were bedded down for the night with no bombs on them. At the early briefing on the morning of the 22nd, we found out why we were in Naples.

In the wee hours of that morning the Anzio invasion had been launched. The 79th Group had the task of low altitude cover over the invasion forces and beachhead—from about 6000 feet on down on the deck. The four Squadrons of the Group would keep P-40s on patrol from dawn to dusk. Other fighters, such as Spitfires, would be at higher altitudes above us.

On our first mission I led Green Flight, the tail-end Charlie crew. As we approached Anzio, the mission leader checked in with a fighter control agency on one of the ships offshore, which was operated by a Wing in our new higher headquarters structure. As we swung in from the water to take up our patrol, the sight below was one never to be forgotten. Warships of various kinds and sizes and many transports and freighters stood offshore, while waves of landing craft churned white wakes as they raced for the beaches.

However, no pilot's eye remained on the sea or beaches for more than a split-second or two; the skies above received full attention for the expected enemy air opposition to the landings. We had barely set up in a patrol pattern of two sections when there was an alerting call of "Heads up." Immediately thereafter the lead section, nearest the coast, called bandits and tore into some 20 enemy planes barreling straight down the coast. We, in the other section further inland, raced to also try to cut off the mixture of FW 190s and Me 109s. We saw a couple of airplanes go down before the Germans reached the landing beach area. The surviving bomb-carrying

An air-to-air role now. (Courtesy U.S. Air Force)

enemy fighters made a quick dive-bomb run and then raced for home.

A wild fight and chase started in the general direction of Rome, and more airplanes were seen to go down. Now the Spitfires dove from above into the chase, cutting off and passing up some P-40s in the process. The chase went on to Rome and beyond. Our squadron shot down several of the enemy, but also lost one plane and pilot. The Spitfires picked off more of the enemy.

Our first day operating as air-to-air fighter pilots over Anzio didn't stay that way for very long. In fact, it didn't last throughout this one mission. When replaced on patrol, on our way back to Naples we took a look along the Appian Way, the coastal highway from Naples to Rome. There we found and destroyed a couple of trucks and an armored vehicle.

These vehicles were headed south towards the scene of some of the heaviest and bloodiest fighting of the war. For the past several days the U.S. Fifth Army had launched strong attacks in the Rapido River area and had met fierce and determined German resistance. Thus we incorporated some fighter-bomber work into this first air patrol mission over Anzio. It would not be the last such combination mission to be flown over Anzio.

The debriefing was an unusual one for us. In the past we rarely had anyone present at a debriefing except the pilots and squadron personnel to obtain the results and handle the required reports. Today there were so many vistors and correspondents around that the pilots had trouble getting to the debriefing tent. Once the debriefing was done (claims were six enemy planes destroyed, one probable, and one damaged) the correspondents took over, obtaining the names, addresses, and next-to-kin for each pilot with an air victory. When the Intelligence Officer brought up the trucks and tank as part of the mission results, the place cleared out as if something offensive had been said. I didn't see a note taken. Obviously the news people were not very interested in trucks and tanks.

For our missions over Anzio, enemy airplanes were certainly our primary targets in the protection of the invasion fleet and beachhead. Our rules were that ammo would be used on trucks and tanks only after the primary mission was over and the ammo was being brought home unfired. In that case, as had happened today, using it on enemy ground targets instead of just lugging it home would become normal procedure.

The initial air fight set a pattern for many more to come. The enemy would see FW 190s and Me 109s together (but not always) with the FW 190s normally carrying bombs and the Me 109s escorting—but either might carry bombs and/or come in on strafing missions. Our job was to completely stop these attacks before they reached the beachhead or ships offshore, but from our patrol positions—almost on top of the target areas—once the first-line enemy fighters reached that point in a determined attack (which they were making), the odds of stopping all of them short of their target were slim indeed. The Germans could not stop the Allies in such attacks right at the target, and it was no different the other way around.

Only a couple of days following our first engagement of attacking enemy fighters, we were faced with a bit different air battle over Anzio. Some 30 enemy fighters came in, but instead of trying to avoid our fighters, they jumped a section of eight P-40s just northeast of the beachhead. This became a turning melee of a fight instead of a running or chasing fight. If the enemy pilots in either FW 190s or Me 109s tried turning with a P-40 a low altitude, the P-40 was reported to have the turn advantage. Our section leader got a 190 that way early in this fight, but the enemy had us outnumbered almost four-to-one, and the rest of the fight was not in neat little individual contests. Airplanes were all over the sky, from about 5000 feet on down to the deck, going in all directions and with heavy streamers rolling from their wingtips.

One Me 109 tried to turn with two P-40s and was losing, but the enemy pilot hiked the nose almost straight up and corkscrewed up on the inside to escape, where another P-40 was in position to run the Me 109 back down to the deck and start a turning fight all over. A few of our pilots had enemy fighters suddenly pop up in front of them, which was good. More of our pilots had enemy fighters pop up behind *them*, which was bad. Then, with both friendly and enemy formations and airplanes generally scattered over the area, six German FW 190s came straight into my element, which led to some reconcentrated action right there. Starting with a head-on shootout, the next several moments involved a very small piece of the sky, but that piece was crammed rather full of cannon shells, tracers, and streamers.

In time, other P-40s patrolling near the coast and some Spitfires got into the overall fight and it all ended up again in a shooting pursuit of the enemy to Rome and beyond. Our claims in this fight were relatively few, but we had lost no one even though there were some damaged planes. Perhaps most important of all, over 30 enemy airplanes had been tied up in the fight and kept from attacking the beachhead.

For the moment we were seeing more rounds from 20mm and other guns being fired at us by German fighters than of 88mm, 37mm, 20mm, etc. being fired at us from the ground. Usually for each round fired at fighter-bombers by enemy airplanes, thousands were fired at them from the

Damage from guns of enemy fighters.

ground. Also, usually for each round fighter-bombers fired at enemy fighters, they fired thousands at ground targets. These situations had been reversed for us—at least for the time being. Even so, we had not gotten away from the ground guns by any means. And when ground guns are mentioned, more than flak guns have to be included—pistols, rifles, machine pistols, machine guns, artillery, tank weapons, and more had all been seen firing at fighter-bombers.

Initially the Bomb Line around the beachhead had been placed out from the landing areas as expected, but it hadn't made any major movements since. It was just a loop right around the Anzio area. On the latest missions our airplanes coming back low-level from Rome after an air fight were picking up considerable flak and noting more activity on the roads. Those patrol missions over Anzio that had not been engaged in air fights and then had used their ammo on the way home for strafing were finding numerous targets. They were encountering more flak as well.

The 28th of January produced an eventful patrol mission. With a section of eight P-40s, I spotted some dozen FW 190s and eight Me 109s inbound just off the coast and headed for the ships offshore. We went after and closed on the bomb-carrying FW 190s as other patrol airplanes took on the Me 109s. That was at about the point the naval forces down below—both American and British—cut loose with antiaircraft fire on the enemy planes. We knew they would, and there was certainly no doubt that they should, but we were getting into position to do some real damage to the FW 190s. I decided to keep going and stick on the FW 190s, and they—and we—went right on into the antiaircraft fire of the ships.

It was thick and all around us. The heavy bursts were bigger but did not seem as bright a fireball as the German 88s, and they left a large, nasty-

Awfully close to the wrong place.

67

looking brownish smoke glob instead of the oily black of an 88. I guessed those bursts were from guns of 90mm size, maybe larger, but on ships they were probably classed in inches. When the FW 190s went into their dive-bomb run, we went down with them into a sky solid with smaller, whiter bursts of antiaircraft fire. I guessed that was our automatic stuff, 40mm and 20mm on ships. The whole mixture wasn't too different from German flak but it was thick and intense over these ships. I had some second thoughts about my decision to fly into Allied antiaircraft fire, but one thing looked promising: If the FWs made it out of the Navy fire, they were not all going to get away. We made it out and they didn't all get away by any means. On their attempts to withdraw, both the FW 190s and Me 109s were swarmed over by Allied fighters.

Air fights continued over Anzio on a regular basis and victories came fairly regularly. On one day the 79th FG downed 12 enemy airplanes. On another, 21 enemy aircraft were reported downed over the beachhead. On some days, such as the 10th of February, the patrols and air fights were under low overcasts in freezing rain and snow flurries. Rarely in a major fight did our units get by without losses too, but they were far below those of the enemy.

The overlap of Spitfires and P-40s in the air fights was a common occurrence and called for considerable alertness by both to keep from inadvertently spraying the wrong kind of airplane with gunfire. Also, the act of flying into friendly Navy antiaircraft fire was not a standard practice or procedure, but some other mission leaders also apparently pressed on into some antiaircraft fire at times when it seemed warranted. Frequently the weather forced all patrol aircraft down to where dodging each other was part of the task at hand.

By this point, not only had the Bomb Line not moved on inland, it was squeezed back around an ever-so-small perimeter of beachhead. The American and British troops therein were under tremendous pressure by the massed and strongly attacking German opposition. While the German forces held strong in the winter lines across Italy, blocking any linkup from there, those surrounding the Anzio beachhead were making a determined effort to eliminate it. Heavy fighting went on around Aprilia and "The Factory" in February, during the strong German attack of 16th-19th, and again with another in March. There was an everyday pounding of the beachhead with artillery and mortars.

While the air patrols continued of necessity, the demand for air support of the beachhead and attack of enemy ground targets was also great. Some of our missions did triple duty. We carried bombs to Anzio and bombed enemy positions, then augmented the air patrol, and if there was ammo remaining afterwards, strafed enemy targets. Some pilots called these "three-in-one" missions.

A particularly strong effort was made against ground targets on a number of days such as the 13th, 16th through 20th of February, and on into March. Our targets included tanks, many gun positions, and enemy troops.

Back on regular ground attack operations, too, against some tough targets such as this. (Courtesy U.S. Air Force)

On these key ground attack days, if the Group also downed a few enemy aircraft (and one or two were on such days), now the enemy aircraft were probably considered secondary in the total results by most personnel. Yet I didn't see any change in the newspeople back at Capo, who still took their notes on enemy airplanes and not much of anything else. Notes or no notes, our unit had several very successful missions on enemy armor and gun positions on critical days of the ground fighting—one in particular against tanks, which were advancing in the open right toward the perimeter of the beachhead.

A small emergency landing strip had been placed within the beachhead at Nettuno (adjacent to Anzio) and it received much use as damaged airplanes that could not make it back to Naples went in for landings there. Unfortunately, not all these landings were successful and some lives were lost in crashes. Spitfires and others flew some operations from there.

The very heavy fighting made our low-altitude patrols more of ordeals than one might expect of a normal air patrol. For one thing, it was impractical to stay solely over the small beachhead, and some of the patrolling was over heavily defended enemy territory, so we were subject most of the time to enemy flak and other fire. (We had one P-40 explode from a direct 88mm hit.) Also, a few Me 109s had come in on the deck strafing. For that reason, when under low overcasts we had some airplanes patrolling at quite low altitudes—low enough to be in the line of fire of incoming and outgoing artillery and mortar shells. The wing of one airplane was knocked off and it crashed before the pilot could get out.

The 79th Group's flying was not restricted to Anzio. We also flew considerable support for the U.S. Fifth Army in the lines above Naples, in the Cassino area, and for the British Eighth Army on to the east. We were in on the bombing of the Abbey of Monte Cassino atop Monastery Hill. From a vertical dive, on pullout I saw my 1000-pound bomb go directly into what remained of the Abbey. Perhaps I would have liked to see it miss, but it didn't and it was only one of many from fighter-bombers, medium bombers, and heavy bombers. We were back to the Cassino area numerous times in following days in support of the heavy fighting there. We would also be there in the subsequent all-out bombing effort to obliterate the place.

The 79th retained ground parties and some equipment back at Madna for a month or so, and we assumed that the Anzio beachhead operation had not been expected to last very long and that we would return to Madna after only a short stay in Naples. There were also rumors that we would go to the China-Burma-India (CBI) theater once Anzio was secure. Neither one came to be. In fact, the ground parties finally moved over from Madna and we stayed at Naples.

We were in a different situation regarding counterpart fighter units in the area. Pilots in squadrons were hardly experts on force structure and order of battle of units, but through daily operations, classmates in other outfits, and news, one could keep up with who else was around. In certain cases contacts were fairly close between units and their pilots—exchanging visits, comparing tactics, etc. In other cases there was little or no direct association. So far, while overseas, about the only other American fighter units I had any contact with were the 57th and 324th Fighter Groups.

Now one could quickly add many more in this area and/or as part of past Twelfth Air Force's operations. My own mental list included the 27th and 86th Fighter-Bomber Groups, and the 31st, 33rd, 52nd, 81st, 332nd, 325th, and 350th Fighter Groups involved in various phases of tactical operations. However, certain of these groups, which had been key elements of P-40 tatical work in Africa and on, apparently had or were headed for the primary roles by transfer to the Fifteenth Air Force and strategic operations or to other theaters of war.

In March, the 79th FG celebrated the completion of one full year in combat. Also Vesuvius, sitting just south of Capo, the volcano that covered Pompeii in an eruption centuries ago, blew its to in another mighty eruption, and we had a ringside view of some awesome and majestic fireworks. the eruption also dumped rock an ash on at least one airfield in the area, destroying almost all of a field full of B-25s. The spectacle of Vesuvius would last many days.

Naples had other fireworks, too. Night bombing raids were not infrequent. Some pilots initially went up on the roof to watch the searchlights, tracers, flares, shellbursts, and now and then a flaming, falling enemy bomber. However, a shower or two of shrapnel raining down around them broke up that pastime. Those who rode out air raids in the club learned to grab their drinks off the bar before the concussion of the big antiaircraft guns firing from an adjacent playground shook them off.

Then, for those who witnessed it from the airfield, came an unexpected and perhaps unreal-seeming display. Axis Sally had singled our unit out for some special treatment in her broadcasts. We were accused of gangster-like and butcherous ways in the air fights over Anzio, shooting already

B-25 medium bomber.

damaged and helpless German planes out of the sky. According to her, the Luftwaffe had some retaliatory plans for us. Whether by coincidence or design, such retaliation came to be—in the form of FW190s strafing Capo at night, using either their landing lights or some rigged for the purpose. It was an effort by a sizable force and resulted in considerable damage. They did, however, inflict most of it on organizations adjacent to us, rather than on the so-called gangsters—but we didn't get off scot-free.

While strongly repulsed at the losses caused, I think most fighter-bomber pilots would have some respect for the efforts of the enemy pilots in such an attack. Even though Vesuvius' fireworks probably helped light up the sky, it was still a considerable feat of combat flying. I, for one, wondered if our commanders might take a clue from this operation and send us out at night to do the same kind of strafing. They didn't.

And as for our alleged gangster-like ways, it is very likely that some of the German planes shot down over Anzio had been damaged by Allied antiaircraft fire before they were hit by our planes, but they were still fighting or heading for home. If they were in dire trouble, they should have bailed out. I knew of no case, report, or even *rumor* of pilots (either Allied *or* German) ever shooting at an enemy pilot in a parachute. And there were numerous pilots seen in parachutes in the midst of these air fights.

The air flights over Anzio slacked off some in mid-to-late February, then came back strong again in March. The weather both over Anzio and around the field were problems quite often. Heavy rainstorms or squalls often had us picking and groping our way under and around them. The Naples area was hilly and rugged terrain for such attempts at threading through and sneaking around the heavy weather. A "sucker hole" could lead to a trap and into a hard rock center in a cloud. To get home, some missions worked their way down over the water off the coast, past Capri, and then in from the south all the way around Vesuvius in order to reach the field over more level terrain.

On one eight-ship mission (now being used instead of 16 for many patrols) I was flying the Number Four spot in the second flight as some new leaders were being broken in. We had spent the patrol over Anzio weaving among showers, and on our return to the Naples area, found ourselves flat trapped out of the field by solid walls of downpours. The young leader tried going in north of the field and south of it with no success. Low on fuel, we were flying off the coast of Naples Harbor searching for any kind of break or light spot that would let us get to the field. Suddenly there was one—we could look under the low roll clouds laying across the crowded harbor and see an open spot on the hill above Naples toward the airfield. I was about to suggest a decision when the young leader made it on his own. Right through Naples Harbor, on-the-deck, just clearing ships, went eight P-40s. Then we went up over the buildings of Naples and on up the hill to quickly slow up, drop the gear and flaps, and all eight airplanes set down together on the big grass field.

Just one more mission completed for these eight pilots? Hardly. Naples Harbor had one of the thickest concentrations of barrage balloons in the war. We had known as we headed across the harbor for the field that we were flying right through those balloons and their cables—which were there to stop low-flying enemy airplanes.

The weather over Anzio helped produce a few special experiences in some of the air fights. One pilot reportedly came out of a cloud and instead of one wingman with him, there were two—the extra one was an ME 109. In the split second or less that it took to start breaking up *that* formation, the fellow apparently had enough time to etch a lasting picture of the Messerschmitt in his mind—one of a very clean, sharp-looking airplane with a mottled green top and light blue underside, with a small painting of a cat on the nose.

My squadron was now in another changeover in pilots. Pilots who had come in around the time I did were reaching 80 missions. Some of them were rotating back to the States; others had chosen to stay longer. A considerable number of them were not present—their tours had ended with entries on their records of Killed in Action, Missing in Action, and POW. Among those pilots going home, the combat missions had left their marks on some. While most pilots remained free of the condition of "battle fatigue"—or, as some pilots called it, "flak happy"—a few of those going home were frank in their admissions that they had existed in fear, and on their latter missions had been all but petrified with it. Yet they went on and flew them and did their jobs—brave men.

We had seen only one total human casualty or failure from the stress of combat flying. One pilot, after some 20 missions, apparently snapped. He was noted to have been playing solitaire one night in the club. The next morning he was still at it, and when asked by friends if he was okay, he seemed to have no idea who they were or where he was. The flight surgeon and CO took over from there and we never saw him again.

I counted missions and knew just how many I had, but I did not count them against any goal; I flew them in turn and didn't really look past the next one coming up. When I flew number 80, the CO didn't say anything, nor did

I. My name came out on the schedule for the next one as usual. It was a foregone conclusion I would stay, as it was with the others who flew on past a normal tour—as was now tradition in this unit. Those who flew on beyond a tour might have been viewed as nuts, war lovers, glory and promotion seekers, or as lacking in some manner by certain of the other pilots, but in the 79th FG there were enough staying that they may have had better claim to being the norm than those who questioned their decision.

Also, they were the mission leaders and it was known that the 80-mission tour would not apply in the future anyway. Replacement pilots from now on would fly 100 missions. In the 79th they would be led by 100 or more mission fliers as well.

At Capo the 79th transitioned from P-40s to P-47s. That was done without standing down and without loss of combat sorties. Two quadrons changed at a time. My squadron (87th) and the 99th were the last in our group to change, as an apparent mass switch from P-40s to P-47s for U.S. units in Italy were underway. The British and others would fly P-40s on through the war here.

When our time came to change, we operated for a while with two sets of airplanes. The P-40s were flown on combat while both the ground crews and pilots were being trained and checked out in the P-47. The P-47 Thunderbolts looked huge and bulky sitting among the P-40s, but they

Both P-40s and P-47s in our unit, Vesuvius still smolders in the background.

73

provided a substantial increase in capability over the gallant old Warhawks in all areas of performance: speed, altitude, and radius of action. Also, the P-47 had eight guns and a 2500-pound bomb or munitions load. In general figures, for the models and series involved, level speeds went up from around 350 for the P-40 to 430 for the P-47. Fighter-bomber missions could vary greatly in load, external tanks, etc. However, based on these models and series with no tanks and a normal munition load for each, if the P-40 could make a radius of around 150 miles, the P-47 could do about 250 miles carrying its greater load. Both could go considerably farther in other configurations and/or with external tanks.

The P-47 had an air-cooled radial engine vs. the liquid-cooled inline engine of the P-40. Hits anywhere in the cooling system of the latter—radiator, lines, etc.—could result in engine failure and in turn put a pilot down in enemy territory. That problem did not exist with the P-47. (Yet experience in the P-40 had not shown its cooling system to be a major problem or concern of pilots in combat.) One thing the big radial engine of the P-47 *did* do was to put a larger frontal area of engine, plus self-sealing fuel tank, between the pilot and enemy guns from ahead and below. Our initial Thunderbolts were early-version P-47Ds in time to be known as "Razorbacks."

I was one of the few pilots in the unit who had flown the P-47 in the States, but I was not assigned the task of training or instructing pilots. Instead, I was given a P-47 to take out and evaluate tactics for it. From that, and discussions with other pilots and units flying the P-47, a few things were changed. We abandoned the vertical dive bombing from altitudes of 6000 feet and under in favor of 60-degree dives from that altitude or above, and dive angles of about 45 degrees for rail and road targets. The P-47 could be considered a "musher"—it could mush or sink on down lower on pullouts than the pilot might expect, so pullout altitudes were raised for it over the P-40. Yet to put all eight guns of the P-47 on a target, the pilot still had to get just about as close to the target as in a P-40. He simply had to be ever alert

A "Razorback" P-47; most of ours had OD paint but a few did not. Group identifying numbers are shown on this airplane; many units used letters instead.

on strafing passes and low level flying in the P-47. For air-to-air work little change was considered, but most pilots were anticipating the use of both the speed and eight guns in any future running, chasing fights over Anzio.

On one of my training and evaluation flights in a P-47 over Naples, I almost managed to intercept a high-flying German reconnaissance airplane, which was leaving a beautiful vapor trail from twin engines—probably a Junkers or twin-engine Messerschmitt. I couldn't *quite* get up to it in time. There was some bar discussion that night as to whether this would have been a combat mission and sortie if I had shot the enemy plane down. On normal missions our rules specified one had to go into emeny territory, plus complete the mission and/or participate in combat there in order to earn a combat mission or sortie. A pilot did not get a mission just because he crossed the Bomb Line and then found it necessary to abort. Technically, under those rules, I guess one wasn't eligible over Naples while on a non-combat flight, even if he shot down an enemy airplane. However, I suspect some other rules would have applied if an enemy airplane went down.

There were firm and unbending rules on the awarding of medals in our tactical air forces in Italy, which were quite different than in some other theaters. No medals were given solely on the basis of completing a set number of missions or completion of a tour. Every Air Medal and all others above that award had to be based on a specific act in combat or in connection therewith. In theory, a pilot could fly 100 missions—or even 200—and not receive a single Air Medal or any other combat medal. Units had to write up and submit each act, and the appropriate higher headquarters had to approve each one.

I seldom went anywhere in Naples, except to get a shower at a central shower unit or once in a while go to the PX. I did not like the place. That had nothing to do with Naples itself, and certainly not the Italian people. It might be said that the Army was its own worst enemy in Naples. If things were not bad, rear area headquarters had a knack for making them so.

We sometimes found a few off-duty diversions that did not involve Naples. Some pilots went up near the lines where they could see something of what it was like close to the front, possibly to take photos of destroyed enemy equipment and perhaps pick up a few souvenirs. A couple of us went over to an adjacent airfield where a higher headquarters kept a few old war-weary Spitfires for pilots there to get flying time. We just walked up and asked if we could fly them. Apparently the decision went no higher than the crew chiefs of the Spits. With their help in starting the engines (plus pointing out that the brakes were operated by a paddle switch on the stick, which incidentally wasn't a stick anyway since it had a ring grip at the top and was hinged for aileron control), we had a ball flying the very maneuverable little machines. We even pounced on some of our pilots who were on training flights in P-47s. These were no contest in a turning fight; the Spits could really turn and the P-47 pilots apparently learned pretty fast that in a play fight with early model Spits, perhaps the best tactic was to back off and

Remains of an Me 109 in a field north of Naples.

make passes trying to run over or fly into the Spitfires. (There was one tale around of a P-47 pilot who spotted a small German liaison or spotter plane—probably a Fiesler Storch—and almost flew into the ground several times trying to shoot the little enemy plane as it flicked and dodged around in the treetops. If the tale is true, that P-47 pilot also tried to run it down as well as shoot it down. And, if the tale is true, he finally shot it down.)

When our CO concluded the squadron was ready in the P-47 (which was only a matter of days after receiving them), the next missions went out in P-47s and the P-40s were pushed over into a corner of the field to become mere relics of the war past. However, six of them were retained in their own little area on our flight line.

Our first missions in the P-47 included the regular patrols over Anzio and air support there and in the Cassino area.

Along with all other units in the Twelfth Air Force, we were deeply involved in Operation Strangle, an extensive effort to completely interdict the supply and support to all German combat forces in Italy—both the German Tenth Army in the lines across Italy and the German Fourteenth Army around the Anzio beachhead. Our ground forces had been held almost totally in stalemate since January.

Strangle involved working well north of Rome and all across Italy, cutting every bridge, rail, and road system and keeping them cut. It also involved destroying anything on rails or roads and keeping traffic at a standstill. Medium bombers (B-25s and B-26s) and light bombers were a major part of the effort on a variety of targets such as bridges, supply dumps, key junctions, etc.

Our operations in the P-47 during Strangle were highly varied. We still patrolled Anzio and provided air support there and in the lines. We had missions of rail and road cuts well north, combining that bombing with armed-recce afterwards. We also had closer interdiction targets such as in the Lire Valley between Cassino and Rome. And we now frequently escorted medium bombers on their interdiction missions. The Luftwaffe stayed active both over Anzio and against the Strangle operations.

The medium bombers made their bomb runs at altitudes of about 12,000 feet. They flew against some heavily defended targets, and did some outstanding bombing. They took tremendous and deadly fire from 88s on many of these. One of the worst scenes of the war for me came during an escort of B-25s on a target well up into the central part of Italy. On the bomb run, in steady formation and receiving heavy flak, one or more airplanes in the interior of the formation exploded in a big ball of fire. I don't know if it was two or three or more airplanes that became tangled in the fireball and explosions, but as falling pieces and parts of airplanes went down, only a few parachutes popped open. If one ever pulled and prayed for more chutes to show, it was done then, but no more were seen.

On some of our deeper interdiction missions we were jumped by enemy fighters. Now, on these missions, as opposed to the air fights over Anzio, we were back to our normal situation of fighter-bomber air fights. First of all, we normally started from the disadvantage of being the jumpees. Also, we were usually carrying bombs, such as a 1000-pounder under each wing and perhaps a tank on the belly.

If these bombs were jettisoned immediately on sighting the bandits, the enemy could succeed in two things at once: They negated our bombing mission, and they could run and probably get away scot-free and not risk the loss of airplanes if they chose. As a result, many such attacks were initially coped with while keeping the bombs on our airplanes—attacks such as feints or quick hit-and-run efforts—after which we could go on and complete the bombing mission. On the other hand, if the enemy came in on a persistant attack and/or left themselves open for us to get to them in force,

A strong effort on interdiction targets. (Courtesy U.S. Air Force).

then the air fight normally became the main effort and the bombs would probably be jettisoned. However, some pretty good air fights were conducted by fighter-bombers *with bombs on the airplanes*—and the bombing mission completed, too.

On one mission, with bombs aboard, we came out of some rather heavy clouds into a big circular clear hole in the weather. Out of the clouds on the other side came some 16 enemy fighters. Instantly the scene looked like one of swarming bees, but then just as quickly changed to one of bees milling around when the enemy went back into the clouds and the P-47s started to regroup. I think after that incident it would be safe to say that certain fighter-bomber pilots fought enemy airplanes without taking the time to do anything about their bombs.

We flew some missions to block tunnels, usually on rail lines. This job consisted of trying to throw 1000-pounders, with delayed fuzing, into the mouths of the tunnels. Since tunnels are never found in good, flat terrain—in fact, a pretty good hunk of mountain on top of them is the only reason they are there—flying down a set of tracks as low as it is possible to get into the face of a mountain may be among the most demanding of fighter-bomber missions. Some pilots said these were "guts" missions. Many bombs were effectively put into tunnels in Italy in that manner, but if a pilot missed the small opening—and some did miss—as the airplane was being yanked up to clear the mountain, the bomb sometimes hit a glancing blow on the face of the mountain and then *passed the airplane* on its way up. Also, the thought of a bomb (even if fuzed to go off tomorrow) smashing head-on at several miles an hour into solid rock right under the airplane was not a fully reassuring one. Fuze or no fuze, one would think it *might* still explode—but we never had one do so.

Then, too, we worked in the Alban Hills just south of Rome, looking for the huge railway guns that were shelling Anzio regularly and trying to find likely hiding places for them in tunnels or caves. Reportedly these were 280mm guns, known to our troops in the beachhead as Anzio Annie and the Anzio Express. Someone said the Germans gave those huge guns names like Leopold and Robert.

When I flew my 100th mission, there was a discussion with both my CO and higher headquarters. They did most of the talking, which went something like, "If you feel like flying more, we would like you to stay." I wrote my wife, and so did the commander of a higher headquarters. I knew what I said—"I plan to stay." I knew what her answer to me would be—in effect, "I don't like it, but I understand." I never knew what the higher commander told her, or what she said in her answer to him. He told me everything was okay back there. He didn't give me any equal assurance that it was all going to be okay over *here*.

I was given a few days rest in Capri again. I went with our intelligence officer, who spoke several languages fluently, and 2nd Lt. Raymond A. Ermis, a pilot who was rather badly crippled from injuries received in a plane crash, but who was determined to get back on flying and finish his tour. His was an amazing case. He looked like he should have been in therapy back in the States, but he had been allowed to stay and try to fly combat again—and he did.

When I got back from Capri, I continued flying. Each mission on the schedule might be one of a dozen or more different kinds. We were going into the Lire Valley on many of them. There, behind the stalemated lines, flak had built up to awesome proportions, and the Lire Valley had become one of the most notorious "flak alleys" of the war.

In late April our veteran Group CO returned to the States. The new Group CO flew two of his first sorties on missions I led. One was in support of Anzio; the other was one of the unpopular Lire Valley jobs. With the change of Group COs I began thinking that perhaps this was an appropriate time for me to call it quits.

I had 115 missions, and was seriously considering the submission of a request to rotate to the States, when the Squadron CO came along with some unexpected news. The Commanding General of the U.S Army Air Forces, MTO, Lt. Gen. Ira C. Eaker, had instituted a trial program of a whole new concept of combat crew rotation. With approval of their COs, pilots and combat crews who had completed tours could volunteer to go to the States for 30 days at home, then return to the very same job in the very same squadron. This program could be an alternative to a permanent rotation for reassignment in the States.

Higher headquarters were taking names of volunteers for the first 30-day leaves at home. Our CO was planning to go and could put two more pilots on the list. My name was entered in one of those slots.

I flew one more mission. Those few P-40s still on our flight line were there for a reason. We flew them in and out of the Nettuno strip on the Anzio beachhead, carrying dispatches and mail. I flew one of these still-yet different missions for a fighter-bomber pilot in my old airplane, No. 99. With the small baggage compartment full of sacks and a couple of pouches in the cockpit, I left Naples for Nettuno. Coming in low over the water, a turn was made over the beach to set down quickly on the PSP strip. The plane was kept moving pretty good until braking at the far end and whipping the P-40 around to head back into the opposite direction. Men ran from positions alongside the strip with sacks and pouches. I threw the ones out of the cockpit and caught the ones thrown to me. A similar swap was underway in the baggage compartment. By the time the ground troops were clearing the wheels and tail on their way back off the runway, the engine was up to full power and the airplane was rolling. The strip was a rough and much-patched little piece of PSP. I took off and made an immediate turn out to sea on-the-deck. The reason these were counted as combat missions was that some pilots had drawn considerable fire on their trips into Nettuno.

By comparison with that few minutes on the ground at Anzio, one could only try to grasp a feeling of the ordeal for those who stayed there day after day and night after night. Perhaps that really sank in during the landing and takeoff at Nettuno, as the wingtip of the P-40 was not very far removed from the tents just inland of the strip — the many tents of the Army hospital on Anzio.

The year was now moving into May and we had been flying in support of the Anzio beachhead since January.

A sendoff party in the club stressed an atmosphere of "see you soon" rather than "goodby," but even so I found myself thinking in terms of more than just signing out to go on another R & R. I felt there was something of a farewell involved — at least to a part of a war. Before departing I took another snapshot photo of the face of the bar. The names of pilots listed there, from original combat to newest replacement — Owens, Rice, Bozzi, Joh, Peterman, Dean, Simmons, Bell, Vaccaro, and many, many more — compiled the best record of any I knew from which to remember service to date with the 79th FG in war.

While P-40s, P-47s, P-38s, P-51s and A-36s have all been mentioned in varying degrees in connection with tactical air, fighter-bomber and strafing missions, it should be further noted that American-flown Spitfires and P-39s/ P-400s were also involved from the earliest days of Northwest Africa on up through Southern Italy.

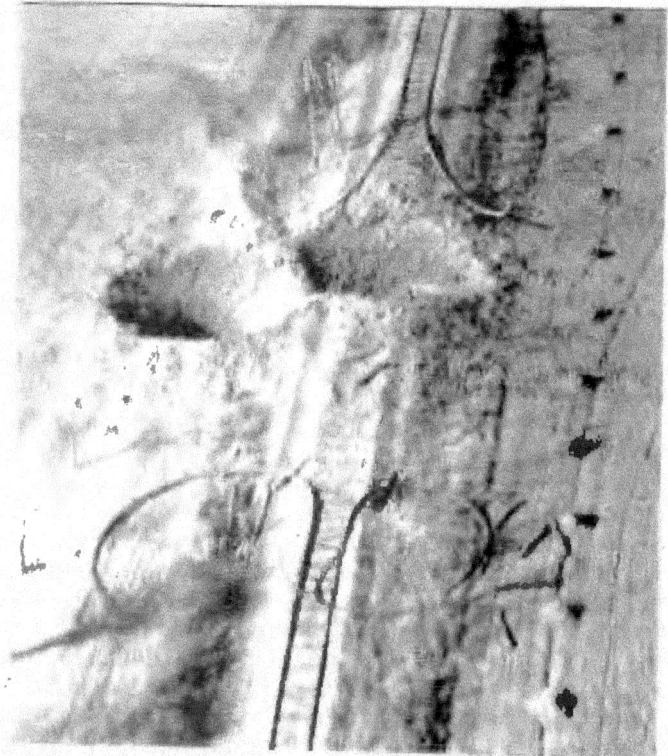

Classic P-47 "rail cut," Operation Strangle (courtesy 79th Ftr Group, WW II)

Chapter 7

Break from War

I had a set of orders sending me on detached service for a period of 30 days, exclusive of travel time. Like all overseas orders they were "restricted" as to when, where, number of personnel, etc. Each of us listed in the orders had an unclassified personal letter from the CG, USAAF, MTO, subject: "Return to the United States for Rest," which explained both where and why we were going.

We departed for the States by troopship in early May. The ship was a big sort of top heavy and tubby-looking vessel, even though such ships reportedly were built as fast troopships. It would not operate in a convoy but cross alone, relying on its speed and frequent course changes to counter enemy threats.

Once on board, rumors that these ships had been designed to carry a maximum number of troops in a minimum amount of space proved to be well-founded.

As a First Lieutenant (and it was often said that rank among lieutenants is about like virtue among prostitutes), I was just another lieutenant bunked in the lower bowels of the ship. The bunks were stacked so close vertically that most people could not turn over in one—it was necessary to get out, turn over, and then get back in. Once the ship was loaded, it was noted with some relief that all personnel were single-bunked—one troop per bunk. On many crossings going overseas apparently the troops were double-bunked—while half the troops on board used the bunks, the other half rode on deck, then they swapped off enmass for the next shift in the bunks.

There was a designated "officer's club" on an upper deck which had nothing in it except some built-in benches for seats and a few butt cans. There were certain authorized deck areas, and quite a few of us spent the first days at sea anywhere we could up topside. Poker games and bull sessions served as a pastime, but if one went to the latrines (or "heads") several times a day and ate the two meals served each day, he had a pretty full day of troopship life. One other thing that could be depended upon was frequent rumors of sub sightings and even torpedo firings that had just missed. The odds were probably in favor of some of those rumors being true.

If there was any satisfying aspect of this troopship operation, it was that the many wounded onboard, both walking and otherwise, returning to the U. S. were given the best the ship had to offer in order to make them as comfortable as possible.

As the coast of Virginia appeared on the horizon, the entire troopship experience seemed to start fading in importance. As the ship steamed into the mouth of the Chesapeake Bay, I doubt if a single mind on board was even remotely concerned with any woes of the crossing. Mine was on two things: One, I was back in the States, which I never really thought I ever would be again. Two, I was living the expectation of being together with my wife again instead of just dreaming about the possibilities of doing so.

At Newport News, the combat crews on 30-day leaves to the U.S. started getting some special treatment. Instead of going through a replacement center or "repple-depple" routine, we immediately boarded a train. It took us to the USAAF's Redistribution Center in Atlantic City, New Jersey, where we were quartered in a civilian hotel.

On arrival to Atlantic City, a message from Italy was waiting that quoted the authority for my promotion to captain, effective several days back. A promotion party here was a bit more expensive than overseas, but I think it was more enjoyable than if it had been held over there.

In a few days we received further orders, train tickets, and some special instructions and authority. The orders attached us to USAAF fields near each returnee's home; the tickets and special authority sent us home (or to desired leave destination) instead of to those airfields. I caught the crack Champion or "streamliner" train going south.

As the train, which did not go through my hometown, pulled to a stop at a very small town nearby, my wife and several members of the family were waiting. I guess that only each individual serviceman returning from war will ever know just what that moment means to him and how he feels about it. I'm sure there is no need or purpose to be served in trying to tell anyone else.

In a small convoy of cars we headed for home. I was perfectly content to just sit quietly alongside my wife and ride, but everybody was chit-chatting about the local scene, from the familiar pine trees outside to the dogs left at home (one was in the greeting party). I had a heck of a time getting any real information on my brothers and my wife's brother as to where they were and what they were doing. Eventually I determined that my older brother was in the Army, where he served in action with a cavalry division in the Phillipines during the war. My younger brother was a radio operator in the Merchant Marine, where he served in action on North Atlantic and Arctic runs to Murmansk and Archangel in Russia. My wife's brother was with an air unit in the Marines and served in combat in the Pacific. Of the young in the family, only my sister, still in high school, stayed at home.

Most families here had sent similar representation to the war—usually everyone in the family who was of fighting age.

As regards the steady chit-chat and reluctance to talk about the family's service activities, I was aware that one could buy little books on how to go about meeting and greeting servicemen returning from combat. Among other advice in them was to allow no extended periods of silence in conversations and not to talk about the war. I was probably one of the few people in the world who actually believed that silence is golden, and I did not know anything of a current nature to talk about *except* the war, but there could be nothing but even more love felt for their efforts to abide by the little book, and I vowed to not mess things up by letting on that I knew about it.

As we drove along I only listened and asked a few questions about local matters and the other dogs. We arrived home at a very nice apartment made available to us by my wife's aunt and uncle, and from then on this was *our* leave in a war, not *my* leave at home.

There were some terrible jokes to be heard about married servicemen returning from the war. One claimed that on reunion with a wife, invariably the *second* act performed was to set down the B-4 or duffle bag. Another theorized how far behind a serviceman could get in the months or years overseas and how quickly he could catch up once at home. But most people didn't talk at all about their own case.

In a few days, even though transportation was available for anywhere we wanted to go, we decided a little more independence would be nice. We bought a 1941 Plymouth convertible, and finally got it on the road after numerous hassles about tires, gasoline, and paperwork. With the car, we interspersed stays in town with short trips here and there. We went to the beach for several days and had a wonderful time, much like days of old—and not the least bit set back that the beaches were now heavily patrolled by the Coast Guard with dogs, nor reports that the food on a German sub captured just offshore had been purchased in a local market.

The local airfield was now a P-40 RTU. Our unit overseas had received a few pilots from here. From what I could tell from them and a visit or two to the base, RTUs were more standardized now. The trainees were apparently getting a bit more flying time, but with little realistic combat training. One reason for that was that many RTUs in the States were now using Grade 91 fuel, while overseas we used the much higher octane Grade 100. The airplanes in the RTU could not be operated at the same power settings as those overseas. For example, in a P-47 the stated normal takeoff power limits in the Pilot Training Manual were: Grade 91—40" Hg., 2700 rpm for not over 1½ minutes; Grade 100—52" Hg., 2700 rpm for not over 15 minutes.

I had heard few gripes anywhere over the fact that RTUs such as this one trained pilots in the P-40 and then sent them overseas to fly P-47s or other fighters. More gripes had been heard in overseas fighter-bomber units about the RTUs not really doing any high-G, treetop, low-level training—the way fighter-bombers flew on many missions. One would have to assume that such flying, even without being shot at, had been considered an unnecessary risk for the pilots in fighter training. That may be quite valid. Pilots in the war didn't practice parachute jumps.

Normally, one would think of fighter aces becoming such only in combat. A pilot at the local airfield officers' club bar indicated they had a potential ace in the making here on the field—if he wrecked one more U.S. airplane, that would make five, and he would qualify as a German ace.

There were many Germans on the base, a fairly large group of POWs. Some people thought they were being treated awfully well, and may have had more freedom on work details than might be expected. From what I saw of them, I guess they were treated well, but rather than complain about it, I'd have rather seen one hell of a lot *more* of them here getting such treatment.

While I was home some monumental events took place in the war. In Italy the Allies broke out of Anzio and the lines at Cassino and all across Italy. Rome fell and the Allies pushed on northward. Also, on June 6, the enormous Allied invasion went ashore in Normandy, opening the long-awaited second front on the continent. While the war had many D-Days, this was the one that would become known as "the" D-Day. Shortly thereafter the Germans unleashed the V-weapon attacks on England. First came the V-1 buzz bombs and many people probably wondered more than ever if Germany would succeed in introducing the so-often-talked-about "secret" or "super" weapon that would swing the tide of victory over to the enemy—a threat Allied troops faced throughout most of the war. The enemy could still win it.

On a wall in town was proudly displayed a lengthy list of men and women from this community who were in service. With it was a special list honoring those who had made the supreme sacrifice—those killed in action and those who died in service. It was not a short list. One could only wonder how many more names would be on it before this gigantic struggle was over—if it was ever going to end.

During the leave, I took part in War Bond rallies, made speeches at civic clubs and schools, and was on the radio and in newspapers more than I probably would have chosen to be. Yet the Anzio actions had drawn considerable attention, as had the number of missions I had flown. Added to this was the fact that I was going back overseas instead of being reassigned here in the States. I was extremely proud and honored to make each appearance.

The "going back" part had become a problem in a number of ways—a few of them probably stemmed from within myself. The leave seemed too short. I was not sure the decision to come home on leave was a good one, but it was a commitment and one under orders. There could be no backing out, and thus that part of the problem just had to be faced. It was much harder to face the other part—that of its effect on loved ones.

My talks, explanations, and pleas about going back would still not change two positions in the minds of some of my family members. One, if there really was such a leave program, why were just a few in it, while all the rest came home for duty in the States? Two, the answer to that question (of this being a voluntary program, which I had chosen to join) didn't sit too well, and could probably lead nowhere but downhill from there because of further emphasis on my deliberate choice to stay away. It didn't help that the officers at the local base knew nothing about such a program, as some of them had said informally to family members and friends. But, in the end, I guess my family members and I were still loved ones as I said goodbye again.

Perhaps my wife and I did much better over it. Both of us realized the hurt to her through the knowledge of both herself and friends that it would have been possible for me to come home and stay on regular rotation. Yet she could recognize it wasn't possible to change things now. She also knew that I might not have been here at all except for the leave program, and we certainly were happy and grateful for this time together. Then too, the whole issue really went back to a decision in December of 1941 rather than one in the spring of 1944. We had agreed to, and been glad of, our marriage in the face of that original decision; we could and would face this one together. Therefore, our last days and hours together were not botched up by arguing over something already done.

There was only my wife and one of her close girlfriends making up my sendoff party as we stood alongside the tracks when the train pulled to a stop. I tried to muster a smile and put on the air of a confident fighter pilot for them and a few others who were meeting the train. If the act was successful, any fool standing nearby would have recognized it as a put-on to cover more sincere emotions. Captains with combat ribbons on their uniforms didn't want to cry in public.

All of us returning from the special leave gathered in Atlantic City again for a few days before moving on to a port. Among those on leave from my squadron of assignment (the CO, Maj. George T. Lee, one other flight leader, Capt. John Beck, and myself) not much was said in attempts to compete in bar tales of adventures and exploits while in the States. All three of us had been deeply moved and honored over the hero's welcome accorded Major Lee in his hometown for his long, outstanding service and extensive combat flying while overseas. Captain Beck and I had experienced an equal reception in heart and spirit by the people at home, if on a lesser scale and less organized basis.

All had not gone well for many while on leave. A good number of participants were full ready or at least willing to go on with the program as planned, but apparently a substantial number had either had changes of heart or had encountered major problems among loved ones at home about going back. One could suspect that the result in certain cases had been the exact opposite of that desired—instead of the respite from war being a happy reunion with loved ones, and a full-hearted, eager crewman returning to combat, the leave had resulted in unhappiness with near, if not actual, disunion with loved ones, and a disheartened, doubtful crewman returning to combat.

Obviously a substantial number of reports of problems reached Washington from either families or participants. When we arrived at Patrick Henry near Newport News, Virginia, reportedly there was a team of officers there to review the program and, I assume, make recommendations on its future.

A few pilots were adamant about going back immediately, my CO included. When queried, I merely said "Continue as planned," and went back to the bar. By rumor, the number of participants supporting a return to overseas was not a majority. However, we were told all *would* go back overseas.

I was given the task of putting some special supplies for the squadron on the ship ahead of our boarding. In the process, I went on board and got a preview of accommodations on this troopship. It was a civilian liner of prewar Caribbean service, and had not been changed at all on the upper decks. All officers would be quartered in regular staterooms and served by the original civilian crew on the ship. When I reported the supply mission complete to the CO, I said nothing about the ship, abiding by the slogan, "loose lips sink ships."

On the ship, I had duties as commander of troops in one compartment, and down there the personnel were packed in like on all other troopships. These troops were replacement infantry soldiers, most quite young, among whom it was rumored were many who had been pulled out of guardhouses and stockades to fill the demand for combat soldiers overseas. There were few if any stripes to be found among them. Thus, an acting first sergeant and NCOs were appointed. They soldiered well all the way, with the compartment in good shape and no problems. Not one of them ended up in the brig on bread and water like some others on board did.

This ship went in convoy, a large one, which was an impressive sight as it assembled. There had been the last sights of the U.S.A. passing by and then fading out behind us as the ship moved out through Hampton Roads, the mouth of Chesapeake Bay, and on out into the Atlantic. Possibly steaming out past the Statue of Liberty or under the Golden Gate Bridge would have been more graphic departures, but I don't think the feeling would be any different if a troopship was launched off a mud flat and that was the last part of the U.S.A. to be seen.

When my CO found he was quartered in a stateroom, with the special supplies safely locked inside, and that he would be eating stateside fare with table service in the dining room, he threatened to have me moved from a stateroom and put in the hold somewhere for not relating the full story on this ship. He didn't, though, and the trip was a surprisingly good one for a troopship. The only things missing from a luxury liner-type cruise were female passengers and a bar, but nothing could be done about the females and in this case a ships' bar was not a necessity.

At the same time, it was certainly no pleasure trip. The sight outside of the many ships and their escorts left no doubt as to why this voyage was being made. Also, this time there were not just rumors of enemy threats; some of the freighters on the outside of the convoy and escorts were involved in enemy submarine action.

On arrival in Naples, the participants in the program who had completed full tours and held doubts about returning to combat were given some options. The three of us were not involved in them and I never knew what they were. Also, I never knew exactly how many crewmembers went on the program, but from observations and our orders, I'd estimate around 165, with about one-third from Twelfth and the rest from the Fifteenth Air Force. From the Twelfth, there were members of about every type of unit assigned: fighter, fighter-bomber, night fighter, bomber, troop carrier and recce. I never knew how many returned to combat, but from personal friends in fighter and fighter-bomber units who did, it was probably a good percentage of pilots from these type tactical units.

I did know from evidence in hand that each one who stayed and had already completed a full tour or more carried from then on an authorization that allowed him to discontinue flying combat and rotate to the States at any time in the future that he so chose. On my critique report on the program, I made some suggestions, but, in summary, my report was that the program had served me well, and should be continued.

If other theaters had similar or special leave programs to the States for combat crews, I was unaware of them. The MTO did in time have a very limited stateside leave program for ground personnel, but no more for pilots and combat crews that I knew.

Chapter 8

Southern France

In a B-25, stripped of its combat equipment and now used by the Group for support flights, we departed Naples flying up the coast of Italy. We passed just inland of Anzio and could look down on the now empty but heavily battle-scarred beachhead. To me, such scenes as here and at Cassino would perhaps serve a purpose if they could be preserved just as they are. That wouldn't show what war is like while underway, but there would be no markers needed to cite that war had come this way.

The 79th Fighter Group was now based on Corsica, at Serragia Airfield. As we arrived over that field, on the east coast about 20 miles south of Bastia, in evidence was a large installation for a fighter-bomber field. P-47 runways were normally around 5000 feet. This one, of PSP (pierced steel planking), was considerably larger with an extensive set of taxiways and parking areas on each side. Toward the beach were the P-47s of another group. It was early July; we had been away roughly two months.

In our processing back into the theater, we could draw a pretty good — if unofficial — picture of the order of battle of the fighter units in the MTO. The Twelfth and Fifteenth Air Forces had long since been established in their respective tactical and strategic roles and organizations. In the tactical Twelfth, all of the known Groups on full-time fighter-bomber operations (27th, 57th, 79th, 86th, and 324th) were now equipped with P-47s and apparently most were located on Corsica. The 27th was on the field with us and the 86th just up the coast, but I wasn't sure about the location of the 57th and 324th. Also, the 350th remained in the Twelfth Air Force in a fighter role. Allied units of the Desert Air Force were apparently the main tactical forces in Italy.

Fifteenth Air Force reportedly had the other U.S. Fighter Groups in Italy. Those known to me were the 1st, 14th, and 82nd (P-38s); the 31st,

Strafing an enemy convoy on crowded roads. (Courtesy U.S. Air Force)

52nd, and 325th (P-51s), and the 332nd (P-47s, changing to P-51s).

In our absence, the 79th Group had been involved in some of the most intense fighter-bomber effort of the war. In May, before the breakout at Anzio and Cassino, they had maintained a complete interdiction in a sector north of Rome. Then after the breakouts and on into early June they, along with other fighter-bombers, had pounded and strafed the retreating Germans—on highways often jammed with vehicles, equipment and troops—in probably the greatest overall destruction of such targets to date in the war. Total claims for ground targets destroyed and damaged by the 79th had grown sharply in this period, and the total of air kills had now

Destroyed equipment lined the roads on the route of the enemy's retreat to Rome and on north. (Courtesy U.S. Air Force)

passed 125 for an "air-to-ground" fighter-bomber unit. The 79th had taken part in the invasion of Elba, and now continued to support the advancing Allied forces in Italy.

If the damage inflicted on the enemy had been great, never before had our squadron and one other in the Group suffered such losses as they did in May and early June. The loss rate in May was such that if it continued over a period of months, the entire pilot force in these squadrons would have to be replaced about every three to four months. Among those shot down was the Group CO. In our squadron, losses included many old friends and newcomers alike—among them was Lt. Ermis, the determined, partially-crippled pilot who had finally returned to flying status.

However, there had obviously been no loss of heart or spirit throughout and the situation had improved in recent days. In the midst of the heavy losses, new records had been set for missions flown per day and munitions put on the enemy. Ground crews had repaired record numbers of battle-damaged airplanes, while keeping the flying going, too.

Even in the face of these grim reports, there was no lessening of spirit shown in "welcome home" greetings for us—or in making use of the "special supplies" during a unit-wide celebration of the return.

While we were away the 79th had moved from Capo to another field in the Naples area, Pomigliano, and then here to Corsica. Along the way, the 99th FS had left the Group, being transferred to the Fifteenth Air Force as part of the 332nd Fighter Group. A first impression of Corsica was one of "back out in the tulies." This was an all-tent operation. A thumbnail description of Corsica would include mountains, beaches, and beautiful scenery—if one had to live in tents, this looked like an ideal place and time of year to do so. Our quarters area was near a clear mountain stream and the weather was pleasant—warm days and cool nights.

While we were away, our squadron had bombed a rather unusual target for figher-bombers—an aircraft carrier. It was hit with thousand-pounders

Most bridges take very accurate bombing to cut. (Courtesy U.S. Air Force)

and rolled upside down in the harbor. As I got the story later, immediately after the eventful mission, the squadron was descended upon by PIO (Public Information Officer) types and correspondents. The young first lieutenant mission leader was the main object of news interest. Apparently, his hits on the ship sent it over so fast that some following pilots bombed the bottom of the upturned hull. If the reports are accurate, he got up in front of the newspeople and indicated there wasn't anything so outstanding about *that*, then went on to say that anybody should be able to hit something that size—a bridge is what takes some *real* bombing to nail. If the last part of the story is correct, the newspeople didn't hang around very long. However, for the record, the unit history of The 79th Fighter Group in World War II carries a definite entry of one aircraft carrier destroyed/sunk.

That same lieutenant, back in the days of Anzio, had rejoined formation after an air flight flying about three-fourths of an airplane. The rest of it had been shot away by enemy fighters, including a good-sized hole in the side of the cockpit. He hadn't bothered to say anything about being hit on the radio. Perhaps *that* wasn't considered any big deal, either.

Seeing an airplane in that shape often brought on bull-session discussions of the merits of the German's extensive use of cannons (20mm to 30mm size range) on fighters versus the .50-caliber machine guns on our first-line fighters.

In the lieutenant's case over Anzio, where those particular enemy cannon shells blew holes in the skin and parts off the airplane, had he been hit with other type rounds or six or eight of our guns with API (armor-piercing incendiary) rounds, they would have gone completely through the airplane and possibly through engine, fuel tanks, and pilot, too. On the other hand, the range of the cannons and their wallop surely scored kills in various situations the .50s would not have. (The U.S. did have cannons in some fighters and other airplanes—in fact up to 75mm in certain B-25s used against shipping and other targets in the Pacific.)

While such comparisons of enemy equipment and our own were invaluable and essential to the development of unit tactics and techniques, I suspect most of us gave such matters little thought, leaving the selection of equipment to the experts and concentrating on the use of what we had. Most pilots seemed fully confident in our guns, and if those guns were put in reasonably good range, the .50-caliber rounds chewed up and burned a wide variety of targets.

I flew around Corsica and parts of Italy on several non-combat flights, getting impatient and probably a bit irritated at doing more of this than I thought necessary. Then, when an outstanding pilot and flight leader with over 130 missions was lost, I went back into that position and combat flying. I flew wing for a couple of missions, which from Corsica could go to any of three general areas. We might fly in support of Allied forces fighting in Italy along the lines south of Florence. We might go on interdiction missions in the broad, flat expanse of the Po Valley, north of the Apennines in Italy. Or

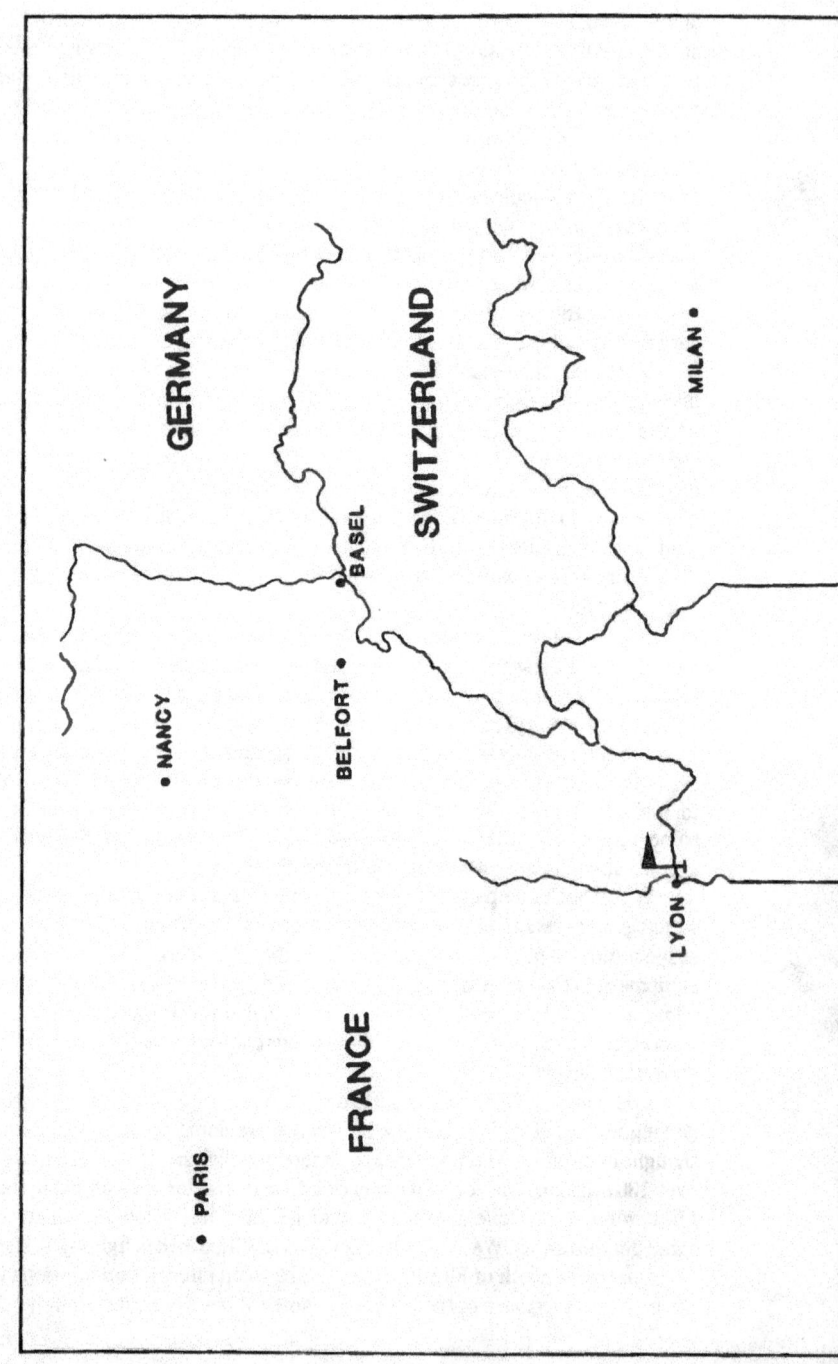

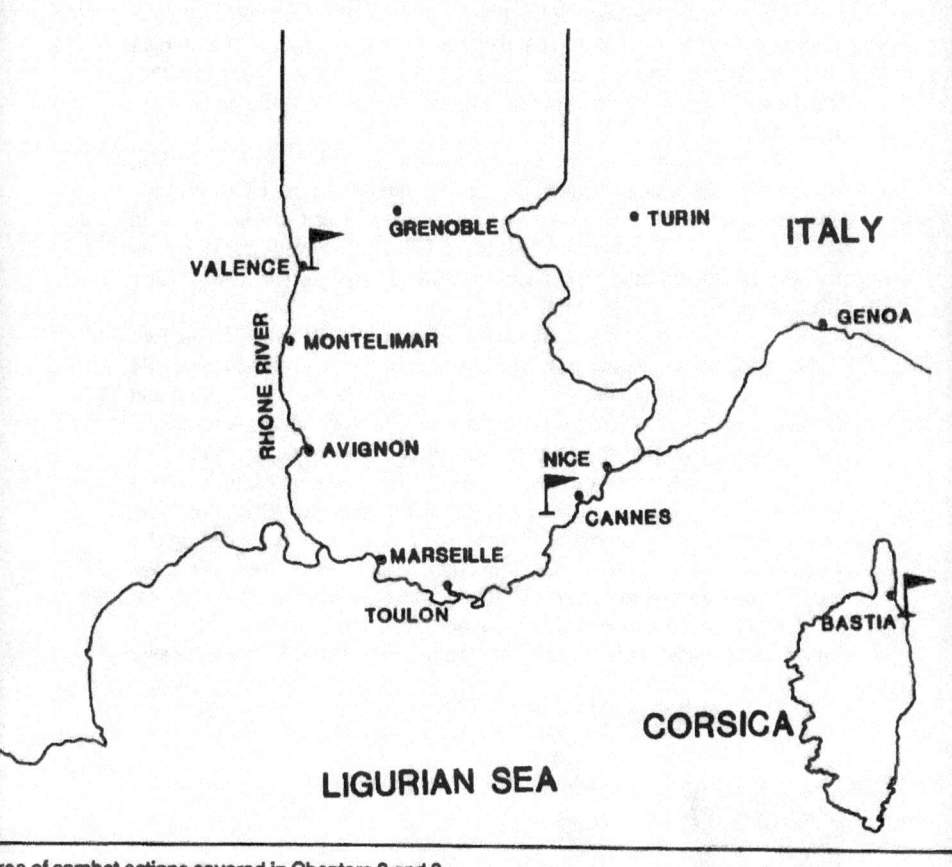

Area of combat actions covered in Chapters 8 and 9.

we might fly missions against the Germans in Southern France.

All these missions involved overwater flights, with those to the Po Valley and Southern France being a pretty fair haul over the Ligurian Sea. The water had saved a number of pilots who managed to get out over the sea in crippled airplanes to bail out, then be picked up by the rescue seaplanes or amphibians, called "Duck Butts." Pilots of of these slow seaplanes pulled downed pilots from the water off the coast of France and Italy—in some cases, from under the nose of the enemy such as one reported incident at Genoa. There were no shortages of enemy guns at Genoa, and the thought of a "Duck Butt" flying and landing in or near the harbor there is rather amazing. That is one more kind of combat flying that I would not want to trade for.

My first few missions went without problems. I had a brand-new No. 99, a P-47D-25, which had a bubble canopy and slightly more fuel than the earlier Razorbacks. I may have flown it twice before it went down in southern France. The pilot did get out, and if he could evade the Germans for any length of time, the chances were pretty good of the French Resistance Forces saving him.

The next morning I had another brand new No. 99. If a unit lost two airplanes, for example, in a day, that night or the next morning there would normally be two new ones in the unit. I assume they were supplied and flown in by the service groups and squadrons that were always somewhere in the area backing up the combat units with supplies and services.

Then, as July wore on, came a very memorable mission. It was a two-squadron effort, 16 airplanes each, taking off in late afternoon. The target was Valence Airfield in France, well inland from the coast up the Rhone River Valley. It was at about maximum range and no bombs or other external ordnance were carried—only our guns. Valence was a known active German bomber base, and some of our medium bomber bases had been hit by night attacks of Ju 88 and other bombers recently. There were also

Republic P-47D-25, with "bubble" canopy.

Strafing enemy bombers. (Courtesy U.S. Air Force)

some fighters reported on Valence.

The plan was to arrive there close to sunset. The other squadron (85th) was "lead," our squadron (87th) was "cover," and there were few doubts among the pilots about whether there would be enemy fighter opposition. On this type of operation you might imagine an elaborate joint briefing and other preparation, but near as I know, the whole thing started in the middle of the afternoon, and any joint briefing held was a talk between the leaders of the two squadrons on a field phone. The pilots to fly the mission were apparently those who were on hand or who could be rounded up the fastest. The CO was to lead Green Flight on the tail end with me flying his element.

As we approached the enemy airfield at a normal enroute altitude of some 9000 feet, the lead squadron started down to initiate the attack. From our cover position, the scene on the field below was perhaps a once-in-a-war sight. It was a beehive of activity by comparison with anything seen before on an enemy airfield. A few bombers had marshalled on the field; some were taxiing and others had engines running in their revetments or parking areas. Obviously they were preparing to launch a major bombing effort.

The flak cut loose, opening what was destined to be one of the most brilliant and savage local shows of combat pyrotechnics in the war. With the first rounds pumped into the bombers on the field by the strafing P-47s, the pace and scope of the fireworks picked up immediately. Fully fueled and loaded bombers, one after another, burst into huge balls of fire or exploded. A P-47 was seen to crash in the middle of the field in a ball of fire, too.

The lead squadron made several passes on the field and parking areas, causing yet more fire, smoke, tracers, and flak bursts to appear. Up above we kept scanning the skies for enemy fighters, but none showed, and when the lead squadron pulled off their strafing attacks, we went down and took over shooting up airplanes on the ground.

Green Flight, in elements, worked over two parking areas somewhat removed from the main field, where the fires and smoke were not quite as thick as over the main airfield. Very shortly we had our own fires and explosions going. Our passes were made between or through tall columns of black smoke from burning airplanes, and amid clouds of smoke, dust, and debris from full-fledged explosions. Streamers could be seen flowing from the wing tips of P-47s as high-G turns were made to put a burst into an enemy bomber in a revetment under camouflage netting, and then send more streamers flying in order to align on another bomber or two on the same pass.

In making the passes, we were swinging around the edges of the city of Valance (which, along with the airfield, was located on the east bank of the Rhone River) and there we saw a sight that might top anything seen on the nearby field. With gunfire and shrapnel flying everywhere, and with some of the flak and our ricochets tearing into trees, buildings, and hilltops in the area, so help me, some of the French people were out on the rooftops, in windows, yards, and streets—waving to, and cheering on, the attacking American pilots.

It was a sort of "sweaty" trip back to Corsica. There were some damaged airplanes, very little ammo in any of them, and not an excess of fuel, either, but all those leaving the target area made it to Corsica. A couple did land at an RAF base on the west side of the island, the closest airfield to France—a fact that caused quite a few visitors from the other side of the island to drop in there occasionally.

Claims for the mission were over 20 enemy aircraft destroyed and others damaged—mostly JU 88s or JU 188s but also some Do 217s, He 111s, and a few fighters and transports. These figures were almost certainly way under the actual kills, but in the Twelfth Air Force it made no difference to individual pilots. We did not get any kind of individual credit for enemy airplanes destroyed on the ground—or for any other ground targets, either. They were recorded and reported only as mission and/or unit totals.

We had a couple of pilots from fighter units of the Eighth Air Force in the U.K. flying with us temporarily. They were flight leaders, here to obtain experience with and from us in air-to-ground operations. While they talked with all key officers and pilots in the squadron, they also flew missions just like everybody else to see for themselves.

Our visitors from the U.K. seemed surprised that we did not get flat on-the-deck to come in on all strafing passes, particularly against airfields. From our unit's standpoint, it was mainly a matter of pilots being able to see more when flying a bit higher and shoot better when making descending strafing passes into targets—that way more targets could be found and destroyed, which was a quite valid objective. If a situation called for deception or surprise as a primary goal, then the lower the better, whether popping up some for the attack or going on through low. We did some such strafing; often it was on repeat attacks against flak guns, and some of the repeat attacks on airplanes at Valence were made while staying very low.

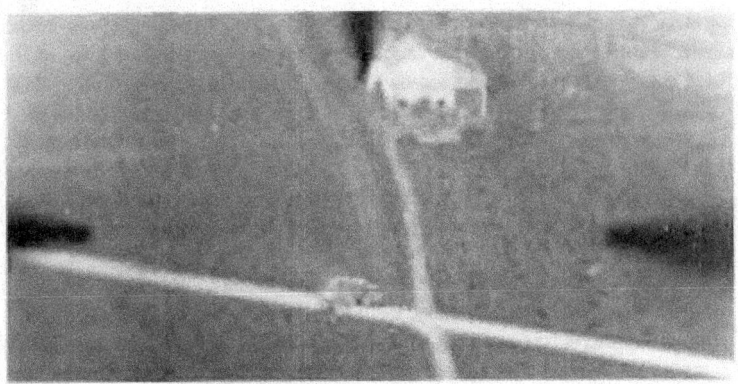

Target. (Courtesy USAAF, World War II)

Yet some of the airplanes there were in revetments and passes on them had to come up high enough to shoot down into the revetments. (Frag bombs could be dropped into revetments, but we were not carrying any at Valence.)

Vulnerability during attacks may have received even more attention in pilot bull sessions than attack effectiveness. On-the-deck might be desirable at many times and places, but flying down there over the water on an open airfield were not among them. The enemy gunners know exactly how high you are and can throw a barrage or crossfire of automatic-weapon flak out in front at that altitude. When operating up off-the-deck, the enemy can see you better and can probably get more guns on the attacking airplanes, but all types of guns might not reach effectively up to the airplanes. Also, incorporating some change in both altitude and direction when possible in at least part of an attack seemed to complicate the gunners' task. However, neither way ever guaranteed anything.

Our guests from England flew P-51s. They also talked about P-51s all the time, and would argue over them, too, if anybody would argue back. I wouldn't. From what little I knew of the P-51, range was its greatest asset.

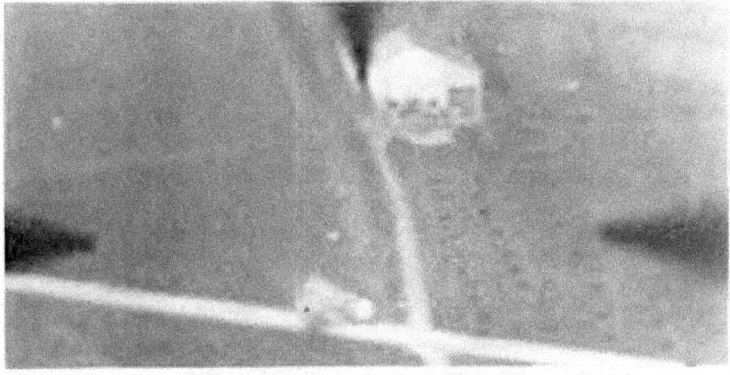

Perfect shooting—not a round wasted. (Courtesy USAAF, World War II)

even though obviously from the record it was making in combat as one of the most famous of all fighters, it had to be a truly outstanding airplane. Both P-47 and P-38 fighter pilots would also argue just as strongly that *their* particular airplane was the better fighter. I don't guess the arguments hurt anything, unless carried to fighting among the pilots, but I doubt that anything was ever proven either way, or that the war effort was furthered to any great extent in the process. The best thing about the matter was that we *had* all three of those type fighters, as well as P-40s and others, for pilots to argue about.

On one mission, with one of the Eighth Air Force pilots along, we shot up a few trucks on several passes, then went back and made a flat-on-the-deck run on the vehicles to see how well the visitor could shoot them that way. They could be hit pretty well by "walking" the bullets through the vehicles, but unless the target is up on a raised roadway or track at least level with or above the attacking airplane (which these were not), then trying to stop the "walking" bullets and concentrate them on the target for even a second or so results in pushing the nose down. Unless that is remembered while flying flat on-the-deck, one is flirting with the world's easiest way to fly into the ground.

We had a P-47 hit in the belly near the wing root area with an explosive round—possibly a 37mm—and the P-47 flew right on out of enemy territory and across the water to home base. One pilot put a sketch of a P-51 on the bulletin board showing what would be missing if it had been hit by the same kind of round in the same place—the coolant and oil radiators, plus the lines to them. Someone said perhaps that's why our friends from the U.K. were interested in flying real low all the time—to keep the bellies of their P-51s protected right next to the grass.

By August, our flying effort turned fully to southern France. Early in that month, most missions were on communications, rails, some airfields, flak positions, and targets of opportunity. Then, in a week or so, our entire effort went against coastal targets of gun positions and radars. Earlier we had flown eight-ship and larger missions; now we were flying four-ship missions in most cases.

Famed P-51 fighter. (Courtesy U.S. Air Force)

Clouds built up over the mountains inland of our field almost daily. To avoid the clouds, most missions took off and went north up the coast and around the tip of the island, and returned by the same route. However, there was a definite gap in the line of mountain peaks, which was directly on course for southern France. When the weather was okay a flight could take off and go straight out on course through the gap without even circling the field. Some days on takeoff a leader could look right through the gap under the clouds and see blue sky on the far side, in which case he might decide to go through that hole. Some did this okay, but one or two got in the gap to find the blue sky was no longer there as the hole closed. Certain of those flights went through the gap on instruments—with mountains not very far away on both sides, but they made it fine. One trip through the gap like that often resulted in two future actions: One, that leader went *around* the island from then on when there were clouds over the mountains. Two, if that leader, in debriefing, mentioned how "we" did on climbout, he had brought up what was sometimes a touchy subject to combat pilots flying element and wing positions. They did not always go for this "we" stuff, such as "we" probably should not have gone through the gap, or "we" should have stayed clear of that reported flak position.

The missions on the coastal targets in southern France were highly unpredictable. Some targets were hit while encountering very little or not more than moderate flak; others brought on intense 88mm and automatic-weapon fire, particularly out over the water. In some cases, I thought these might be among the roughest missions I'd flown. If it was practical to hit the target from the inland side, I'd choose to do so from that direction and withdraw that way, too. However, many of the targets were blanked by the rugged, rocky coastline and/or hidden by tall trees and could not be sighted or hit effectively except by approaching them face-on from the water.

It was just such a mission, on a radar station nestled in among the rocks on a small point, which saw a record end for me—one I was extremely proud of. Until now I had never lost a pilot from any element, flight, or mission of which I was the leader, but while strafing and destroying that radar station (in the Frejus-St. Raphael area between Toulon and Nice), my wingman was hit and crashed into the water. Apparently there were not great numbers of enemy guns involved, but their positions along the coast, the crews could concentrate very effective fire on a particular airplane. On this mission, we encountered such accurate fire that it was one of the few times to date I doubted it possible to fly through the stuff. We did not have pilots assigned as a regular wingman for each leader; any of the line pilots might fly wing for any leader.

In certain spots along the coast, airplanes flying right above the water produced a very nasty sight indeed. The automatic weapons sent out a sea of tracers across the wave tops of the sea below, as well as sent rounds flying in crazy, mixed-up patterns as they hit and richocheted off the water. The big 88mm rounds burst just above the waves, churning a froth as blast and shrapnel hit the water, and also sending up large geysers of water from those rounds impacting in the waves.

We, along with all other units, received orders to do some extensive non-combat flying, and of a scope unheard of in the past. That was night flying. Each pilot was to get at least one flight, and we had two nights to accomplish the job. At first glance, such a task should be no problem for any unit, but a closer look at the situation presented a different picture. Airfields (like all other facilities, towns, etc.) were completely blacked out at night—there were no systems or features showing on the ground for navigation or to even find the field again. Dust covered this field during heavy operations, which was no major problem in the day but could blank it out completely at night. Worse yet, at the time there was no moon to shed any light on the task at hand.

The portable runway lights were readied and checked out. They provided a minimum of light to pilots for takeoff, approach, and landing, but didn't really show from the air otherwise. The ground personnel received extra tasks of stations along the runway to repair broken wires or lights, and to back up the light system with flambeaus. The use of water trucks for dust control, vehicles and other light sources to augment the runway lights, provisions for potential loss of the tower, and numerous other measures were considered. Some units put a flight leader or other experienced pilot in the tower or along the runway with radio contact to pilots to try to keep them on the runway if necessary. Many of the combat pilots in these units had not flown at night since training days.

Once the airplanes began taxiing out on a pitch-black night, with two full groups feeding the runway from both sides, any blackout protection was down the drain for the time being, since the airplane lights clearly showed the airfield. I caught one shift in the tower, which was very close to the runway. The experience was worse than either flying at night or combat.

Early in the game, an airplane on takeoff took out many of the lights on the tower side of the runway. The men replacing them or putting flambeaus in their place had to dodge some airplanes in the process. Part of the tower crew bailed out of the 20-or-so-foot frame platform as an airplane bore down on it. The dust blocked visibility of both the tower and pilots. Little help could be provided, except as the airplanes were almost on top of the tower. One was so far off at that point that the tower crew stayed quiet as the pilot took off on the dirt behind the tower.

When I flew, the next night, things were a bit better for dust. My flight got off fine and joined okay, which was no easy chore, since the lights on a P-47 were not much to talk about and an OD airplane blends in quite well with a pitch-black night. We were using "silver" airplanes in all leader positions where possible and placing the turbosupercharger controls to dump the engine exhaust out the wastegates on the lower nose of the airplanes to light them up a bit more. (Many of the airplanes arriving overseas now were left with their natural aluminum finish rather than painted OD).

I believe the field lost three airplanes in the non-combat night flying, two on takeoff and one during flight. The latter involved one of the most amazing and miraculous incidents of the war. For whatever reason—disorientation or other problems—the pilot (from a sister squadron) bailed out at some 6000 to 8000 feet. His parachute did not open. He impacted in a swamp just south of the field—and received only minor injuries. In any flying event of such an epic nature there were sure to be sidelight stories. One was a rumor that the pilot had been flying along in formation in the dark when he became convinced the entire flight was flying upside down, so he rolled over to be rightside up, after which things went to pot pretty fast. Then there was the old joke about parachute riggers and their promise that if a chute doesn't work, "Just bring it back and we'll give you another one." Here was a case of a pilot who brought one back, but if the story is correct, he wasn't interested in exchanging it for another of like kind.

On the night of August 14, the reason for the night flying became known. The next morning, units throughout the theater put up missions well before daybreak in support of the invasion of southern France.

For many airplanes participating in the invasion, there were established blocks of airspace and routes for various kinds of operations (i.e., troop carriers and gliders, medium and heavy bombers, etc.), but there would be many of them in those blocks of airspace. There would also be a control system through an agency on a ship offshore, with specific time frames for various air functions. For example, early on D-Day morning there was a period of four-ship missions of fighter-bombers over the beaches to dive-bomb any guns seen firing, then one for small formations of bombers and fighter-bombers to attack special gun positions, then another period of dive-bombing on gun positions, then one for bombers to hit beach defenses, finally followed by continuing patrols of fighters and fighter-bombers on call as needed.

The takeoffs on the morning of the 15th involved a few additional considerations. A large number of airplanes would be going off at very close intervals—once started, they could not afford to stop, and they would be carrying bombs. While losing a bomb or tank on takeoff was rare in a P-47, it could and did happen, in which case the lost stores could be on the runway in the dark. A crash could also block the runway. Provisions had to be made to know the runway was clear, and, if blocked in any way, to quickly clear it—as well as be prepared to takeoff on the dirt along either or both sides if necessary.

From the ground there were several unforgettable sights. First was the overall movement of airplane lights from every far parking area on the field in a mass migration toward the runway. Then set after set of those lights went roaring off into the night, one set right behind another, each set now augmented with blue-white exhaust glows. Those sets of lights gathered into four-ship missions and moved out in streams, joining more airplanes moving out in streams from other fields on Corsica, and in turn joining streams flowing overhead from Italy and possibly Sardinia. Once into solid streams, one observer said there were simply too many lights too close together to think of them as individual airplanes—it all looked more like gigantic flows of lava moving across the sky.

From a pilot's view in the cockpit, staying on the runway during the takeoff roll was the first major hurdle. Then joining up into flights was a unique challenge. There were sets of airplane lights everywhere. Some pilots later said they quit trying to dodge other sets of lights because doing so just sent them even closer into yet another set. Instead, they just pressed on, more hoping to avoid other airplanes than really trying to. However, no airplanes were seen to explode from midair collisions, and none were known to have been lost that way.

When it began to get light, the sight down below off the coast of southern France was probably the most striking one yet of the three major Allied invasions I had been involved in. And there was one new aspect in the air support of this invasion. It had often been said that while the U.S. Navy and Marines were deeply involved in air support in the Pacific, they were not a regular part of the tactical air war in Europe. Off southern France were several aircraft carriers (relatively small ones, assumed to be escort carriers) and we had been brushing up on aircraft identification of both the U.S. and Royal Navy planes operating from these carriers. Both U.S. and British Navy Air elements were involved in the invasion of southern France.

Most all missions went well and with few losses; we did fighter-bomber work rather than air patrol. By the end of the day we were accustomed to Navy planes operating in the same skies—and, I guess, vice versa. Each had looked the other over a time or two as being potential boggies, but otherwise the strange airplanes in the skies caused no problems at all.

The next several days, many four-ship flights were flown in general support of the highly successful landings in southern France. In less than a week, our advanced ground parties boarded LSTs and went ashore across

LST, our ground echelon's transportation to France. (Courtesy U.S. Air Force)

the beach there. One week after the invasion began we landed our airplanes in southern France. The airfield was a very dusty one with a PSP strip, just inland from the coast at St. Raphael near Cannes on the Riviera.

The officers were quartered in very nice villas, sitting among tall pine trees, right on the beach. Yet the sight in that direction was not one of inviting waters and sunning beauties. Our ships still stood offshore and the beach was marred with various obstructions, and lined with warning signs depicting skulls and crossbones and the words "Achtung Minen."

Trenches linked the villas to a command post, storage bunkers, and gun positions. Two dead German soldiers lay partially covered with rocks in the trench out front. Just beyond the garden wall of the main villa sat an 88mm flak gun, with two others in the adjacent trees. Built into the rocks down at the beach was a concrete emplacement containing a 20mm flak gun system. There were half a dozen or so machine guns still in positions spread around the area. Inside the villas were uniforms—some hanging neatly in closets, others thrown about—and various other personal belongings of German troops. There was food in the kitchens, and even dirty dishes in the sinks. Obviously, the previous occupants had left quite hurriedly.

Except for the 88s, which were missing the breech locks or mechanisms, all the other guns were fully operational, and there was a tremendous supply of ammo for all. Of a sidelight interest on the ammo, the ground machine guns had both regular ammo and wooden-bullet ammo, the latter rounds painted bright red. Had we found guns like these at some past isolated base such as Madna, the CO would have been besieged for permission to let us fire them to our hearts' content—more likely, he would have led the shooting. Here there was no place to shoot safely because of endangering the populated areas and installations along the coast and inland, and the Navy was still sitting off the beach—no one in his right mind was going to do any shooting in *that* direction. Thus, the ammo was separated from the guns and the guns relieved of firing components, after which we were free to play flak gunners if we wanted to.

Most pilots did not concern themselves to any great extent in the technical aspects of flak guns, such as their exact sizes or German nomenclature (Flak 18, Flak 30, Flak 41, etc.). While we had seen automatic flak guns listed from 15mm to 37mm, some of us still talked in terms of 20mm to 40mm sizes. Any of them could easily do a fighter-bomber in with a good hit. Of greater importance was knowing the general capabilities and where and how they might be installed, carried, mounted, and encountered. (On the other hand, some pilots said there was a simple answer to all that: "If the Germans are there, the automatic weapon flak will be there.") There was one aspect of flak capabilities that many pilots and intelligence officers never did seem to see eye to eye on. That was the effective range of the German guns. Of course, anything larger than about 37mm could effectively reach above the altitudes that fighter-bombers flew on most missions. It was the automatic-weapon flak where the differences of opinion existed. For example, if pilots were told the "effective range" of certain of the guns

Always more strafing. (Courtesy USAAF, World War II)

was 5000 feet, and then saw rounds from those guns at 9000 feet or so, many of them said to hell with whether they are "scientifically effective" up here; more important was the simple fact that they could shoot this high. Other pilots discounted the entire business of studying facts and figures on flak guns, their theory being that where we flew much of the time, a kid could throw a rock and reach us.

The 20mm flak position outside our villa had considerable impact on

Whether through firsthand examination or intelligence reports, very little about German flak weapons, such as the Flakpanzer here, was reassuring. (Courtesy U.S. Air Force)

some pilots. The guns were mounted in a powered turret, much like an airplane turret with a similar gunsight. Ammo was fed to each of the four guns by chutes from a supply down below. Some eight spare barrels were in racks alongside the guns. When one barrel burned out, it could be dumped overboard with the flick of a lever and another slapped in place and locked in position. Tracking airplanes or birds with the system was extremely smooth and easy. Some pilots who operated this system said they wished they hadn't—it was better not to know that such guns were being fired at them. Some—perhaps wisely—stayed away from the guns.

Also, while this little complex of guns had not been destroyed, other gun positions along the coast on both sides had been—as had a radar station just down the beach. These destroyed positions were among targets we and other fighter-bomber pilots had attacked in the recent past. It was a curiously morbid situation to sit behind the guns in the turret and realize that these very guns had surely been fired at you—and, in my case, quite possibly were the guns that shot down my wingman on the radar station mission.

Chapter 9

The Rhone River Valley

August 28, 1944, was a clear, sunny day in southern France. It was late afternoon; flying was over and most of the pilots and flight vehicles were already at the quarters. The airplanes from the last mission were being tucked in for the night. Another pilot and I were sitting on folding chairs in front of the Ops tent on our field at St. Raphael; a third pilot was around somewhere. All three of us had been updating our personal maps. Once finished, instead of calling for transportation to the villas, we were waiting to catch a ride with the Intel officer, who was finishing his reports.

Our flying for the last few days had gone extremely well—good results on missions, with little flak and no losses. The war had not folded up around us by any means; on the contrary, there had been very heavy ground fighting in Toulon and Marseille areas since the Allied landings.

Also, from the airfield, many of the gliders used to bring troops in during the invasion could still be seen in nearby fields. In these fields the enemy had erected numerous tree trunks and other poles as obstructions to glider landings. Because of such hazards and the normal ones associated with combat glider operations, many wrecked and damaged gliders were strewn throughout the area. On such operations, once the pilots accomplished their powerless flights and landings in the big, heavy gliders, they ended up in the ground fighting. (That was one *more* type of combat flying that I would not be the least bit interested in making a trade for; nor would I volunteer to trade a fighter-bomber for one of the troop carrier airplanes that towed the gliders in and also dropped paratroopers at low altitudes over enemy territory.)

Yet, despite the recent heavy fighting and various signs of war still strongly in evidence, the action may have seemed a bit removed in time and distance from the scene on our field at the moment. The airplanes were just quietly sitting and the few pilots around were doing the same—both apparently done for this day's part in the struggle. Then a clerk dashed from the tent, shouting that the Group wanted a mission *right now*.

That mission was put together on the spot. The three pilots on the field would make up the lead or Red Flight. A call was made to the quarters for four pilots to man a second or White Flight. The few ground crews on hand headed for the closest airplanes and a call went out for more crews to handle the second flight. Airplanes without bombs, scheduled for strafing missions in the morning, were picked in order to avoid messing with fuzes or dumping the bombs. Our orders for the mission were to "go take a look north of the Bomb Line up the Rhone River Valley."

We were airborne in minutes. I was leading; Flight Officer Russel K. Jennings, a very impressive and well-accepted young pilot with about 10 missions, was flying my wing. The third pilot was widely recognized as one of the very best in combat ever to come along and had been a mission leader from a very early stage, 1st Lt. Philip Bagian. He was flying as a one-ship element. Our quickly planned route was grease-penciled on a map and left for White leader's use in joining us along the way.

We flew westward to pick up the main road and rail routes leading north up the valley from Marseille. As we flew north up the Rhone River Valley, this mission of three pilots, followed by four, found the bulk of the entire German force in southern France moving north up the valley—and made initial air attacks thereon. Word of the find was passed back to White Flight, led by 1st. Lt. John T. Boone, to relay on to any ground agency they could reach. Then, to sum up the mission, Red flight attacked the very spearhead of the column, where the concentration of enemy armor and automatic weapons took a terrible toll as both Red Two (Jennings) and Red Three (Bagian) were shot down, and Red One (me) limped home in an airplane that was scrapped on the spot from both extensive flak and airplane fire damage. White Flight attacked a few miles back in the enormous enemy column with excellent results and all its pilots returned safely. While some 50 vehicles were reported destroyed and more than that damaged on the mission, more importantly, the detection of the German column allowed other attacks during the night, and the next morning most of the German force was still trapped in the valley. Tactical air pounded it incessantly for a couple of days (in time, artillery did, too), leaving one of the greatest single scenes of destruction and carnage in the war.

While the end result of that air operation is well known, little is known about how it started, except by those involved. Thus, I am going to give a step-by-step account of this mission in the air. Of course, it will be from my viewpoint and experiences, which will be highlighted along with my decisions as the mission leader—and some of the latter can certainly be questioned. Yet the story of pilots Red Two and Red Three, who were subject to those decisions, is the thing to keep in mind—there is a story of soldiering that should be known.

On that mission, as we flew north, from the Bomb Line on there was traffic in evidence, some speeding along. Further up the valley, from the area of Avignon on, the traffic thickened and it appeared the speeders were trying to catch up to those ahead. In time, the sight of military movement along the main highway on the east side of the Rhone River grew to proportions unseen in the past.

The Bomb Line had never been wrong, but what we saw now made us wonder a bit about such a possibility. Often, when looking down on our side of the Bomb Line, the roads were full of vehicles and equipment. On the other hand, rarely was that the case on the enemy side unless something beyond normal operations was involved. A major switch in traffic patterns was being observed today, except that all the movement on the enemy side was to the north. One might wonder if the entire Allied force in southern France—the U.S. Seventh Army and French forces (which I had heard identified as both the French First Army and French Army "B")—had broken out completely and was rushing north without the Bomb Line keeping up.

Yet, that latter situation would never happen, and certainly not as far north as we were now. I moved in a bit lower and closer from our position of about 3500 feet above and just east of the highway, where I saw that the column simply did not match the image of an Allied or U.S. operation, which was always made up of strictly GI equipment. Down there was a wide variety of vehicles, from first-rate tools of war to horse-drawn wagons. I moved back out a bit and went on north alongside the column.

White leader had checked in on the radio and was cutting across slightly north of our original route to fall in behind us going up the valley. While the sightings were relayed on the radio, no instructions or other word was ever received back from any ground agency, and we were now out of contact with them anyway.

As we went on north, what we saw below became downright hard to believe. Now vehicles were moving north side-by-side and even three abreast for some of the smaller types. In time we had flown past about *thirty miles of solid traffic*. While we could not make out the rather small black-and-white crosses usually painted on German armor and armored vehicles, there was little doubt that they were there. There was also little doubt that a good part, if not all, of the German forces in southern France were moving north. Reportedly, that was the German Nineteenth Army. But the number designation of the army was well down the line in our thoughts at the moment. Perhaps foremost in my mind and probably of the other pilots as well were thoughts involving strafing—and what we would find when we reached the spearhead of this enormous column.

The valley we were flying over was narrow, with steep slopes and hills on each side. Those on the east were covered with vineyards. There were rail lines and a highway on both sides of the river in the valley, but with few if any alternate or side routes out. Perhaps there were none that the Germans could afford to take without risk of eventually being cut off by our ground forces. In any event, where the column was now, they surely were going to try to keep it from being stopped—and so far, not one enemy vehicle had pulled over or the personnel taken cover as we flew alongside the column in full view. They just kept moving along.

It was reported that the German Army in southern France had at least one armored or panzer division, which I believed had been mentioned as the 11th Panzer, but whether it or other specific armored units were part of the column, or separate somewhere, probably wasn't going to change things too much. When we reached the spearhead there would surely be no horse-drawn vehicles, but instead, a solid mass of tough stuff, and all the automatic weapons that could be gathered—which would be a bunch, perhaps an unprecedented collection in one spot.

With that in mind, I eased back in closer to the column a time or two—perhaps closer than we should have been—looking for certain types of vehicles. Those were fuel trucks, and I had seen a number of vehicles spread along the column which appeared to be just that. Then too, any of the regular trucks found among armored vehicles and artillery might be hauling Jerrycans of fuel as well as ammo. Thus, when we reached the spearhead, any trucks among the panzers were to be kept in mind. Roaring fires and explosions from such support vehicles might offer the best bet to delay or slow the movement of this monstrous target.

We reached the spearhead near the town of Montelimar – actually on the highway north of Montelimar. I gave the briefing over the radio on the first sighting of the spearhead. Red Flight would attack the very lead elements and attempt to get some good fires going. White Flight would attack a few miles back in the column, and strafe to the maximum to destroy as many vehicles as possible and put a real cut in the column at that point. White Flight acknowledged, "Roger, Wilco" (received/understand, will comply).

As I drew almost abreast of the German lead elements off my left wing, I had moved out and up slightly. We were in great position for a good strafing pass, but also close enough for every gun down there to be tracking the airplanes every inch of the way. I was sure it would make no difference what I did now. If I tried to turn out further, or fly on by as if we had not seen a thing, or have the wingmen (who were spread into attack intervals and positions away from the column) break off even wider, I'm sure the reaction from below would have been the same—every enemy gun would have cut loose. And, while knowing full well that was coming, in the last second before our next move was made I couldn't help thinking what a tremendous sight of war we were seeing there on the ground. I wondered if anyone other than God and we three pilots had ever seen anything like it.

I rolled in on the attack and the expected reaction from below came—quickly and strongly. I was partially dazed, but recovered enough from the shock and blast to realize my wings were still near vertical. I could see a huge hole in the right wing where the gun and ammo bays had been. The wing panels of both bays were gone, and so were two of the guns. The barrels of the remaining two inboard guns were twisted like pretzels—one pointing straight up, the other right into the cockpit. I saw the last of the linked ammo in the wing go slithering over the trailing edge and aileron and fall free of the airplane. Clear blue sky was visible through the entire gun area and part of the ammo bay area of the wing.

That round hit the wing before I ever completed the roll-in. There was also some shrapnel damage in the fuselage, but the P-47 still flew reasonably well, so I continued the attack. When about ready to fire (while having a flash thought that perhaps the bullet in the curved gun barrel could come through it and into the cockpit) I was hit again up front somewhere. The blast of another explosive round was felt, but more so was a sort of sickening, solid thud and shudder through the airplane as if it had all been stopped for an instant in the air. My pass was disrupted to the point of being ineffective except to get a very close look at the enemy force, to call and (perhaps needlessly) confirm the column as German to the other pilots, and give the location of what appeared to be a fuel truck among the spearhead vehicles.

The other two pilots made effective passes and a small fire or two burst out among the enemy vehicles. Neither pilot made a transmission on the radio, but from the number of guns I saw firing from vehicles, troops with small arms, and other gun positions in the vicinity, the chances of them not receiving some damage were absolutely nil. My plane was still operating but without full power available.

Immediately after the pass, because of airplane damage, thoughts flashed into my mind of changing what had been planned at this point. Now, to withdraw immediately, we might be able to go up and out over the high hills on the west side of the valley, or turn left and go down the west side as far away from the column as possible, or take the better-looking option of turning right and going out in front and away from the column. Regardless of what we did, we were going to receive a lot more of the ungodly accurate automatic-weapon fire in the process.

The decision I made was none of these, but rather to stick with the plan held in mind from the start. That was to quickly come right back on another strafing pass and try to inflict more damage on the head of the column—then go out through the much closer and lower hills on the east side of the valley and get behind them for protection in withdrawing.

This time I had a good pass, putting all the rounds I could from my four operating guns into the hoped-to-be fuel truck and other potential "flamers" nearby. The fuel truck was in the open on the west side of the convoy, where it had been shielded some by armored vehicles on our first pass. I came through the pass cleared the hills to get out of the valley, but with additional hits, I was in trouble now with more power loss and heavy smoke pouring out of the airplane and filling the cockpit.

Red Two and Red Three both completed their passes with good strafing, pressed on to the point of barely clearing the enemy equipment— and surely, that was done in severely damaged airplanes. Then Jennings, Red Two, called that Bagian, Red Three, had crashed into the hillside, and advised that he had dire problems and was low and behind me. I tried to maneuver to pick him up, but by the time I did, he had crashed. White Flight, hearing these transmissions, called that they were on the way to our position. Now I was back in the field of the fire of the column again, as any attempt to cover the crash sites were going to be. I told White leaders to stay away and use all their ammo on cutting the column where planned.

How I made it back is certainly not essential to an account of this mission. The performance of Jennings and Bagian in the face of the tremendous enemy firepower and overwhelming odds against them is the story of this action. Still, the performance of the P-47 I was flying may be of some note in itself. The amount of smoke pouring from the engine compartment surely had to be from a fire rather than something just smoking. It could not be a major fuel tank fire or everything would have gone up at once; perhaps it was a fuel line leak or oil leak into the engine exhaust system. The oil pressure was all but gone. I opened the canopy, unstrapped and squatted in the seat. If the plane exploded, I might be blown out. I also switched the turbo controls to see if the different exhaust pattern would affect the situation. The smoke lessened.

I had enough power to climb slightly, but not with much airspeed. Various small-arms and fragment holes, acquired since the original flak hits, were in the wings. I headed away from the valley and towards mountainous areas to the southeast, where a bailout might be made over base areas of the French Resistance Forces, or the Marquis. The engine continued to run, with the smoke lessening even further, and chances of such a bailout looked better. I probably should have gone over the side as soon as I got high enough and over the first such likely area reached, but with the engine still running I went on, even though the oil pressure was now zero and the engine temperature was starting to climb a bit.

Limping alone, still under 2000 feet, I could not go over the mountains on a direct route to home base. Swinging more to the east, I crossed the other main route north from the Riviera, which went up to Grenoble. I'm sure I felt the explosion of every round of the six or so 88s that encircled and engulfed the airplane, further riddling it with shrapnel and buffeting it to the point I was thrown almost completely out of the cockpit—more out than in, fighting to hang on and pull back inside. Once succeeding at that, I had serious doubts about the wisdom of doing so. The next salvo would surely blow the airplane and me away. Seconds went by, then a minute, then another minute, and the next rounds didn't come. They never came.

With White flight now enroute to join up, I was over territory that offered a good chance of French assistance on the ground. While I was using every means of engine cooling I could think of, amazingly the engine had not overheated severely, and it kept right on running. It did so all the way to home base, where the gear surprisingly came down and locked. Only on final approach just off the edge of the field, when the power was reduced to idle, did the engine clunk to a halt, leaving the big four-blade prop sitting still in the air.

A count of holes in the airplane was started, but after it passed 100 in

Strafed enemy vehicles burn in the streets of Montelimar. (Courtesy U.S. Air Force)

the fuselage, an exact figure did not seem essential to the decision and report declaring it beyond repair. The fire had, among other things, burned the engine firewall out of the airplane. That P-47 (like numerous others and other types of airplanes in World War II) had flown home after it was technically totalled.

The losses hit hard with the Squadron and, in particular, with the CO. There was also the unusual circumstance of a mission debriefing being a one-man report for the actions at the spearhead. White Flight could verify the presence and location of the enormous column, the orders given, radio transmissions, and their observation of fires on the ground at and around the spearhead of the column, but the details of the attacks and flak there were known only to what remained of Red Flight—me—and the Germans on the ground.

When the Allied ground forces moved up that valley in a few days, it was heard that the U.S. Seventh Army reported some 2000 enemy vehicles destroyed along the valley in the Montelimar area. Our advanced ground parties moved out on September 1 for Valence, which was to be our new base in keeping pace with the rapidly advancing ground forces. Our convoys went up the Rhone River Valley on Highway 7—the same highway taken by the Germans, which route, and the recent combat action thereon, would become known as "The Road to Montelimar." Here is what one entry in the 79th FG's war album had to say about that trip:

> As we travelled up the Rhone Valley the destructive powers of fighter-bombers became apparent with a grim clarity that none of us had ever fully realized. For a distance of

Destroyed enemy equipment and carnage left on the "Road to Montelimar." (Courtesy U.S. Air Force)

roughly 30 miles, centered on the little town of Montelimar, was a shambles that may well have had no counterpart in this war. Here had been created a bottleneck of traffic, lined bumper to bumper, that had been ceaselessly attacked for days on end. Vehicles of every description were blocking each other until all fell victims to Allied air power. There were great diesel buses such as once were used for passengers on the streets of Berlin, there were tanks and horse-drawn carts, there was in actuality everything that could move on wheels, and all were now abandoned in flight. Only the odor of decaying bodies, animal and human, remained to connect this spectacle with the part it had once played for the Wehrmacht. The debris had been cleaned from the road to the ditches alongside by a bulldozer which was still thus occupied as we hurried on northward.

On the rail lines in the valley was further evidence of earlier fighter-

More of the "Road to Montelimar." (Courtesy U.S. Air Force)

Some devastation was left on the rails, too. (Courtesy U.S. Air Force)

bomber work. Some seven trains, carrying mainly ammunition, and four or so huge railway guns lay dead on the tracks.

Not all of the German forces in southern France had been trapped and destroyed in the valley. Reportedly, considerable armor and some other equipment escaped (whether by other routes or from within the valley) and the bulk of the troops walked out. Still, the overall loss of equipment to the enemy forces in southern France and in the Rhone River Valley was tremendously high.

The welcome received by our personnel along Highway 7 and in Valence was a once-in-a-war experience in several ways. First of all, when one element of a convoy was halted by a destroyed bridge, they forded a stream and took another route. In the process, they apparently entered an area that had either been bypassed by our ground forces or not yet reached by such forces, and were welcomed as the first Americans on the scene.

The trip to Valence was characterized by warmth and friendliness of welcome throughout. Once the airplanes arrived, the welcome in Valence

Valence Airfield was a scene of destroyed enemy airplanes. (Courtesy U.S. Air Force)

More of such a scene. (Courtesy U.S. Air Force)

took on rather incredible proportions. The French people, who had risked life and limb as spectators to our attack on the airfield there, recognized the airplanes as those making the attack. Our commanders were faced with the situation of either having to call out the troops to shoot local men, women, and children, or let them keep coming as they descended on the field, many bringing flowers, food, and wine. At Valence, we became accustomed to operating in an "open house" setting of civilians on the airfield.

We also had a chance to look around this huge airfield complex, which the Germans had left only a day or two before our arrival. The destruction of airplanes on it was extensive. The claims for our attacks here had been far below the actual destruction inflicted that day.

Then came a wonderful surprise. We were shocked and overwhelmed—most joyfully so—when Lt. Bagian, Red Three of our initial attack on the Road to Montelimar, walked into the squadron area. He wasn't merrily hopping and skipping along, but rather hobbling in with the help of a homemade crutch. Even so, he was a most welcome sight.

He had survived the crash into the hillside. Although having considerable injuries, he had pulled himself free in time to escape fire and/or explosions, and crawled on into a grapevine in the vineyards. He subsequently endured an ordeal that can only be imagined. First, German search parties looked through and poked bayonets and shot machine pistols and other weapons into each grapevine. This was not a quick, one-time effort; it went on until they were forced to move on out ahead of the oncoming Allied forces. Some of the bombs dropped on the nearby enemy columns, particularly at night, came down very close to his grapevine. The mass of German troops walking out of the valley came through the vineyards and hills to avoid the air attacks on the road below. They walked by, sat, rested, ate, etc.—and searched all around and even in his grapevine until the last of them went on by.

Finally, the French farmers or vineyard tenders in the area came on the scene. Bagian was taken in, provided nourishment, treated for wounds, injuries and insect bites, and provided a crutch that was handcrafted from a tree limb on the spot. He made his way down to the highway and caught a ride with advancing friendly ground troops. And, in time, he went on to fly many more missions, becoming one of the most decorated, renowned and respected fighter-bomber pilots and mission leaders in the war.

Red Two, F/O Jennings, however, was found to have been killed in action, joining so many others in making that supreme sacrifice for his country. Of all who did—and of those who lived—in my view, none could have reached above and beyond the call of duty any higher than this young pilot flying as Red Two on August 28, 1944, on "The Road to Montelimar."

If we had become accustomed to visitors on the field at Valence, our first Sunday morning brought a massive exodus of men, women, and children from town and countryside to spend the day with us. A few airplanes had been set aside (away from the dangers of munitions, turning props, and other flight line activities) for the public to examine. They were attractions, all right. Women and young girls preferred sitting on the wings, dangling their legs over the leading edge around the gun blast tubes. The men seemed more interested in the cockpits, while the favorite spot of young boys was up on the nose and engine cowl. As for potential damage to the airplanes, someone said the French public did better than some of our own people in obeying the "No Step" sign on the flaps.

The Group flew its first missions into Germany proper from Valence. I led one of these, flown on the Sunday of the "airshow" crowds on the field. Each airplane was cheered along by the visitors on its way to the runway and as it roared past on takeoff. This mission was an armed-recce effort to the Freiburg-Mullheim area, just east of the French border and north of the Swiss border. In fact, we had to make sure we skirted wide of Switzerland enroute to and returning from the target area.

We strafed two trains and then turned to strafing barges on the waterways in the area. I had strafed a few barges in the Po Valley, which were small agricultural area types, probably pulled from shore by work animals. These in Germany varied in size by included some fairly large ones; many seemed to be self-propelled types. We religiously dodged the main population areas and plotted flak positions and flak was about nil otherwise. We strafed barge after barge, setting a number of them on fire.

I had a definite feeling as we crossed the border flying into Germany itself. Now we were hitting the enemy in his homeland instead of battling him in countries he had occupied. I guess I was also quite anxious for a first look at Germany. I'm not sure what I expected to see—perhaps some sort of tremendous fortress of a country and countryside. What I did see—in addition to targets—was some picturesque towns and villages, and very

With each move, more scenes of destruction along the way. (Courtesy U.S. Air Force)

pretty and green countryside on the fringes of the Black Forest.

As the sun lowered and flying ended for the day, our French visitors departed with many waves and goodbyes passed between them and the personnel on base. The French people did not come back after that; the visiting on base apparently was over. We didn't stay but a few days more before moving on to Lyon; the unique experience and relationship between the town of Valence and the 79th FG was over except for memories and history.

The reception in Lyon may have been even more welcomed by some. Here was friendliness on a city style instead of a farming community approach. Shows, cafes, and nightlife held forth. We lived in the manor of a large estate just out of town; the men of another squadron were camped in a park in the city, surrounded by apartment buildings—they may have had the best quarters arrangement of any unit in the entire war.

After the mission at Montelimar I had about decided to go home, with the move to Valence, it was obvious we could fly into Germany—and I wanted to do that at least once. Now that had been done, and it would be the last mission I would ever fly with the 79th—but the way that came to be had nothing to do with going home.

Chapter 10

Po River Valley

Captain Beck, the other flight leader who had gone home on special leave, and I sat and listened as the Squadron CO said that both of us were to assume command of squadrons. It was rather unusual for two officers in the same unit to hear that at the same time. However, Colonel Bates, our old Group CO from the days of Sicily and Southern Italy, was back overseas commanding another Group in Italy. He had arranged for the transfer of some experienced personnel from the 79th FG to boost the experience level in his outfit. As near as I knew such transfers between groups were quite rare. Anyway, our squadron CO, LT. Col. Lee, was being moved there to become Deputy Group CO and a squadron CO was also needed in that outfit.

Thus, one of us would take this squadron and one would go take a squadron in Italy. Which of those it was could make a big difference in many ways to a new CO. Here, the new CO would know everybody in the squadron and they would know him. He would know this unit's operations and procedures both in the air and on the ground. A senior flight leader moving up to CO in his own squadron was a normal and expected way for a unit to acquire a new CO. And this unit was in France, in the mainstream of the war, and among quite pleasant surroundings for a combat zone.

On the other hand, the new CO in the other unit would be among total strangers. He would be starting from scratch as far as that squadron's past operations and procedures went. Also, a young flight leader coming into a unit from elsewhere to command was unheard of as far as I knew. And that assignment meant returning to Italy, which some had said was the forgotten war—and in Italy it was always possible to end up in another isolated mudhole as home base.

I guess I suspected from the start which of us would go where, and may have been searching in mind for some kind of reason, however slim (such as

Beck being a bit older and more senior in grade), that would make it best for me to stay here. But the CO went on to brief us on what level of command, and just who at that level, had approved and ordered these new assignments, and had done so by name of those involved. Once aware of that, I didn't put forth any reason against, or make comment at all, when told that Captain Beck would stay here and I would go to the unit in Italy.

Actually, any opportunity to command a squadron far overshadowed considerations of which of these two it would be. Also, the assignment in Italy had one strong point in its favor: I might not know anybody else in that outfit, nor they me, but I knew the senior commanders I would serve under, and they knew me.

It was realized that the next mission schedule I faced would not have familiar names in the slots next to mine as in the past—names such as Cassiday, Balega, Brittian, Tichenor, Lincicome, Shuttleworth, Benito, Ac Moody, and many others.

The next day we were in the B-25 on the way to Italy. And there were now three of us going. Lt. Boone, the experienced and outstanding pilot who had led White flight on the Montelimar mission, was to take a flight leader's position in a squadron of our new Group. As the B-25 flew along on its normal noisy, breezy flight for the passengers, my thoughts were mainly on a new role in the war—one which would actually make it a new war for me. It was often said that the best job a fighter pilot could ever have was to be a flight leader holding the rank of captain. There he was a commander and leader in the air. He was deep into tactics and techniques, and in the development and performance of his pilots. His world in that position centered around flying and fighting. I had been in that position and that world since the early days of entering combat. Now, as a squadron CO, there would be another, equally important world—the world of all the ground operations and functions that made the flying and fighting possible.

Of course, with all the Group COs I knew—and certainly the one I was going to serve under now—a squadron CO's world does not change regarding flying and fighting. He flies and fights as first and foremost among all his pilots in the primary exercise of command of his unit in combat. He commands all the rest at the same time, with the sole objective of getting that combat mission accomplished.

That was the principle used by most of the higher commanders in the overseas theaters. The majority of the squadron and certain Group COs were now officers—some quite young—selected from the in-theater combat pilot force rather than by transfer from the States of more senior and experienced officers in terms of past military service. Certainly, there were exceptions. Many veteran officers from training commands (or elsewhere) came overseas, flew a while in combat, and then assumed command of units, and some were highly successful and effective. But the general trend was to fill CO vacancies with the best combat pilots and mission leaders in the units, regardless of their rank or overall military background.

These young combat pilot COs had much in their favor as commanders.

They were proven in combat. They knew the war at hand, and knew combat squadrons and groups from living and serving in them. Also, they knew and had a close tie with ground personnel. That was a knowledge and bond forged through duty in combat together, rather than by study of men at war from afar. And they fit well into the overall mission—which was not one to meet certain specified standards or criteria, or to prepare for future events and service, but rather a mission to fight and win World War II *now*.

The specific backgrounds of these COs, and those considered as the best potentials as COs, seemed to make little, if any, difference. Many had no college and no military training prior to the war, and came from various walks of life and civilian pursuits. The common denominator came in performance in the sky on the other side of the Bomb Line. Being a "hot" pilot in itself seldom led to a CO position, but if an officer and pilot could successfully and effectively fly, lead, and command missions in the air, making the decisions required there, he apparently could do the same thing on the ground. If it was possible for one to command effectively on the ground but not do the same in the air, I certainly did not know; I personally never saw such an officer get the chance in the war—at least not for very long.

In my own case, I suspected that my time spent as an enlisted man and a corporal before getting into cadets could not hurt things. Perhaps being in the ranks for a short while doesn't do a great deal toward knowledge of all the things a CO needs to know and do, but any enlisted service can leave memories and probably a few strong feelings on certain things a CO should *not* do in regard to the troops under him. And perhaps having been an enlisted man reinforces in mind the all-important part played by that other head man in the unit—the First Sergeant

On the way to my new unit I had some thoughts of home, too—mainly, that I could forget about going back there right away. However, my wife still wrote daily, and except for our being apart, things were okay at home. There had been no bad news about any of the family members in service. With my transfer back to Italy, the mail from home would be interrupted until I forwarded my new address and APO number, but it would all show up—and probably without undue delay. One of the amazing feats of World War II was that performed by APOs, FPOs, units, ships, etc., in delivering the mail to millions of servicemen and servicewomen throughout the many movements of units and personnel all around the world.

The B-25 landed at Grosseto, just inland from the west coast of Italy and about 80 miles above Rome. On the airfield were the P-47s of my new outfit, the 86th Fighter Group. The 86th FG was a well-known fighter-bomber Group in the theater. They had entered combat with A-36s, flying missions into Sicily, from a field in North Africa in July of 1943, and had come on up through Sicily and Italy supporting the U.S. Seventh or U.S. Fifth Armies most of the time. They flew from Corsica in support of southern France, then returned to Italy. As I understood it the 27th, 79th and 324th went into France after the invasion, while the 57th and 86th did not.

The 86th had flown the same varied fighter-bomber missions as all other units of this type in the MTO and covered most of the same campaigns and major battles, and they had inflicted their full share of destruction and damage on the enemy all along the way. They first went into Italy in support of Salerno, while their base (Sele Airfield) on the beachhead was still under enemy fire. A battery of U.S. artillery, 155s or "Long Toms," had been located between the field and the beach, sending outgoing fire over the airfield. From the field, ground personnel could watch their own airplanes making dive-bomb runs on enemy positions just a short distance inland. Among the unusual missions flown by this unit while in Italy was the dropping of food and other critical supplies to beleaguered New Zealand troops near Cassino. These were delivered in special containers at minimum altitude while under fire from German positions on Monastery Hill. Excellent results were reported by the grateful friendly troops. In other words, the 86th FG was a veteran fighter-bomber combat unit, not newcomers or converts from some other type of mission.

In a few days I was commanding the 86th's 525th Fighter Squadron. The other squadrons were the 526th and 527th. The 525th FS was a top-notch military outfit. It was fully manned, with well-qualified officers and NCOs who, along with all personnel, had been performing this mission a long time. They knew what had to be done to keep the unit going, and how to do it. Even in my initial observations it was obvious they did that extremely well. Thus, for a start, why not leave them alone and let them do it?

In a very brief talk to all personnel, I said I was very proud to be here, but did not say where I came from or why. In fact, *I* did not really know why except that I was following orders. The crux of the orders and guidance to me by my new Group CO could have been put in the form of a question: "You know what I want?" I knew *exactly* what he wanted. That was passed on to squadron personnel as my sole goal and purpose while Squadron CO: We would continue to fight the war to the fullest, to the best of our abilities and capabilities, and help end it as soon as possible. There were also assurances of no planned major changes or shakeups, of an open-door policy to see me, and a few other items. From my own experience as an enlisted man, I doubted that the troops would always believe the "no changes" business, but this time it was meant to be—at least as long as everything went okay.

My next step was a visit to each of the sections in the squadron. Riding with the flight surgeon to the squadron medical facilities (in tents on the airfield) we rounded the end of the runway and a P-51 whistled overhead and crashed on the field. It came to rest not far from some of our squadron personnel. They immediately rushed to the burning airplane and pulled the pilot out of the cockpit. As the pilot was taken to the medical section, I had the impression that a body was being handled, but after a short while the

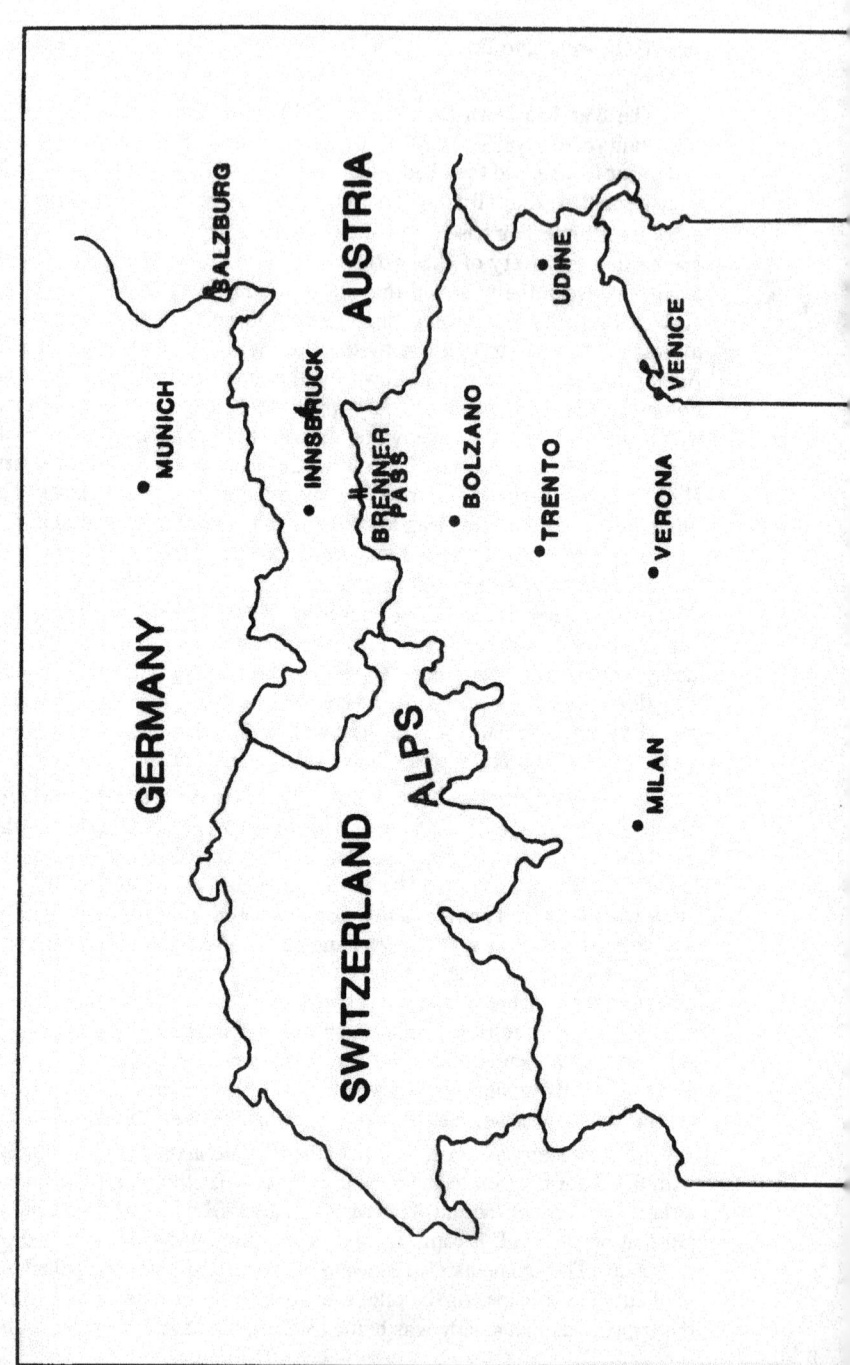

Caption: area of combat action in Chapters 10 through 13.

"Doc" and medics brought out a cleaned-up and very much alive pilot, who had relatively minor injuries. Right away I had seen a little of how *this* unit performed. And while not all rescue attempts were as successful as this one, such heroics in crashes on airfields were a frequent part of unit ground operations.

My approach to flying operations was a bit different than for the ground activities. While I wasn't going to personally try to run engineering, armament, transportation, the kitchen, or any other ground section of the unit, I most definitely *was* going to run the flying and fighting. Initially I had advised the Operations Officer to keep the flying going just as they normally would. Then, before turning attention to those operations, I went to visit a veteran CO of a squadron in another group, mainly listening as he discussed their current combat operations in Italy. Then I came back and listened for a long time as my Ops Officer and flight leaders discussed the flying operations in this squadron. I also flew a couple of missions, just like any other newcomer.

We were facing a major change in the pilot force in the 525th. Most of the veteran pilots were nearing rotation back to the States, while the rest of the pilot force consisted of two large groups of mainly young pilots. One group averaged about 30 missions and the other was just starting out. Except for a few pilots with instructor experience, all these younger pilots were products of flying schools and RTUs. In the very near future, the bulk of all flying operations in my squadron would be done by these young pilots.

Meetings in most combat units were very rare, but we held a series of pilots meetings at night and went over every aspect of combat flying: tactics and techniques, situations, and anything else on flying that I could think of. Then it was open for anything about flying the pilots wanted to talk about. Once the young ones got warmed up in eagerly talking with their new CO (who now had 140 missions), the meetings could have gone on indefinitely. They were discontinued very shortly, but the talking of flying never did stop in the 525th. It probably never stopped in any unit.

Beyond a doubt, the informal (and in some cases constant) talk of flying added many details of experiences and happenings (both good and bad) that were not covered in training. Of course, any informal discussions in meetings or elsewhere was only an adjunct to a squadron CO's number one task of commanding and calling the shots on the flying and flying in policies, tactics, techniques, judgments, decisions, and all the other factors that determine results on missions—and can play a major part in losses, too. If a squadron flew only one or two big missions a day, they could all be led by the most experienced pilots; however, we flew many small missions each day, and half the pilots or more in a squadron had to be leaders. Those small missions take all the same judgments, decisions and actions as a large one. Thus, while a CO naturally dealt in channels through the S-2, Ops Officer, and Flight Leaders to assure all missions had current essential information, a lot of pilots—from the CO on down—led missions and needed to know all they could about this highly diversified business of fighter-bomber combat flying. And since there was no standard "book" on it, the main means of communicating knowledge on the subject was word of mouth. In actual experience, many pilots had found that something learned in a bull session could come in just as handy in saving a mission or one's self as if learned in formal training.

I made no real changes in ground functions in the unit or in general operations and intelligence procedures. The latter I liked better than in my old unit. Several changes were made in combat operations. I modified the basic AAF combat formation flown by this squadron, spreading element and wingmen out slightly and also bringing them forward a bit. I asked that the harmonization point of the guns be moved out a couple hundred feet as the airplanes went through the next boresighting. Also, some tactics were modified, such as entry altitude for various attacks. I talked long and hard on close support and "100 percent sure" and many other subjects. Among them were weather criteria, some "dos and don'ts" of armed-recce, more "dos and don'ts" of dueling flak guns, and a pet peeve of mine against burning out gun barrels by firing long bursts at nothing in particular but rather at enemy territory in general.

I didn't dwell very long on discipline, or on concentration in combat, because (absolute and total) both in the air and on the ground were the only degrees of these we had to know.

Perhaps the best-received comments of all by certain of the pilots were those made in a general summary of how we would fight—and try to stay alive, too. The fighting had to be done, and the nature of that leaves absolutely no room for a timid or cautious approach—which, in fact, is a very good way to get killed. The fighting would be extremely aggressive and determined. We would fully fulfill every combat task called upon and/or presented, barring intervention by God and Mother Nature—and the enemy was specifically *not* included among any potential bars to completing each mission. To try to stay alive, we would rely on winning the war and getting it over with.

What I had done so far was enthusiastically received by a high percentage of the young pilots. Also, the "old heads" in key positions had cooperated fully. The biggest boost of my first few days as a CO came when two pilots, widely recognized throughout the unit as the most outstanding and strongest combat pilots among the "old heads," asked to stay and continue to fly combat instead of rotating back to the States.

And with that overall brief period of transition into this squadron, our full attention was turned to fighting the war and the day-to-day tasks thereof.

If Italy was considered a forgotten war by some, apparently it wasn't by the enemy. They kept a force of some 20 to 22 divisions facing a comparable force of the Allies in that country. The result was a very tough and bloody struggle. The Germans had now fallen back in positions along the Apennines, setting the stage for possibly another defensive line across Italy from the Pisa area on the west to the Rimini area on the east. Heavy fighting was underway as the Allies made efforts to advance, especially on the east end of the lines and with a major push in the middle directly toward Bologna.

Our flying was of two main types. One was in direct support of the ground fighting, particularly of the U.S. Fifth Army. The other was in an all-out interdiction effort in the Po River Valley north of the Apennines and on up into the routes leading through the Alps from Germany. That involved keeping all bridges across the Po and Adige Rivers cut, as well as keeping cuts in the main transportation lines. It also involved destruction of supply points and dumps, and always the attack of vehicles and personnel in the transportation systems.

In southern France we had seen little of the Luftwaffe, but in the Po Valley enemy air units were reported to be active on a number of airfields. These included Aviano, Vicenza, Villafranca, Ghedi and Udine. Periodic attacks on these installations were also involved, particularly Villafranca and Ghedi. Opposition by German fighters, as well as some Italian types such as the Macchi C.202 and C.205, was to be expected on missions into the valley.

Our most common missions in the Po Valley were rail cuts, the dive-bombing of railroad tracks, perhaps the most unglamorous of all fighter-bomber missions. On the surface, it might appear that some of these would be relatively uneventful as well, but rarely was that the case. It certainly wasn't if the cut was made in or near Bologna or any other city in the valley, and many cuts were made in such locations. On those missions in or near cities, the 88mm flak gave dive-bombers a fit during the approach and roll-in on the target; as usual, from there on the automatic weapons were the main problem.

When the rail cuts were made out in open countryside, where the 88s might not be a major threat, the light flak often still was. Also, on a rail cut on open tracks, most units released their bombs from absolutely the minimum altitude to clear the bomb blasts. That technique gave the best accuracy, but sometimes put holes in airplanes, too.

A rail cut. (Courtesy U.S. Air Force).

A Po River bridge, fall of 1944. (Courtesy U.S. Air Force)

Another primary type of mission was dive-bombing attacks on bridges. While some of these were initial attacks, most of the main bridges had been previously hit by medium bombers of fighter-bombers. However, these could be repaired or have bypasses constructed by the enemy, and the fighter-bombers often got the job of recutting them or keeping them from being repaired or bypassed. One bad thing about bridges was that many of them were in cities, which again meant operating in both heavy and light flak, and almost always in intense amounts. Bridges are hard to hit and cut anyway, and the pilots had to press on into and through the flak to quite low release points in order to achieve the best accuracy possible on each attack.

Another kind of mission that sent us into cities were commonly called "clean-ups." After the bombers hit a marshalling yard or other major target in a city, the fighter-bombers were frequently sent into clean up specific remaining targets that might be spread around within the general destruction area of the bomber raid, such as still-upright locomotives, freight cars, switching control facilities, power stations, etc. These could be rather sporty strafing missions.

Then there were bridges other than the fixed or permanent ones — mainly pontoon bridges. Some were in cities and other heavily defended areas; others were not. In fact, they could be almost anywhere, sometimes

This locomotive needed no follow-up work after a bombing attack. (Courtesy U.S. Air Force)

popping up overnight in places where there were none the day before. In that respect they were somewhat like targets of opportunity, yet most missions on them were pre-planned, scheduled missions. I liked to dive-bomb pontoon bridges. The pontoons and framework across them could be sent flying into the air along with walls of water, and in turn many loose pontoons and debris would go drifting downstream—where they could be shot to pieces with the guns. A bad thing about pontoon bridges was the enemy's ability to replace them rather quickly; then the new ones had to be hit, too. Fighter-bombers waged a long-running battle against pontoon bridges on the Po River. There were some ferry points, too, which at times

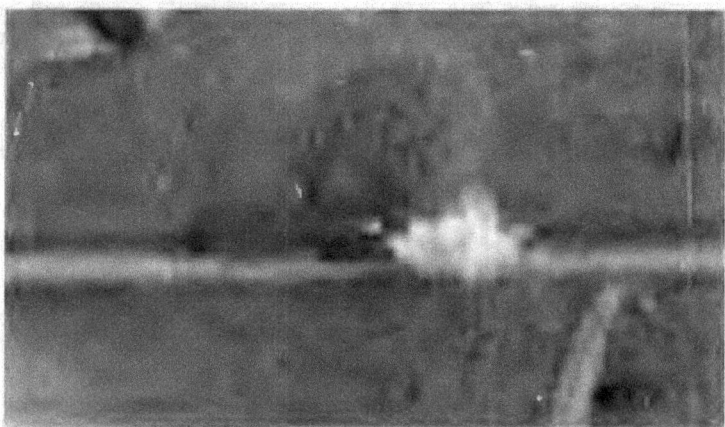

Vehicles attempting to hide under rather sparse cover. (Courtesy USAFF, World War II)

offered good strafing targets of vehicles in the area.

The immense Po Valley of flat, open, and apparently fertile farmland, with extensive road and rail networks throughout, was also very fertile territory for armed-reconnaissance and strafing. Seldom were large concentrations of targets found, but there was almost always some general traffic movement—and little in the way of places for the enemy to hide or take cover. Overall, it was probably a strafer's paradise (if anything about strafing or anything else in a war can be viewed in such a light). On almost every mission, after bombing a primary target we turned to armed-recce and strafing of targets of opportunity. We destroyed substantial numbers of vehicles on a regular basis.

Even more sought-after targets were found on the extensive railroad system in the valley. From my very first missions into the Po River valley, I had a keen interest in that system. I had asked Intelligence for all the information available on the rail networks in northern Italy and on up through Austria and into Germany. As a result, I had studied the routes and lines and found an absolute maze of rail lines crisscrossing the entire Po Valley.

From the beginning of our flying in the Po Valley, many trains were spotted and strafed as they operated in the open during the daytime. Yet my curiosity had first been triggered by the substantial numbers of freight cars seen sitting on tracks and sidings each day in so many small towns and villages. It was obvious and well-known that much heavier railroad operations went on at night and in bad weather, when our fighter-bombers were not overhead. There had to be a tremendous number of locomotives in that system.

And, as I figured it, for them to get into effective operations at night and bad weather, the distances were too great for the bulk of the locomotives to be hidden in the major cities or in tunnels (such as the huge one north of Genoa) during the day. I made my own evaluation that many of them had to be out in that flat, open valley in the daytime—many more of them than we usually saw in operation.

We went into a program of looking for locomotives on missions after our primary bombing target was attacked. Like all other units, we always kept our eyes open for moving trains on the main routes, but now, in addition, we really concentrated on the secondary or connecting lines in searching for locomotives. On these routes in most areas we could operate relatively free of flak—in many cases completely free of it. In those areas, instead of flying the armed-recce at 3000 feet or higher, we were down under 2000 feet—often much lower—where we could get a closer look along all the tracks. We found and strafed locomotives almost everywhere we searched. Many were in villages on sidetracks or on spurs among buildings, etc. Our number of locomotives destroyed rose dramatically.

When flying missions in support of friendly ground forces, as opposed to operating in the Po Valley, we were again in an area of much "sameness" of features among the hills and valleys of the Apennines. Again the mission

Napalm. (Courtesy U.S. Air Force)

leaders had to ensure a positive location and identification of targets in that "sameness" of features, and the flak was becoming perhaps some of the thickest for direct support operations of the war. That was especially true in front of the Allied attacks in the center of the lines.

A new fighter-bomber weapon was introduced into the war in Italy in the early fall of 1944—napalm. This was a fire bomb of jellied gasoline, carried in external tanks with a grenade and fuze to ignite the mixture on impact. Napalm had some deadly and nasty characteristics for the enemy upon which it was dropped. It produced a sudden large fireball on the ground, fed by a gluey fuel mix that would stick to anything it contacted as it spread forward with impact.

In the mountains, we normally delivered napalm in fairly shallow dives, tumbling the tanks into enemy positions. These drops created more-or-less round globs of fire on the ground. When used in the Po Valley or other fairly flat terrain, it was usually dropped in level flight at absolute

Napalm tank filler cap and grenade shown below blast tubes of the guns.

minimum altitude. These drops created long swaths of fire on the ground, which could be rolled into enemy positions, buildings, etc. Some pilots referred to such attacks as "wiping the tanks off on a target." Some pilots figured they were accurate enough doing that to throw a napalm tank through a particular window of a building—and some probably were.

My squadron had some rough losses in October. One of the outstanding veteran pilots, Captain Richard G. Oldham, who volunteered to stay instead of going home (and who incidentally had been on the special leave program to the States) was lost on an airfield attack. Oldham was hit as the attack was started, and chose to continue on leading the mission through the attack in a badly damaged and burning airplane. He did this with excellent strafing results, but crashed immediately thereafter. He was awarded the highest medal of any member of the 525th FS in the war.

One of the other veteran pilots, who had also been a stalwart leader in my early days as CO, was lost shortly before he would have rotated home. And one of the youngest pilots was hit on a close support mission and crashed back on our side of the lines. He was hospitalized with grave injuries, went into a coma, and later passed away.

Everyone flying knew there would be losses, but keeping them as low as possible was what had to be always in mind and strived for. And losses among pilots in squadrons were never viewed as statistics or rates; they were felt as deeply personal in nature.

Most missions in the Po Valley were not spectacular in nature, but they combined into rather spectacular total results. And there were many that *were* thrilling and noteworthy. On one mission in October we added a large number of freight cars destroyed in one sweep as a marshalling yard went up in a series of fires and explosions, scattering cars and parts in all directions. (That scattered the strafing airplanes in all directions, too.) I

A war on trains in the Po Valley. (Courtesy U.S. Air Force).

also requested and received permission to fly a couple of extra missions over and above our normal schedule. These were pure strafing missions on trains and each of them destroyed nine or ten locomotives and damaged about the same number, along with numerous cars. While the bombing and close support results and the total of targets of opportunity were the basic achievements, in September we destroyed some 28 locomotives with about 30 damaged; October results on locomotives were building toward more than double those figures in each category.

How those figures on locomotives compared to other squadrons outside the 86th FG in the MTO or in the ETO, I had no idea. But, from them, our sister squadrons, this the 525th FS picked up a nickname that would be with it for a long time—the "Locomotive Wrecking Company" of the Po River Valley.

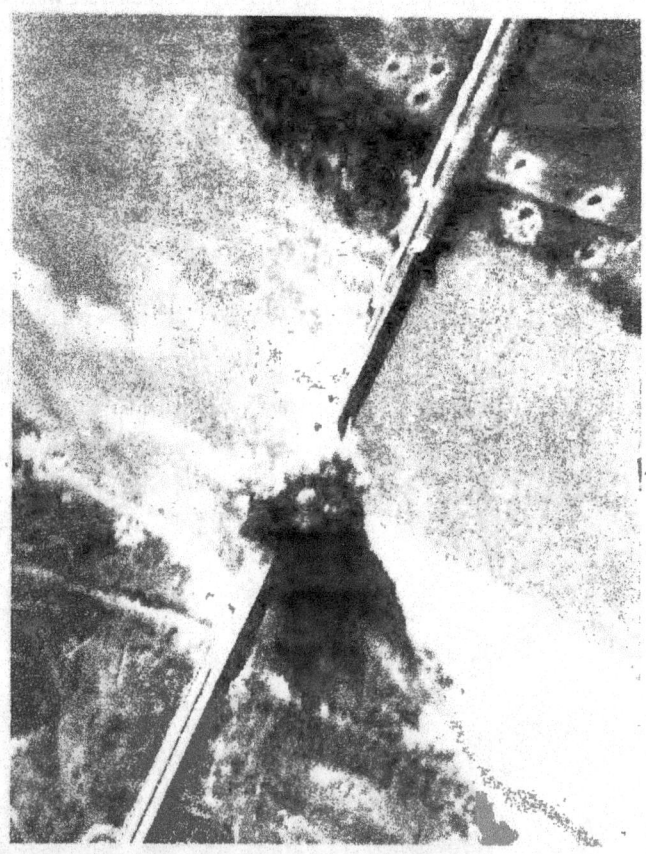

Yet, "wrecking locomotives" was only one element of our multi-mission job. Here, P-47s dive bomb a bridge. (Courtesy 79th Ftr Group, WW II)

Chapter 11

Winter Lines of 1944-45

By late autumn, Allied ground forces had pushed the lines across Italy to the north of Pisa on the west and above Remini on the east. In the center, our forces were below Bologna, still engaged in heavy fighting, where they had come within some 10 to 12 miles of that city but were unable to break out into the Po Valley. While winter by the calendar had yet to arrive, perhaps another situation of enemy winter defensive lines had.

In late October, we moved. The 525th FS was ordered to Pisa, while the Group and other squadrons would stay at Grosseto. This was one of the rather rare cases in the MTO of a planned separate squadron operation, except for certain initial operations on invasion beachheads. However, where we were going, the enemy wasn't much farther distant than on some of the beachhead airfields—well under 20 miles away. As someone said, by *miles* that sounds like a fairly safe distance, but if a pilot looks down on the length of a 5000-foot runway from the air and pictures the enemy as being less than 20 of those away, then they seem very close indeed.

The move was made amid a full-fledged flood. Part of a convoy got over a bridge before the bridge was swept away, stranding some of the vehicles and men on the wrong side of the river. Once in Pisa, the Arno River had inundated much of the city. To get around and set up operations on the field, a DUKW or "Duck" (amphibious vehicle) was borrowed from the ground forces. It was also used to rescue some of the public from flooded areas. In a couple of days, the unit and airplanes were operational on the Pisa airport.

The field had been heavily bombed and we were generally set up among wreckage and remains of buildings. However, there was enough of the terminal left to have the unusual luxury of an Operations office overlooking the ramp and airport, with the control tower left fairly intact upstairs. For quarters, we were situated in some rather majestic and

Pisa Airport, with our Group's "grasshopper" or liaison airplane buttoned up in a parking spot.

historic surroundings—buildings of the University of Pisa. The men and squadron headquarters were in school buildings just outside the city wall, directly across the street from the famed Leaning Tower. The officers were in a main university building in the city.

Now I was a base commander, too. Also, the squadron now had many of the functions of a Group staff simultaneous with squadron operations, but we had a few Group people with us and full support from the staff at Grosseto. Naturally, security was a major consideration. USAAF fighter groups and squadrons had no MP or special security troops assigned. The ground forces secured the general countryside (cleared it of the enemy) and conducted military police functions in the area. For unit and airfield security, the air units used the age-old military system of officer and seargeant of the guard, with guards detailed from among the troops. Otherwise, all officers and NCOs controlled everything and everybody in the unit area as a function of command channels and authority in the face of the enemy in combat. MP armbands were used at times by the guards on the roads into the airfields.

From Pisa we could fly missions well up into the Alps—to Austria and the Brenner Pass area, almost into Germany itself. Many of our missions were directed on the main transportation route from Germany to Italy through the Alps; however, most of our targets were south of the Brenner Pass itself, involving interdiction of the rail lines between Bolzano and Verona.

One overall interdiction program of tactical air apparently was to knock out the power stations and electrical facilities in the Brenner Pass routes to eliminate the use of electric locomotives and force the use of steam power on those mountain routes. Both bombers and fighter-bombers were involved. We hit some power facilities, but mainly we cut rail lines and strafed locomotives. Usually on this route it wasn't necessary to work hard at searching for locomotives—they were normally out on the main lines chugging away.

Flying in the Alps brought forth quite vividly a few new aspects of fighter-bomber work. One was flying among the cables strung from peak to peak and across most of the passes and valleys in the Alps. In some areas the cables were thick enough to be a definite hazard. We logged and plotted cables on our maps, and looked for patterns in cable altitudes in order to try to fly above or below most of them. We also descended and climbed out fairly steeply in order to reduce exposure time to cables. But we still had an airplane hit one. When it did, there was an eerie bluish flash across the sky, and then the cable was gone. The P-47 went on to complete the mission— with a large gash in the wing leading edge extending back to the bomb rack (which apparently snapped the cable). While extremely happy about the outcome in this case, no one was overjoyed when examining the damage to the airplane's wing and the evidence there as to the diameter of the huge cable. The odds of an airplane withstanding the next encounter with such a steel cable appeared very slim.

Naturally, this critical transportation lifeline through the Alps, from Germany to the enemy forces in Italy, was well defended with flak, both 88s and automatic weapons. That wasn't new to us at all, but when flying in the valleys it was different to see more flak coming *down* on the airplanes from nearby mountainsides and peaks than was coming *up* from the valley floor below. The enemy gunners did not seem to be the least bit shy about shooting into the countryside below as they shot down on our airplanes.

At the southern end of the main Brenner Pass route, as the hub of rails and roads branching out into the Po Valley, was the city of Verona. That is a rather lovely name, and it was probably a very lovely city. However, most fighter-bomber pilots probably never took the time to appraise its beauty from the air—even if they could see it through the clouds of flak that came up from there, and from miles around it in most all directions. It was not a nice area in which to do fighter-bomber work, and when we went there the emphasis was on hitting the target and leaving without undue delay, and with no appreciation at all for the scenery or hospitality.

On missions deep into the Alps, up near or in the Brenner Pass, we religiously avoided flying over Verona and the main rail lines until reaching our target area. Usually that was done by flying just to the west and over Lake Garda on the way north. Small boats were on the lake at times, but on one mission we saw a large vessel cruising right down the center of the big, scenic lake. We flew on and hit our target, and on our way back the large boat was still underway on the lake. We had enough ammo to shoot it to pieces and leave it engulfed in a roaring fire. I was not sure just what kind of vessel it was. In earlier years it may have been an excursion or sightseeing vessel, but in the war it was assumed to be a ferry.

From time to time other boats were destroyed on the lake, too. One or two more fairly good-sized vessels were strafed, but the most interesting shooting was at speedboats. When caught out in the open on the lake, they ran around maneuvering at full speed while our pilots tried to outmaneuver and outsmart the boat operators. Usually the pilots won and destroyed the boats, but it is probably a minor miracle that none flew into the water in the process.

By early November, most all of the "old heads" among my pilots had departed for the States. With a captain in the Operations Officer spot (and as my deputy) and one captain in a Flight Leader spot, the rest of the key positions were filled by young lieutenants. Picking flight leaders and assistants had been one of the roughest tasks I had ever faced. That was not in trying to find capable ones; it was because there were too *many* capable ones and not enough Flight Leader or assistant Operations Officer positions for all of them. From the beginning, the performance of those picked and all of those leading missions was exceptional in every respect—and there had been no way to slowly work them into leading missions; they had simply been sent out as leaders.

Also in early November we faced a major threat to the entire unit that had nothing to do with combat flying. The Germans made a strong attack in the lines to our north, apparently breaking through and rolling towards Pisa. The Ops officer was given control of the airplanes and pilots, with instructions on getting them off on missions and/or evacuating them back to Grosseto. Classified material and some equipment was loaded onto vehicles to move out to Grosseto as well. Per previously established plans and orders, I and the rest of the unit prepared to join any other available forces or troops in the area and fight on foot to attempt to defend the bridge across the Arno River at Pisa. While the prospects of an air unit—equipped mainly with individual weapons—tangling with German infantry was not very promising, the personnel of this one were ready to do just that.

Fortunately, it never happened. The Germans were stopped just north of the city, reportedly by a division that had recently been relieved in the lines but was still located between Pisa and the enemy. Regardless of how stopped, the Germans were also almost immediately pushed back to the vicinity of the original lines. And we turned our attention back to fighting the air war.

In the locomotive wrecking work, certain pilots seemed to get a special kick out of cases now and then where they completely knocked a locomotive off the track or had one derail and wreck when they strafed it. Through pure luck, I had that happen on a couple of the very first missions flown with the 525th. However, some developments while strafing trains up in the Brenner Pass and Verona areas had us thinking much more about how to destroy locos *at all* in that area, rather than on how spectacular the kills might be.

First of all some of the locomotives appeared as if they might be carrying armor plate on the sides of the boilers. Certain locomotives were much harder to "blow." That might lead to a need for shooting them from the rear, through the cab. But, at the same time, on some recent missions, pilots had been committed into their strafing passes, only to see the sides of one or more would-be freight cars fly open to expose the blazing multiple

Doing this gets much tougher when there are flak cars on the train. (Courtesy U.S. Air Force)

barrels of automatic flak guns, with armor or concrete protection for the gunners. The term "flak cars" joined many others based on the word "flak" (such as flak traps, flak towers, flak alleys, etc.) in the language of fighter-bomber pilots. Some pilots called them "flak wagons;" either way, they were bad news for the strafers of locomotives and trains.

Our tactics to cope with surprise use of flak cars against already committed airplanes was to have the flight and element leaders turn on the flak cars in a shootout with them, while the wingmen went through to destroy the locomotive. That worked okay (if *anything* about a shootout with flak guns was ever okay) when we could come in from 90 degrees or so on the trains—that way, the flak cars did not get a good shot at each airplane. If we had to come in down the tracks either from behind or ahead of the locomotive, then the flak cars had a good shot at each airplane unless we knocked out the flak guns. Either way, it was tough business.

As the days went by, we found trains with more than one or two flak cars. Also, sometimes there was no attempt at disguising the flak cars—rather, they were just sitting out in the open. And now the term "flak train" joined that of "flak car" and the other "flaks" in pilot talk and reports. Leaders had to start evaluating before an attack if the train below was in fact a train hauling cargo, or if it was out there running in the open for the purpose of enticing fighter-bombers into a flak trap.

All mission leaders had long been alert to flak traps of various kinds. On airfields, such as Villafranca in the Po Valley, one or more old wrecks of Ju 52s or some similar bait might be set out in the middle of the flying field to lure fighter-bombers into good range for the automatic weapons there. Unless some movement of airplanes or activity around them was evident, close-in investigation and/or unscheduled attacks on enemy airfields was bad business.

While not necessarily flak traps, many trucks along roadways were burned-out wrecks and were a waste of time and an unnecessary risk to strafe. Some leaders kept tabs on the location of many of them, as well as looked for telltale signs of past fires on the roads from which the wrecks may have been pushed aside. Again, movement or some sign of activity around vehicles was the best clue of a valid target. Also, if locomotives, sitting isolated on sidings or spurs, didn't produce immediate clouds of steam when strafed, they were highly suspect as being derelicts of the rails.

All leaders probably followed the rule of not going into areas of known intense flak unless ordered there or worthwhile targets were clearly seen there. It was a poor gamble to go just on the chance a target might be found. The old argument of whether or not one truck was ever worth a strafing pass was always around. Yet, as could be pointed out, if no one ever strafed single trucks, the enemy could send them singly down the road every 15 minutes or so and get a tremendous amount of supplies through in unchallenged and unattacked trucks. Strafing single trucks, or small numbers of them, was part of fighter-bomber work—it was simply best to do so in areas where the odds of being shot at from the ground were slim.

When we first moved into Pisa, our airfield was the most forward base on the west side of Italy. As a result, we had many airplanes from other units land there with battle damage and emergencies. Our ground crews were involved in a number of rescue efforts on crashes, and in removal, repair, and service of many of the transient airplanes. Our own battle damage was high, and while keeping a base as well as a squadron going, the 525th FS at Pisa was surely one of the hardest-worked flying units in history.

Of course, we had communications with higher headquarters, and forwarding mission reports on the visitors, as well as putting some of them in contact with their units, was also a small extra chore. At any rate, our rather numerous visiting pilots at Pisa highlighted a couple of things about the nature of life in an overseas theater. One, a pilot with a parachute over his shoulders—especially if it had been used—had no trouble at all hitching a ride back home. Two, as some of the visitors contacted home bases, friends, or whoever with calls of various kinds, one could be amazed at the field telephone system. You could pick up a field phone and, in time, talk to just about anyone desired, anywhere in the theater.

Most of our missions continued to be on routes in the Alps or northern part of the Po Valley. We did fly a few escort missions now and then, and participated in a concerted firebomb effort on fortified German positions in the Apennines.

These varied and far-flung operations (spread over a wide range of terrain, population densities, and enemy activities) had considerable impact on the actions taken by mission leaders in the event of a downed pilot. A pilot bailing out over German positions in the front lines, over an airfield or other heavily defended areas could hope for little beyond capture by the enemy. One going down over the main routes in the Alps faced almost certain capture, too, and one going down in the deep snow of the Alps away from populated areas probably faced little chance of survival at all. In certain areas—mainly in the northern part of the Po Valley—local authorities and others posed a threat and a pilot would be better off turning himself in to the German military. On the other hand, some areas of the valley—particularly along the southern edges—offered good chances of evasion through the assistance of friendly Italian partisans, and the flat farming areas of the valley could offer some hope of assistance by partisans or local farm families.

Thus, each case of a downed pilot and his situation had to be weighed by the mission leader. If a pilot went down in known partisan territory and had been seen to be okay and take cover, then the leader would probably not further pinpoint the pilot's position by circling overhead, but rather would check on any possible movement of enemy forces from elsewhere toward that general area. If a pilot was down in an open field in the valley and seen running for the nearest cover, any enemy positions or forces nearby would surely be attacked to keep them away from him until he could reach cover or possible assistance.

In due course the rest of the 86th Fighter Group moved up to Pisa and took over functions at the base level. The 86th's airplanes now sported a distinctive paint job of bold red and white candy-stripe tails. (Those in my squadron had been painted as one more of the varied tasks while at Pisa.)

Then we were joined by another unit on Pisa. This was a P-47 squadron of the Brazilian Expeditionary Force. As both outfits shared the airfield and off-duty life in Pisa, the presence of the Brazilian troops presented an unusual situation for American troops. The latter were widely recognized as the best-paid troops among the many Allies in Italy—and the biggest spenders, too. While that was true mainly because the other Allies were not paid much of anything, the Brazilians were paid more than the Americans.

One day I was told that a general officer, chief of staff of a higher

Some of our airplanes had artwork on them; shown here is Miss Tennessee.

Even on a city airport, some things didn't change from "field conditions" for us and our allies.

headquarters, wanted to visit and spend a full day with one of the very youngest and newest of the COs of a fighter-bomber squadron. I thought that sounded like an excellent idea, until I heard the rest of it—the squadron was *mine* and the day was *tomorrow*. I was on the early mission, and frankly was a bit superstitious about changing flying schedules. In fact, swaps or trades among pilots were not allowed, and no changes were made after the schedule was posted unless absolutely essential. However, the general had no objections to my flying the first mission. He would be present for the debriefing.

Due to the nearness of the mountains and the enemy north of Pisa, instead of climbing over the field and then crossing the enemy lines, most all our missions into the Po Valley took a route to the west out to sea after takeoff, climbing there and turning north to enter enemy territory across the coastline. As long as Genoa, La Spezia, and a few other defended spots on the coast were avoided, we could go to and return from the valley completely free of flak. Our mission on the morning of the general's visit was a fairly long one, a rail cut along Lake Como north of Milan. The weather was not good; clouds were built up fairly solid to the west. We climbed over the field and took a route staying over land all the way. An exceptionally strong tailwind was clocked enroute to the target. Once there we had excellent results in rail cuts, and made one strafing pass on a small convoy of trucks on an adjacent road. On the way back, where we had been over scattered clouds going out, we were now over a solid overcast—and having to climb to stay there. I almost had to force myself to fly the extra time to allow for the strong winds. When we reached a point where the Arno River Valley and Pisa should have been showing clearly just ahead, we were at 14,000 feet, barely on top of the clouds, and with nothing but cloud tops showing in all directions.

Some penetrations and letdowns in clouds had been common while at Pisa. Most were while going and coming over the water, but we had made them in the Arno Valley, too, when the Apennines were in the clear and a positive position could be determined. Today we didn't have that positive position. I fudged a little on the time, flying a bit further south, and then one airplane went down through the weather. The report back wasn't good, but it was much better than no report at all. That plane broke out in the valley near the coast but under a ceiling of only a few hundred feet, and visibility was not good underneath. The rest of the mission penetrated and broke out over the water, coming back on the wavetops for a landing at Pisa. There were seven pilots involved in the formation penetration, and some iron-willed and exceptional flying was accomplished in order to have it succeed in weather that thick, solid, and low.

The general was on hand and did stay all day. While I had expected to be involved in explaining our flying operations most of that time, after the debriefing he never mentioned flying again. The day was spent discussing everything *except* flying in the unit, and much about the military in general.

I could see my Executive Officer, Adjutant and First Sergeant really sweating out this operation. They were surely looking on it as an extremely important and critical inspection if conducted by a general officer. And with a new, young CO showing the inspecting general documents (such as the personnel rosters, morning reports, etc.) and answering all the questions thereon, they could surely envision many nights of work trying to answer the kind of "write-ups" that would be in this inspection report.

They were probably feeling like I had at a recent ceremony on the ramp as a general officer awarded medals to pilots. A few dogs had ventured underfoot of some of the principals—in fact, almost knocking the feet out from under the Adjutant while he soldierly pressed on, reading a citation as if there were no dogs in all of Italy. I was sure no good was to come of the episode, but there had been more smiles than anything else. And, as it turned out, on the general's visit with me there was to be no inspection report to answer; when I saw the Group CO that night, he indicated all was well and fine.

However, all had not been well and fine on the mission that morning. While little had been said in debriefing about the weather except to report it unsuitable for any more flying, we had another little debriefing on the mission and weather. In this one, it was specified that I should never have gone on to Lake Como. Once in the air, seeing that much weather west of the field, I should have bombed the first main rail line we came to in the valley, and then returned to land immediately. And while some bad weather was common in northern Italy in fall and winter, neither I nor the other leaders ever put ourselves into quite that much of a weather bind again.

We were given a new type of mission to both design and fly—flak suppression for the medium bombers, who apparently were taking a real pounding from flak over many of the targets in northern Italy. With our first such mission scheduled for the next morning, I was asked to brief both my Group CO and, in turn, higher headquarters on how we planned to go about it. I didn't know, but assumed other groups and squadrons were probably doing the same thing. Anyway, I gave them our plan and received no orders to change anything for the upcoming morning mission.

I had the target, route, length of bomb run, altitude, and airspeed of the bombers, and of course the radio channel, but otherwise no briefing between them and us was necessary. In the air that morning, with eight airplanes, we made a normal rendezvous as for an escort mission. The fighters were positioned with one flight of four on each side of the bombers, my flight slightly forward of the second flight. As the bombers began their bomb run, I started the fighters down in a shallow dive. Our goal was to be looking down on the area surrounding the target and in position to start firing as the bombers approached the critical part of their run prior to bomb release. Then, as the flak guns opened fire, we would try to pick up firing batteries and press on in to the deck, keeping fire on those batteries as the bombers released their bombs and broke off from the target.

On this first mission, that worked out well. We picked up some firing batteries of 88s and were able to not only suppress but knock out some positions. Leaders were briefed to go after tracking and fire control equipment, while wingmen shot guns and gun crews. Then, when on-the-deck, we flew on through the target area to avoid the now-falling bombs. However, we did not keep going on out of the area. Each flight made a turn on-the-deck to come back on already spotted gun positions to work them over again just after the bombs hit. And from then on we made repeated passes shooting guns, gunners, and fire control systems as the bombers withdrew.

That first mission was considered highly effective and we used basically that same system on and on while flying this type of mission. In some cases the flights were staggered slightly more, and even with one or two more flights trailing the first two. In most cases we didn't really fly out from under the bombs, but rather just avoided the immediate target area and kept on strafing as the bombs impacted.

One of these missions produced an incident worthy of lasting "war story" status. One pilot, flying on-the-deck, made an extremely tight turn

Cold day on the ramp as a napalm mission is launched and a GP bomb serves as a footrest.

back to try to shoot the crew off a firing 88mm gun, which he saw just off his wingtip as he made a first pass on that battery. As he came back, he got the sight on the crew and blasted away, but he needed just a wee bit more time of concentrated fire there to get all of them. Well, as previously noted, that "wee bit more" on-the-deck can cause a pilot to fly into the ground. This one knew it would cause him to brush some trees, and that he did. However, he didn't fly into the ground—he flew into the *gun*. The barrel cut a neat outline right through the tail of the airplane.

Once that airplane was on the ground, I was in position to make some decisions. One was to cover up the outline of a gun barrel in the airplane with a tarp, field jacket, or something. Another was to report the damage as caused by an 88mm flak gun, without going into any further details. I had a particular interest in both the airplane and the pilot. It was my airplane, No. 39, and even closer to heart was the fact that I had just now stepped down out of it. My efforts to keep the incident "under wraps" were successful in official channels, but were a complete failure among my pilots and other personnel locally.

(The 525th FS had the lowest number of the three in the 86th Group, thus had the lowest numbered airplanes, Numbers 10 through 39. Normally a CO would probably pick the lowest number, or some special number such as 11, but when I came in No. 39 was unassigned and I decided to stick to the highest number in the unit as I had in my old squadron. ("Thirty-nines" among the P-47s here hadn't done much better than my old "Ninety-nines;" I was already on the second one.)

The Group CO suggested I take a short break from combat and accompany him to Capri for a few days—and when such suggestions are made by such COs, that is what one does. When we arrived there, apparently the international social set on the island were traveling again. My civilian friends were at Rome for the season or some other non-war related reason. The island seemed overpopulated with permanent party and Naples-area types. I didn't do much of anything except walk up and down mountains, sleep, eat, and wait for the R & R to end.

When I returned to Pisa, the Group CO presented me with a set of major's leaves and the orders promoting me to that rank.

As November came to an end, our results showed sharp increases in vehicles and gun positions destroyed, and in ammo expended. The locomotive kills were still up but a sister squadron was pressing us some for the title of "Locomotive Wrecking Company," as well as in total results. Yet a strong point had been made for mission leaders to avoid making judgments or decisions based on any kind of a contest between squadrons on strafing results. One contest—that with the enemy—was the only thing to keep in mind. Some losses had continued, and I had lost a pilot to flak from the high cover flight as my flight was making an airfield attack. The cover flights, flown as protection against enemy airplanes, and now used only in certain areas and situations, had sometimes taken as much or more flak than the strafing airplanes down below.

Pilots kept right on going to the valley to shoot up trains and track. (Courtesy U.S. Air Force)

Even though technically winter had still not arrived, the weather for it had—and so had the establishment of the German defensive positions across Italy, this time known as the Gothic Line. Pilots could start to picture another winter of stalemate—and an ever-continuing buildup of even more flak in the Po Valley, as had been the case in the Liri Valley last winter.

The Po Valley already had its own war song, which, among other things, mentioned:

> *Oh, I went to the Po River Valley,*
> *Many wonderful sights did I see,*
> *But the one that will live in my memory*
> *Is the flak that they shot up at me.*

The song also mentioned going to the valley to shoot up some trains and some track—after which many pilots added their own lyrics of being damned lucky to get back.

Chapter 12

Forward Air Controller

After the Group moved to Pisa there was a grand opening of a new mess and club, and both were rather plush for a unit that was supposedly in the field. Tablecloths on the tables and strolling musicians in the room added considerable atmosphere (even if not otherwise changing the same old rations on the plates). In the club, a roaring fire in the huge fireplace and nickel drinks at the bar warmed one's body as the Group's band played stateside dance music. And there was an excellent show of nurses and WAC officers present, many invited from Leghorn and Florence. Our fighter-bomber living facilities and social activities had come a long way from the days of sitting under a bridge listening to a hand-cranked record player—and, with another long winter facing us, we would probably be very glad for such surroundings.

However, I wasn't there very long after the grand opening to enjoy them. The close air support system had also come a long way since the very first missions were flown on which the pilots talked by radio with personnel among the ground forces. The terms "Rover Joe" and "Rover David" had come into the fighter-bomber pilots' war, usually recognized as the identity of "spotters" on the ground for close support operations. Now a system was incorporated to put well-qualified operational pilots in the front lines as decision-makers on strike requests and controllers of close support missions. The higher commands in Italy attached such importance to this program that the selection criteria for these controllers were that they be highly experienced in combat, be squadron COs, and hold the rank of major or above. An assistant controller, who accompanied each controller, had to be a highly experienced flight leader. And, while not in the published criteria, there was a strong rumor that a commanding general up the line was personally involved in the picking anyway.

A "Rover Joe" position for communications with fighter-bombers on close support missions. (Courtesy U.S. Air Force)

However done, I was selected by someone. In turn, I chose one of my more experienced flight loaders, 1st Lt. Richard B. Moyle, who was also one of the more rugged physical types among them. Perhaps neither of us knew exactly why we had been picked, but we both knew we had not volunteered for this tour of duty. With a jeep load of field equipment, we headed for Florence for a briefing at a higher headquarters before going on to the front. We still wore the .45-caliber pistols as standard practice and had augmented these with a bit more firepower (one .45-caliber Thompson submachine gun and one .45-caliber M3 "Grease Gun") from the rather sizable collection of extra weapons in the unit.

Moyle and I reported to the Commanding General of the TAC (Tactical Air Command) in Florence. During my service in the Twelfth Air Force, fighter-bombers had first operated under an Air Support Command, then a TAC (XII), and for a short while under a Fighter Command. Now they were back under a TAC (XXII) again, which had become the standard intermediate command under the tactical air forces in Europe to handle fighter-bomber operations. I knew this CG, Brig. Gen. Benjamin W. Chidlaw, and had been extremely impressed with his knowledge of the stick-and-rudder air fighting and his ability to talk flying details with the pilots, which he apparently liked to do. Most of the briefing and guidance came directly from him and his A-3 (operations chief). Our orders were quite specific on rules and procedures regarding requests for air strikes and safety of friendly ground forces. The key object was to have targets received, evaluated, and acted upon right there in the front lines. Situations in which we would contact the TAC CG for decisions were specified, and when those situations came up, he left no doubt that is what he wanted done. Yet, at the same time,

I gathered that he didn't want to *be* the forward air controller—that's what *we* were going for.

We pressed on toward the ground war, traveling for awhile on a main highway, following a map and directions received from a ground force liaison officer at the headquarters. In time the scene around us changed considerably, now with few if any civilians seen and many signs at intersections pointing off to various unit locations. Then, per our directions, we turned off on a mud road and started a winding climb up a mountain. In time we were held in a row of traffic, mostly "six-bys," as a line of vehicles came down the mountain. The truck driver behind said we were waiting our turn to cross "the bridge." He also said to "Watch it going on up, the road gets bad and a jeep could slide over the side." When our turn came to travel the one-way section of road and cross the bridge, the truck driver's advice proved to be very sound.

I was busy following that advice and only had a glimpse of the bridge as we crawled up the mountain toward it. There may have been the core of an engineer-type steel bridge in the structure (Bailey or otherwise), but if so, it was shrouded pretty well with many tree trunks. Those timbers seemed to be propping the bridge up along a sheer rock wall. Then, with a span over a small but deep gorge, it appeared tied the same way to a rock wall on the other side.

With MPs starting each vehicle across, and instructions to hold the interval, across we went. As we did, Moyle glazed down and made a remark that there was "enough room down there to split-S a P-47." That may have been as astute, flying-oriented observation for a pilot to make, but I had trouble seeing how it contributed much to the task at hand. (And I made a mental note that if we ever got back to our airfield, to send Moyle up here in a P-47 to fly a few split-Ss under this bridge—at night!)

A road to the front in the mountains of Italy, traveled here by elements of British forces. (Courtesy National Archives)

were in an area of British troops. That's as it should be, since we were not joining a U.S. division, but rather the British 78th Infantry Division. We found their division headquarters, while proceeding rather cautiously to prevent finding some of the enemy first. It was set up in a few war-ravaged stone houses in a small village—a perfect picture of a headquarters as might be seen in a war movie. However, on checking in with our hosts, one of them mentioned the damage to the houses had not been left over from earlier fighting as the war passed through, but rather had happened two nights ago in a German artillery barrage. Now the setting did not seem to have any connection with a movie at all.

We stayed at the Division that night, being welcomed by and meeting the staff and various key combat commanders—and that was mainly the business of the evening as compared to going into briefings on the combat situation, our duties, etc. The entire atmosphere was one of glad to have us, appreciative of the air support, and welcome here at the headquarters and mess anytime we could get back in for a night or so. One could conclude that the relationship was one of our hosts knowing what they were doing and giving us credit for knowing what we were to do. The closest any real talk of fighting came was when one officer asked if we had encountered any incoming fire on our trip in. As we indicated we had not, I tried to completely blank out any thoughts of such a thing as being shot at on that bridge.

If the lines in Italy were in a general stalemate, this certainly was no "phony war" situation of both sides sitting idle, waiting for spring. In early December the Allies had reportedly launched yet another offensive to take Bologna. It had been met by fierce resistance and strong counterattacks. This kind of action continued, with the Allies fighting forward, or to establish a beachhead across a river or stream, only to be met with a counterthrust by the enemy. As we arrived on the scene to be forward air controllers, it was early December and our position in the lines was almost directly in front of Bologna.

Before daylight the next morning we were met at the Division by a captain, a company commander, who would escort us to the control position in his section of the front. He was a very rugged individual, fairly young, who gave a strong impression of being what a combat infantry commander would be. At the same time, he showed more pleasantness and good nature than one would ever expect in a person who had fought as long and hard as we understood he had. However, he went right into the subject of the war rather than dragging out the initial courtesies and protocol.

First off was a check of what we were wearing and had for equipment. We had thought of bringing fur-lined flying equipment to counter the winter weather in the mountains, but I had nixed that in favor of GI field equipment. That was fine, and just what we should have. Specifically checked was that we had no German weapons, helmets, or other souvenirs, and no slick or fancy boots of any kind. The captain explained all this. He had Gurkha troops (the famed soldiers from Nepal), who had a habit of crawling around at night with some extremely good knives as they felt for certain things in the dark. If the rough finish and buckles of U.S. and British combat boots were felt, all was fine. Also, if the rough finish of a U.S. or British helmet was felt, all was fine. However, if the smooth finish of either German boots or helmet was felt, throats were cut in a flash. The same was true if any German weapons or other enemy equipment was identified on or near a corpse-to-be.

In a very short trip in the jeep, we came to a sign indicating "Beyond This Point You Are In Full View Of The Enemy." We pulled off to the right from the road, which led on to the left around a definite ridge, and parked the jeep among the rocks near a couple of tents nestled at the base of the ridge. That was our base camp, manned by a few British soldiers. The captain led us up the sharp backside of the ridge, pointing out a route that would keep climbers from the view of the enemy; yet, obviously from a better path over to the left, some people were going up and down in view of the Germans.

Near the top we stopped at a shallow cave, which was our duty station and quarters at night. Our escort pointed out something I had been eyeing off and on all the way up—about eight fresh shell craters just below the cave. Obviously the Germans could put artillery on the position. I assumed they could hit it with *nebel werfers* (multiple barrel-rocket launchers, or "screaming meemies") and perhaps mortars, too. The main point made was that the Germans did outnumber the Allies in this area and were quite active on patrols at night. Patrols had ranged well beyond our position; thus, whether up here on the ridge or back at Division for a shower, *don't go roaming around at night*. The captain added that if we wanted to do some ground fighting over and above any that might come to us anyway, he would take us out to do it.

I was now smoking about two packs of Chesterfields a day, and there might be a little strain in refraining from lighting up at any time from sundown to sunup. Yet, as it turned out, the incentive for not flicking a lighter and showing a flame for somebody to shoot at was quite adequate for me to break the habit at night.

On up, on the very top of the ridge, was the control position. It was a hole among the rocks with an entranceway to crawl in from the back side, which also was a drain for rain water and melted snow. There was room for about three people, a couple of VHF radios, a bank of field phones, and a ground radio. From there, peering out to the north, we could see an identical ridge a short distance away—which was held by the enemy, with the front lines in the valley between these ridges. However, by looking left or right of the adjacent enemy ridge, we could look down on enemy-held valleys where much of the air support would be used. The valley to the right was a large one, leading on into the flat expanse of the Po Valley. On a day of good visibility, we could almost see into the valley floor in the Bologna area.

I was relieving a lieutenant colonel, a veteran squadron CO in the 57th Group, with combat experience going back to the days of North Africa. We watched as he and his assistant, working with a British major (intelligence officer) processed a couple of target requests and controlled the air strikes. Then we took over the duties as the ex-controllers headed back to their home base and the air war.

Naturally, there were rather extensive and firm rules on procedures, weather conditions, etc. Included were normal safe distances for various munitions. GP bombs—mostly 500-pounders—were a standard munition on many close support targets, but we had used 250 and even 100-pounders in the past on such targets. Strafing in the bomb run was a normal procedure on these targets by many units, and voluntary second or repeated passes were often offered by mission leaders. They were normally quickly accepted by the controllers, too. On the other hand, rarely was a second or repeated passes requested of mission leaders, but they were in some cases of urgent need, and those were usually quickly accepted by the mission leader.

One ground rule was that air strikes were not to replace artillery. Attempts had to have been made to take out targets by artillery, or reasons given why they couldn't, before we accepted and sent air strikes on them. The British major had direct contact with an artillery battery to mark targets with smoke shells when needed.

Requests for strikes came from the combat commanders through Division channels to the British major at our position. We quickly evaluated them for safety of friendly ground troops, weather conditions, munitions of the available airplanes, etc. Then, if all was well, the strike was executed. By radio, each mission was given the target by exact location and physical description as well as the type of target and situation involved. Confirmation and agreement from the mission leader had to be received through these means. Then, if considered necessary, the target was also marked by smoke. Yet never was smoke alone depended upon as a sole or primary

Using a smoke shell to help identify a target (Courtesy U.S. Air Force)

means of target identification. The enemy threw some smoke shells around too, at times.

Usually we had some allocated number of missions coming to us at time intervals during the day. In my own experience, we always had targets for those missions, and we had a direct line to the TAC for decisions on any problems encountered as well as to request airplanes for special needs. However, that line to the TAC usually stayed silent and the close support system in this area operated from a hole on a mountaintop in the front lines.

Yet it did not operate in isolation. As the sun set on our first day as forward air controllers, the line from the TAC was used for quite a while. The CG called for a discussion of the day's operations and much in general about us, procedures, relationships, etc. Such a call and discussion with the CG or his A-3 would be a regular evening event before we closed up the control position each night.

There were other regular events each afternoon as the sun started to set. Down in the little valley behind the position, where our base camp was located, there had been little activity during the day. Some troops and vehicles had moved back or forth on the road going on around our ridge. Occasionally, when a vehicle went around, there would be an outburst of more than normal gunfire as a result.

Now, as sunset neared, there were more troops in evidence. In particular were the Gurkhas, who were in little groups here and there. From what we heard, they did not eat with other troops or in field messes. They were given their own food or rations, and went off and prepared it themselves in special utensils. I remembered that back in southern Italy, the Gurkha ack-ack gunners on our airfields had seemed to live right in the small gun pits rather than in a base complex. They were regularly seen cooking their own meals over a fire on the ground near their gun positions. As they grouped around here I was quite pleased to see them, because otherwise we seemed pretty much isolated and alone up on the ridge.

Instead of crawling in the cave with some K or similar rations, we had been served a hot evening meal, as we had at lunch and tea. The few British troops of our support camp maintained the communications gear, cooked and brought meals up to us, took care of laundry, etc. We didn't get comparable treatment anywhere in our service. And as the sun went down, searchlights popped on throughtout the front to reflect off the almost ever-present clouds to provide "artificial moonlight" for the night war. Contrary to what I had anticipated, I slept like a rock among the rocks I was sleeping on.

Time passed quickly during days of good weather and flying operations. On the days of low ceilings, rain, sleet, and/or snow, time drug by as we sat and waited. We spent some time watching the German ridge, where on occasion they might be spotted looking back. Far more time was spent watching even the most routine of events in the little valley behind us. Right at 10:00 each morning a jeep carrying mail and laundry made a dash around the ridge to the forward positions in the line. Reportedly it seldom if ever was shot at by the Germans, and each day's trip was awaited to see if the record would hold.

The close air support missions went along effectively day to day—the kind of operations that receive little news coverage except perhaps in the form of a note indicating "Fighter-bombers flew so many sorties in support of ground forces." There might also be mention of some number of our planes that failed to return. From a forward air controllers' view, those losses were not seen only as numbers. They were seen as airplanes with fellow pilots in them that burst into a ball of fire or that failed to pull out of a dive. And if a day went by without one or more such loss, that was a most welcomed part of that evening's discussion on the day's operation.

Not all operations were routine, nor did they all fall neatly into a package of missions flown "by the book." In several cases we had worked out means of getting strikes in on targets in special situations. However, none of those approached a case we were hit with in mid-December. We received a request to put an air strike on German forces that were only across the street, in a small town, from friendly troops on the other side of that street. Our rules did not cover hitting targets only 20 or so feet away from our troops.

The request was not just thrown at us without explanation and reasons therefor. An Irish company had attacked and entered the town; a much larger German force had counterattacked, and the Irish were now pinned down and trapped in one part of the town. The Germans held the rest of the town and surrounding area. Without help, the Irish company would be annihilated.

I had to reply that we could not do it with bombs and give any assurance of safety to the Irish, but we probably could strafe the enemy without endangering friendly troops. The answer came back from the Division as a personal one from the commander of the Irish company—again a plea for air strikes on the Germans in the buildings across the street. The Irish commander and his troops were aware that they probably would be hit, too, but they were under constant fire from all around and could not pull back to a safe distance. They had no chance without the air support; they would rather have it, regardless of the consequences.

Strafing alone surely would not do enough against troops in stone buildings. Thus, when I quickly briefed the CG at the TAC on the request, I kept right on going to request eight airplanes with napalm, then eight more to back those up. Napalm was not even in the rules for use in very close proximity to friendly troops, but with the general's immediate decision, it came into the rules. It was also agreed that pilots from my squadron would know exactly who they were talking to on the ground. Thus, the first eight airplanes would be from my squadron.

The British sent us all the information possible on the exact location of the enemy and the Irish troops in the town. The single small highway through the town was the dividing line. The pilots needed to hit everything on one side of it and nothing on the other side. The Irish CO was notified that our bombs would be the deadly gasoline fire bombs and we did not know if the mix could splash back across the street from the enemy-held buildings or not. The reply was to the effect of "Thanks ever so much for the planned mission—and come on with the fire bombs."

In studying the surface wind on the floor of the valley in which the town and target were located, its direction should blow the dense black napalm smoke off to the side of the desired attack route. Had it been blowing into the direction of the attack, the smoke might blank out the target to some of the following airplanes during the attack.

The airplanes checked in on the radio less than an hour after all this started. I recognized the mission leader as 1st Lt. John P. Botten, one of the young but now experienced flight leaders. He, as well as the others, had come through exceptionally well in leading some very tough missions. He sure had one today.

With the target and task at hand briefed on the radio, each pilot in turn confirmed that he fully understood the instructions, and that one side of the street was enemy while the other side of it was friendly. Even though the nature of the mission had been passed to the unit, unless it could be confirmed that each pilot received the instructions, some of the airplanes would have been held off the attack to ensure that a pilot without a radio receiver did not go in on the attack—he might just drop his napalm on the wrong side of the street simply because everybody *else* was dropping theirs on the *other* side.

The airplanes took good intervals, making long straight-in runs, holding steady in the flak, on down to minimum altitude. One after the other the pilots sent their sets of napalm tanks into the buildings across the street. Not one set was short for a disaster, nor was one set long and completely off the buildings on the far side, either. They engulfed the German side of the town in napalm fire.

The mission leader asked to make a strafing pass. While Lt. Moyle gave instructions on strafing certain areas around the town, I picked up the phone to the TAC and I don't think I said anything right then except "They did it!" The napalm of the following mission was used on other enemy positions in the area. That night we were advised that not only had the Irish company survived, they took the town. (And, in conjunction with other forces in the area, never gave it up again in the war.)

I received a call and message from the commander of the Irish company, which I was sure would always be among the most treasured memories of the war for me—when and if I ever got out of it. The next morning there was a personal message from the Commanding General of the Division. He did not send or call it, he came to pass it on in person. He was an older but most professional and distinguished officer in physique, bearing, and manner. In an immaculate uniform, he spryly hiked right up to the top of the ridge and into our partly muddy and partly icy little hole at the top. That event was to be an always-treasured memory, too.

While weather conditions allowed some flying on most days, the

A napalm attack, but not the one described in this chapter as "across-the-street." (Courtesy U.S. Air Force)

conditions on the ground became terrible. Between rain, sleet and snow, freezes and thaws, all the roads near our position became unusable. Pack animals—mostly donkeys, led mainly by Italian soldiers—became the main means of moving supplies forward. There was one other way, too: by the legs and backs of men. Apparently, only ammo and food were going forward. Coming back were the dead and wounded and some enemy prisoners.

I was ready when we were relieved as forward air controllers a few days before Christmas, but Moyle wanted to go on a patrol. The British took him, and he came back looking like something the cat drug in. There were some indications that, over and above quite a physical ordeal, getting back *at all* had been of some concern during the night. I did not go so far as to ask to go on a patrol.

In Florence, at the TAC, we had a fine meeting and debriefing with the CG and I had a lengthy personal talk on close support and other tactical flying which was to be a treasured memory, too. We were given a clean jeep and put up in a set of luxurious VIP quarters, which in turn were put to use in doing some cleaning on ourselves. I followed my recently acquired habit of going to bed with the chickens—this night in a huge, extremely soft down or feather bed. I had nightmares, and awoke tired and sore. Probably my GI cot back at Pisa would be hard enough to allow more relaxed sleeping, I thought, but if not, I might have to find a few rocks to sleep on for awhile.

At Pisa, reports on the squadron operations were excellent. Results had been outstanding with no losses recently. From about the 16th of December the squadron had been involved in a strong interdiction effort in the Brenner Pass area. That effort reportedly had a goal that was the exact opposite of previous efforts there. Instead of keeping Germans out of Italy as before, this one was to keep them *in* Italy and prevent movement of troops and equipment to join the German forces in the critical Ardennes offensive, or the Battle of the Bulge, up in the ETO.

I flew a mission on Christmas day, and not long after I did not come very far from killing myself. On an early morning strafing pass in hazy conditions, I didn't see the steel tower sticking somewhat above others along the rail line until too late. I was watching as the tower cut the right wing off just about midpoint of the aileron. I had a bit of a struggle with the airplane to keep it from rolling, but managed to fly it on up in a climbing right turn. The water-injection system of this engine, and war emergency power, gave some 2300 or so horsepower instead of the original 2000, and I was using all of it. (With water-injection, one would hear of cases where the engine manifold pressure was adjusted well on up beyond the normal maximum of 52"Hg. Some reports of 72" Hg. were heard; others indicated a more moderate boost to 62" Hg. or so. My thoughts on this were that what's best for the engine will be best in the long run for pilots who fly single-engine airplanes over enemy territory. And even with the normal maximum manifold pressures, water-injection made a P-47 a much better performer.)

As we headed home, this airplane did not fly as well as my badly damaged one at Montelimar. That one had a whopper of a hole in the wing,

Little travel was done without crossing engineer-constructed bridges. This one appears to be by British forces in Florence. (Courtesy National Archives)

My P-47 looked pretty good from this side after the belly-in job.

but this one (in addition to the amount of wing missing) had only half an aileron—and *that* was partially jammed. A section of loose skin and ammo bay door were sticking up in the breeze. On the other hand, I still had an operating airspeed indicator and aileron trim system, since both the pitot head and movable trim tab were on the left wing. Had the same cut happened over there, both of these would have been lost.

Back near Pisa, I "felt out" the airplane to see how it might handle for landing. The result was that the touchdown would have to be quite fast. I took very little time debating what to do and decided to belly it in.

I sent the other airplanes in to land, then flew around awhile as a couple of missions took off. When the tower said it looked like a good time traffic-wise, I bellied it in on the runway—actually I flew it into the runway. There was a little sweat on contact as to whether it would go straight ahead or not, but it did—all the way to the overrun on the far end. The only moment of horror came as I was sliding along and a B-25 at the far

It didn't look quite as well from the other side.

end started to taxi out onto the runway. I could envision sliding into the airplane, knocking the gear out from under it, and having it all fall right on top of me. Fortunately, the rescue crew at that end stopped the two birdmen in the cockpit before they got all the way out onto the runway. That night, a couple of the young pilots came by with the suggestion that if I was going to slide under the nose of any more B-25s on a belly landing, it would be better to cut off the wing on the side *next to* the B-25 instead of the one on the side *away from* it, as was the case today. I told them I would keep that in mind—as well as who suggested it.

December 1944 was a month of tremendous combat results. The 525th FS set all-time records in destroyed and damaged equipment. Both vehicle and locomotive figures soared up into the hundreds, and we went far out ahead of any potential competitors in the locomotive wrecking business. Best of all, losses were down—well below other squadrons we had figures on.

A forward air controller's view of a close support dive-bomb attack. (Courtesy U.S. Air Force)

Chapter 13

Special Missions

Starting in January, we received fewer close support missions; more of our flying was on interdiction. In a period from late December to mid-January, over 400 rail cuts were reported in the Brenner Pass lines to Germany and those further east from northern Italy to Vienna, Austria. We, along with numerous other units, were heavily involved in putting them there. Missions in the Alps now worked over heavy snow throughout the mountains and valleys. The Po Valley was also frequently blanketed with snow. It might be said that a general trend in our operations on into the winter was one of cutting icy railroad tracks.

It was only a general trend at best. Some close support continued. Flak supression missions came regularly, as did some escort missions of medium bombers and a few of accompanying reconnaissance airplanes. And there were quite a number of missions of an unusual or special nature. A few of this last category came to be by happenstance, but most were planned for a special purpose or task.

For several months we had flown past Genoa, staying wide of it, but able to see the flashes of welding equipment as ships were worked on in the harbor and yards there. One very large warship was involved. I guess the high-level plan was to let them work away repairing ships until one or more was almost seaworthy again, then send some airplanes to re-do the damage.

Anyway, we flew a mission into Genoa. We had good results on the designated target with 1000-pounders, but in later informal talk there was more said about the flak than the bombing. It was among probably the thickest 88mm fire I had seen put up against a dive-bomb mission. There were a few holes in airplanes. Missions like this helped contribute to a single month's total of 54 cases of battle damage to airplanes in our squadron. While a few may have been scrapped, most were repaired—and that is a lot of sheet metal and other work. The fact that 54 airplanes returned from missions with battle damage, while only two were lost in that same period, again re-emphasizes the ruggedness and toughness of the P-47. Many pilots gave credit to those features of that fighter for their survival in the war.

We flew one escort mission that was different in several ways from normal escort. That was for a single B-25, which did not bomb a target, but rather made a landing and takeoff in enemy territory—on a makeshift strip in the Po Valley foothills of the Apennines, north of La Spezia.

For another special mission, I was asked if my squadron could go to a certain location and take a photograph. Naturally, a few questions popped into my mind, such as, "Why not send a recce airplane?" However, I had not been asked for any opinions on doing the mission—only, *could* we do it? It was a long haul, but we could get there. Whether we would get there and *back* when the time came might be less of a sure thing.

Fighter-bombers were in the photography business anyway. All of our squadron airplanes were equipped with gun cameras and they were used on all missions. All of the 16mm movie film from those cameras was developed, reviewed, and studied. However, what invariably happened on very spectacular missions, such as an ammo train exploding or a major airfield attack, was that the Group headquarters would want to see the film. Often that was the last we ever saw of it, or at best it would come back with all the good shots missing. The better footage was apparently sent on to yet higher headquarters, and in turn to Washington for review and probably PIO use. What was left in the squadrons of the surplus unclassified film was eventually given to the pilots (if they wanted it) or it was discarded.

Every so often we had carried special cameras of some kind, usually in attempts by higher headquarters to get good-quality negatives and prints and/or color photography, which the gun camera black-and-white positive movie film did not provide. We had even mounted big movie cameras on a pylon to take color footage for movie uses. Those cameras had not been too popular because usually the pilot with the camera needed to follow along behind or make an extra pass or so trying to get pictures of "flamers," good bomb hits after the smoke cleared, etc. I had not been too enthused about getting a pilot shot down while taking PIO pictures. We did get some good photography, but I would not have rated us as high when taking PIO photos as when bombing and shooting.

However, this particular photo mission was different. One would assume that it was not a PIO project. We would use a special camera to take a photo of a particular bridge—a photo which was wanted by higher headquarters, but we were never told why. The bridge was a fairly small one, located in Austria, all the way across the main part of the Alps, and almost to the area of Salzburg on the German border. I needled the project officer, who brought the camera to us, by suggesting that if we were going that far to take a picture, why not also load a bomb and try to knock the bridge down at the same time? His reaction made it obvious that only the photo was

159

wanted; he did not seem the least bit interested in having the bridge destroyed. Yet from where he wanted the picture taken (from almost point-blank range and level or slightly below), there was some chance of the *airplane* knocking it down.

With the camera installed on the left pylon (a summary investigation had been made on its effect on range), two airplanes took off to go take the picture. It was one of those exceptionally clear, cold days that usually followed after a heavy cloud cover moved on out from over the valley and Alps. On such days when flying over the Alps, one feels he could actually see forever.

Enroute, as on all long missions and many others as well, we went through the experience of running the belly tank dry (and then, sometimes, the auxiliary tank, too). Even though the pilot knew about when each tank would run dry, that moment of the engine shutting off over enemy territory was still a sudden attention-getter. Running tanks dry was not a recommended procedure in training manuals, but most combat units did it in order to utilize every drop of gasoline on board. Then too, most pilots were pretty fast in reacting and switching to a tank with fuel in it, and we never had a case of an engine failing to catch and continue operating after running tanks dry.

As I passed near the 12,000-foot-plus peak of Gross Glockner, our checkpoints leading to the target showed clearly, and once across the main Alps we descended into the low-level run on the bridge. I snapped the picture and pulled up over the bridge—then turned full attention to a problem that started just before I took the picture. The engine had suddenly begun to run very rough, and it wasn't from a tank starting to run dry. I was on the main tank and all the fuel on board was in that tank. For a moment, my only thoughts were on whether it would keep running, and in surveying the immediate countryside for a place to set down or get out.

The engine kept running—no better but no worse either. If it continued to do so, I should be able to climb high enough to cross the main part of the mountains again. Then there could be a choice of continuing on toward home base or going toward the Adriatic Sea to get over water and possibly onto a field on the east side of Italy. Both destinations were some 300 miles away. The course to home base was over enemy territory all the way except the last few miles. The alternate route to the sea was about half enemy territory and half water. However, to reach the Adriatic Sea, the course would be directly through enemy fighter fields in the Udine area.

In the end, I chose not to divert to the Adriatic, but rather to try to avoid the fighters at Udine by staying in the Alps on down to the area of Verona, even though from there the whole Po Valley would still have to be crossed. The engine ran rough all the way, but we made it back to Pisa. One round—probably from a machine gun—had caused the problem. However, the engine would most likely have run forever. I wish I had known that in the air on our long trip home.

Something else that was not known all the way home—or at debriefing, either—was whether we had taken a usable photo. Perhaps that is why I would rather have carried a bomb—then you know you either hit the bridge or missed it. In any event, we were not sent back and in time we received word the photo—whatever it was for—was fine.

On a clear and cold February day, following a heavy snowfall in the Po Valley, we had a mission on a train that did not have any flak cars, but the situation made the mission one of a somewhat special nature. As we flew over the valley I may have done a double-take or two because of what we saw below. A rather long passenger train, pulled by a big, sleek locomotive, was running at high speed down the tracks as if there was no war going on—or else we had found a high-priority troop train or military train of some kind. Naturally it was considered to be military or in support of the war, otherwise it would not have—or *should not* have —been out there.

We immediately attacked the locomotive, blowing it, and sending the fast-moving train skidding down the tracks for a couple of miles or so before coming to a stop. Then many human forms began pouring out of the cars, probably several hundred of them. However, they sort of froze into a mass alongside the cars. Apparently the snow had drifted up along the tracks and the people on the train were bogging down in it and could not either flee or disburse. They were all wearing dark-colored clothing, and presented a picture of troops on a troop train.

Anything about the rest of this mission would have to be viewed as war in one of its uglier moments. With no real challenges or heroics required in the air, a training type of gunnery pattern was used to strafe the cars and the deep snow alongside them until every round of ammo was gone.

In the past, a squadron that used 150,000 to 200,000 rounds of .50-caliber ammo a month was doing a lot of strafing. In recent months, we had been doubling that range of figures, resulting in a wide variety of targets destroyed and damaged in proportion to the ammo expended. Among those

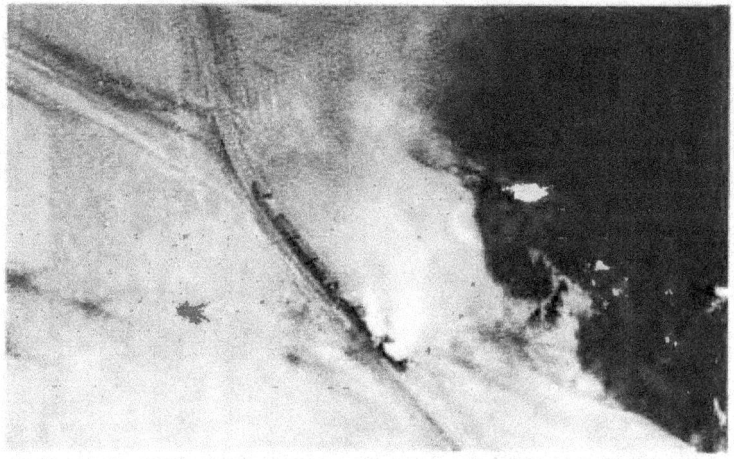

Another train attacked and stopped in the snow. (Courtesy U.S. Air Force)

targets was one where just a small mission sent some 13,000 plus rounds of ammo into a train and its full load of people trapped in the snow.

Yet another program of missions were identified as "Specials," and one of the special aspects of them was that they never came out on our regular daily mission orders from higher headquarters. They originated by me picking up a field phone and calling the Group CO to request permission to fly a "Special." If agreeable (as I understood the system), he in turn called the CG at the TAC with the same request. If I received a call back with approval, the mission was flown.

These were bad-weather locomotive busting missions. They were requested and flown only after adverse weather in the Po Valley had forced cancellation of regular dive-bombing and other interdiction efforts. Their beginning went back a few months to the start of the seasonal period of fall and winter weather in northern Italy.

On certain days, when flying above the cloud cover in the Po Valley, one could see an amazing sight. While the mountains both north and south might be clearly showing in bright sunlight, the entire valley floor would be covered with a solid layer of clouds. The tops were so consistent and level that there was an illusion of the undercast being a slick surface. Those tops were usually in the vicinity of 3000 to 4000 feet and there was never a gap or hole—it was always 10/10 solid coverage. That naturally blotted out every target area in the valley and halted regular ground attack operations.

Early in the game of encountering such days of cloud cover, our squadron had found out something about the *bottoms* of these clouds—they were just as flat and level as the tops. The first time I had been under them the ceiling was around 2000 feet and the visibility was excellent—and the railroads in the valley were operating at full capacity. We came home with a

Another Po Valley rail cut. (Courtesy U.S. Air Force)

very impressive kill of locomotives for four airplanes.

When I first proposed flying special missions on such days there had been some questions on how I knew so much about the bottoms of the clouds. Once *that* little discussion was over, we got back to the proposal. As a result, the Group CO obtained permission for me to take one mission up in such weather. In effect, it would be a test, on which the Deputy Group CO would go along. If it worked out as I planned it—that we penetrated and broke out where I briefed and the weather underneath was as I thought it would be—then other missions might be considered.

The next time that particular weather situation existed we flew the test "Special." The Apennines were in the clear, and so was Genoa. With only a short flight over the undercast from a positive checkpoint, we let down and broke out right where planned, over farmlands and away from main routes and any flak. The tops and bottoms of the clouds were slightly lower than before, but with plenty of room and excellent visibility. We racked up another impressive kill of locomotives.

After that, serious consideration was given to a program of such missions. Both my Group CO and the TAC CG were involved, which is how I learned about the extensive knowledge of that CG on the nuts and bolts of combat flying. I was already well aware of that fact about the Group CO. I had to convince both of them that we could fly the "Specials" without undue risk of a disaster such as losing an entire mission. The Deputy Group CO, Lt. Col Lee, my old squadron CO, was a major factor in this being done. No one in the theater was more highly respected as a combat pilot and commander, and he was a strong supporter of this proposal. We convinced them, and the program was approved by the Group and TAC with a set of firm rules.

In essence, the rules were that the missions would be flown by volunteers only. I had to lead each one, and if I aborted, the mission would abort, too. Missions would be flown only in the particular weather situation of flat cloud cover in the valley, not in a heavy system of clouds built up over the valley, mountains and home base, and with a set minimum altitude to descend in the clouds while trying to break out underneath. The rules included the provision that it was up to me to evaluate the weather conditions on a stand-down of regular flying, and to take the action to initiate a mission when and if I thought one could and should be flown. It was not mandatory to fly one just because the conditions were right—only if I chose to.

In time, the CO of the 526th FS, our sister squadron, was included in the program with the same ground rules for him and his unit. If other squadrons in the theater were involved, I had no idea; however, while on these missions we never saw any other Allied airplanes, nor did we hear any radio transmissions from other airplanes in the Po Valley.

In my squadron, we flew about nine or so of these "Specials" in the fall and winter of 1944-45. We moved them around in letdown point and armed recce areas, with most all flown in the western half of the valley. The missions each averaged 9 or 10 locomotives destroyed and an equal number damaged, and some freight cars and military equipment on flatcars were strafed as well. We did not encounter flak except a few instances of isolated automatic-weapon fire. We had no damage to airplanes and no losses on any mission. We never aborted one, nor ever failed to reach the desired target area.

As for the pilots flying them, the volunteer list was the same as the roster of pilots—and few lists have ever been checked more closely by those on it to ensure that no one got an extra turn.

While the "Specials" were steady contributors to the total of locomotives destroyed and damaged, the regular missions never slacked up on shooting trains, either. One of them (which pressed on in bad weather) on a armed recce in the Turin area put a top score on the board for a four-ship mission of 13 electric locomotives destroyed.

On February 14, our advanced ground echelon boarded LSTs at Leghorn on a move to France. The 86th Fighter Group and at least one other from Italy were being transferred to the war in the ETO. However, that other group was not my old one, the 79th. It was the 27th, going to France for a second time in the war. Where a very few of us had once been "felt for" by friends as we left the old squadron in sunny France to return to Italy, no perhaps the two of us remaining of those transferees could "feel" a bit for our friends in that squadron who were destined to stay in Italy.

Something told me that France wasn't going to be very sunny or that anything else about it would be very rosy this time. At least we were not changing theaters as individuals again, and Colonel George T. Lee had moved up from Deputy CO of this Group to be its Commanding Officer. Thus, for the second time in the war, I was serving under him. Also, this

Trains stalled by rail cuts in the valley. (Courtesy U.S. Air Force)

Fighter-bombers would continue to leave their mark on the enemy. (Courtesy U.S. Air Force)

time we were leaving the Twelfth Air Force and its long-time and highly respected CG, Maj. Gen. John K. Cannon.

We continued to fly missions in the Po Valley and Alps as we awaited the time for moving the airplanes to France. I had been flying missions there now for five months; the rest of the 86th Group and others in Italy had flown combat there much longer than that. Any number of pilots had come to Italy, flown a tour, and gone home—with their whole war flown in the Po River Valley and surrounding area.

My last look at the valley was as we flew out of it on the way back to Pisa—returning from another "rail cut" in the Po River Valley.

Chapter 14

Push on Germany

We ferried the airplanes to France, on February 23, which was the only day of the war since I first arrived overseas that my unit of assignment had no scheduled combat missions. We had until the following morning before flying combat again. Our new field was at Tantonville, near Nancy, in the northeastern corner of France, some 45 miles from the German border. The USAAF airfields in France—and there must have been hundreds of them—had designations of A-1, A-46, etc.; some had designations such as Y-1, which this one did. Yet we were accustomed to calling airfields by names and this field was always Tantonville to us. It had one of the roughest PSP runways we had ever encountered.

There may have been some doubts associated with just what air force we now belonged to initially. It was assumed we would be assigned to the Ninth Air Force, the strong U.S. tactical air force on the continent. I think we were for awhile, or maybe we were all along in a roundabout way, but we settled down in France as officially operating under the First Tactical Air Force (Provisional). Reportedly that was an organizational arrangement to handle the tactical operations of certain U.S. units along with counterpart French units. In any event, we were under a TAC (XII) and would be flying the same type of tactical operations as the Ninth Air Force units, whether we were in the Ninth or not.

Apparently, our TAC—and now we,—worked mainly in support of the 6th Army Group, made up of the U.S. Seventh Army and the French First Army. These were the same TAC and ground armies I had flown with in France the previous summer. These armies were located on the southern end of the massive Allied Force undertaking the push on Germany's Western Front. The French First Army was southernmost, next to Switzerland, with the U.S. Seventh Army adjacent on the north and in turn flanked on *its* north by the U.S. Third Army. I also understood that among the German armies facing these Allied forces in the south was an old enemy from last summer, too, the German Nineteenth Army.

The tactical air war in the ETO, which we were joining, was one of immense proportions by comparison with most any other theater. In addition to the First Tactical Air Force and the U.S. Ninth Air Force, the strong British Second Tactical Air Force was supporting Allied ground forces in the northern part of the lines. A stalwart of the 2nd TAF fighter-bombers was the powerful British Typhoon, a renowned counterpart to the P-47s of our 9th AF and 1st TAF. Many other airplanes types were also involved in the total air-to-ground effort.

Both before and since the invasion of Normandy, Allied fighter-bombers had applied strong air pressure on the German forces and supporting systems in Western Europe. Back in June of 1944, the German Commander-in-Chief in the West had issued a memorandum to his troops to the effect that "The enemy has succeeded, by concentrated and ceaseless attacks from the air, in disorganizing our supply to such an extent and to cause such losses of railway rolling stock and vehicles that supply has become a major problem." Another report indicated captured enemy soldiers had stated that even dispatch riders could not be depended upon to get through. If they did, it was usually after one or more close calls and much time spent hiding in the woods, ditches, etc., while Allied fighter-bombers strafed anything enemy seen on the roads.

From June of 1944 on, one could cite numerous major and key events in tactical air operations across France and the Low Countries and on into parts of Germany. For example, by mid-June the rail and road bridges over the Seine River were reported as completely interdicted and unusable. The Falaise Gap or Pocket, in August, was among the truly massive kills of enemy equipment and personnel by tactical air and fighter-bombers in the war. Other such operations could include the Rhone Valley of France and German withdrawal in Italy in May of 1944. At Falaise, a German army, which I understood was the Seventh, was completely devastated. In other action, for one week in August it was reported that Allied fighters destroyed 600 locomotives in France and Belgium. Then, when the bad weather that had persisted in the Ardennes over the Battle of the Bulge cleared on December 23 or so, the door opened for a series of massive kills on the strong enemy forces been employed there. At least one came immediately, and others followed to include that of the Dasbury area in Germany in January 1945.

The Ninth Air Force had long used forward air controllers, including special emphasis of controllers with armored units to make up the famed air-tank teams. Controllers had reportedly been riding tanks or accompanying tank columns since the breakthrough at St. Lo and during the thrust across France. As I understood it, these controllers, who directed air strikes against any and all types of opposition to U.S. armored forces, were predominately young pilots with the rank of lieutenant or perhaps captain.

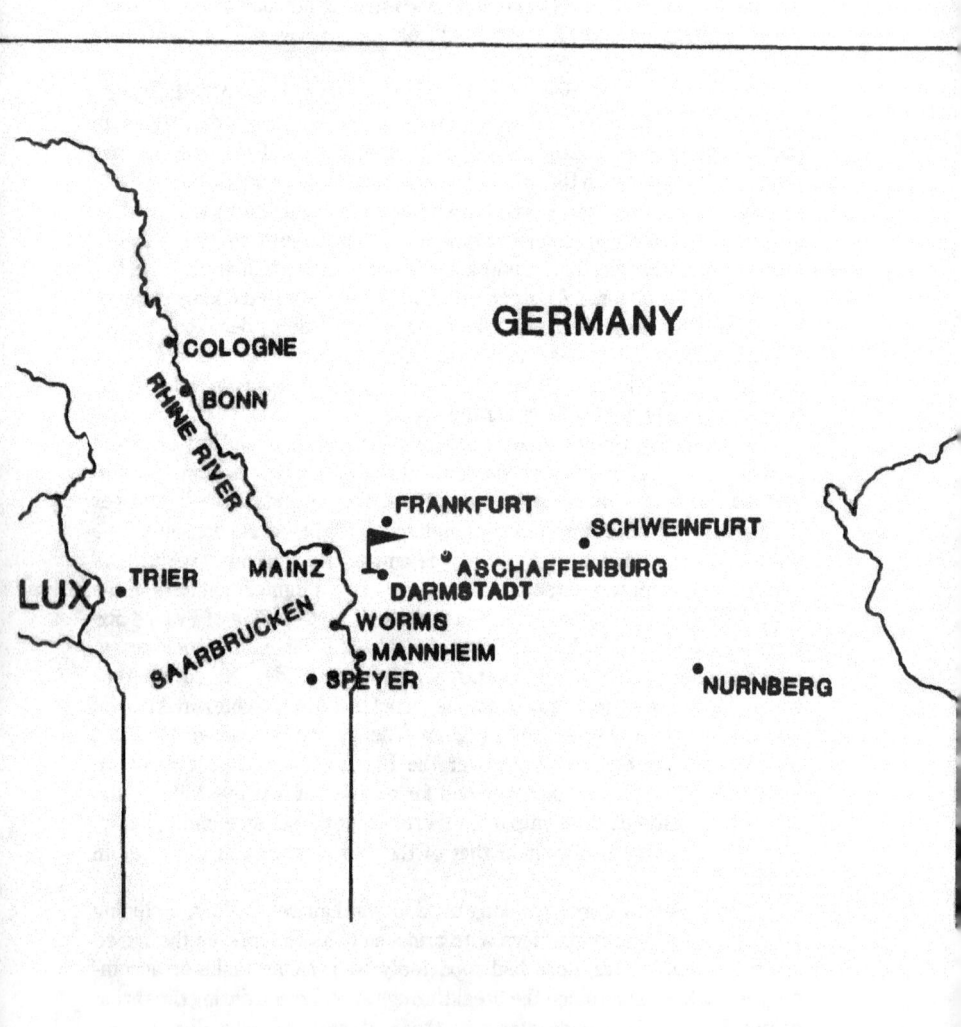

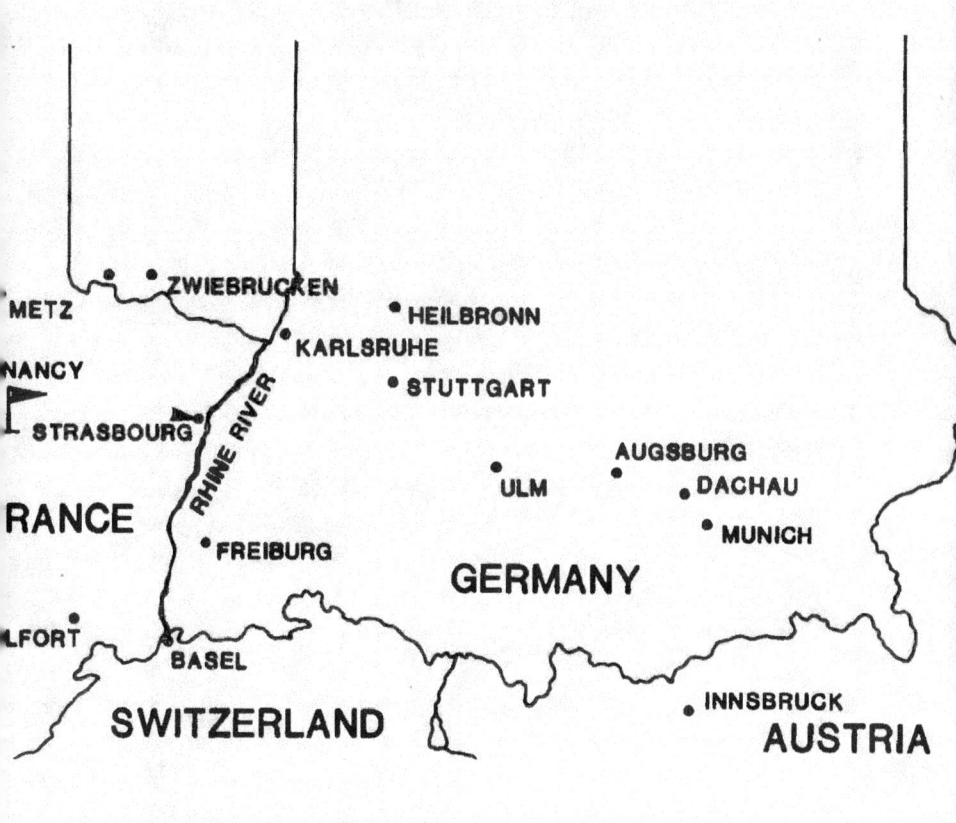

ny, area of combat actions in Chapters 14 through 16.

Trains and track were shot up all over this theater, too. (Courtesy U.S. Air Force)

Part of the aftermath at Falaise Gap. (Courtesy U.S. Air Force)

The Allied fighter and fighter-bomber pilots in the ETO had also flown many missions against some very heavily defended airfields, and they had been involved in attacks on the German V-weapon sites, the launching facilities of the V-1 buzz bomber "doodle-bug" and the supersonic V-2 ballistic rocket, sometimes referred to as "silent death." Some of these pilots had chased and shot down some of the V-1 flying bombs, as the air defense forces in England were employed regularly to do.

While I was quite familiar with our counterpart fighter-bomber units in Italy, I had little idea of either how many or which Groups were in that role in France and/or the ETO. By distribution and addresses on various documents and orders, it appeared that we in the 86th (and the 27th) from Italy had joined at least the 50th, 324th, and 358th Fighter Groups (all flying P-47s) here as the American fighter-bomber force under XII TAC, and I guess in the First Tactical Air Force.

Ninth Air Force had some three TACs and 18 or 19 Fighter Groups as its normal fighter-bomber strength during the push through France, and even more at times on loan from the Eighth—plus the light and medium bombers and all the rest. In past months I had pictured all the fighter units in Ninth Air Force as flying the P-47, but there were two Groups of P-51s and three of P-38s in that total of 18 or 19 fighter-bomber outfits. My count of units showed the following Groups as being in Ninth Air Force at this point in the war (after formation of First Tactical Air Force): 36th, 48th, 354th, 362nd, 363rd, 365th, 366th, 367th, 368th, 370th, 371st, 373rd, 404th, 405th, 406th and 474th. Obviously the 50th and 358th had been Ninth units—and might still be, and the 363rd had converted from fighter to recce along the way.

Our squadron was set up in tents except for the officers, who were quartered in a small hotel in Tantonville. Probably never has a squadron had a more ideal building for a self-contained squadron operation. While none of the civilian help were retained (we never used indigenous personnel in our squadrons), the hotel did have a kitchen, dining room, bar, and lobby that would have made a perfect squadron club and mess. However, we were still on a Group club and mess basis, even though there wasn't a building in the area (other than a few manure-floored barns) that was large enough for such a facility. That problem was solved by finding and erecting a circus tent in a field on the edge of town.

I called the entire squadron together (which was a very rare event for us) to discuss protection from air attacks and security of the unit. In Italy we had not really been hit with air attacks since Naples, but up here the Luftwaffe had made a strong effort against Allied airfields at the first of the year. Major damage was inflicted on a number of fields; thus, we were going to do considerable "digging-in" on this base. There were also reports of German paratroopers being dropped in the area for sabotage operations, and security measures were reviewed and stressed.

In combat flying operations, numerous interdiction missions could be expected in support of the massive Allied offensive. For us, much of that

Scenes of destruction were seen by the ground echelons in France as in Italy. (Courtesy U.S. Air Force)

would probably be in connection with efforts to isolate the German forces on the west side of the Rhine River—on the rail and road networks of the Saar-Rhine areas. However, many missions might be expected in coming days against the German forces themselves, including tanks, other armor, gun positions, fortifications, bunkers and personnel—some of the real dirty work of fighter-bomber flying. Also, since the heavy fighting at Strasbourg and elimination of the troublesome Colmar Pocket on the southern end of the lines, the main emphasis seemed to be on the northern sector of the lines within our area of operation. We could probably expect more close support missions there, as the U.S. Third and U.S. Seventh Armies worked together in the Saarbrucken and surrounding areas. Much cramming of current details on situation maps was done on our first night at Tantonville, but we had been studying the aeronautical charts of these areas for several days before departing Pisa.

We would have a new control procedure, which we had not used in Italy except temporarily during some of the invasions. After takeoff, each mission would check in with a ground control facility. In most cases, we could expect to merely be sent on to complete our preplanned and pre-briefed mission. However, we might be diverted to another mission or—quite likely—instructed to contact a specific forward air controller for a close support mission. On all missions we would check out with the ground control agency on our return from enemy territory and before landing at home base. In Italy, except on close support missions, we seldom talked to anyone on the ground other than our own control tower.

Our missions would be over Germany itself. The situation there for a downed pilot offered little or no chance for evasion. Becoming a POW under the German military, who were recognized as in general compliance with the Geneva Convention on treatment of POWs, was about all a downed pilot could hope for in most areas of Germany. Thus, the basic guidance to pilots was that if shot down over Germany, attempt surrender to the military, or Wehrmacht, and preferably to the Luftwaffe if possible. Various past actions by the other pilots on a mission (capping, strafing, etc.) could not actually keep a downed pilot from being captured. In fact, they might backfire and cause him to be killed and/or other pilots on the mission to be lost without achieving anything. Pilots flying over Germany, at this stage of the war had to face the fact that, whether tried or not, there was no real help to be had from the air in most cases if they went down.

Our first mission from France was an innocent appearing rail cut and armed-recce on the east side of the Rhine near Karlsruhe. It didn't turn out that way. Flak had been expected but not reported as extremely intense, and in the air we had not observed really intense enemy fire. Yet after the rail line was bombed, and while a train seen underway a few miles away was being strafed, two airplanes in the cover flight were hit almost simultaneously by flak. One dove steeply and crashed into the ground. The other presented a very shocking sight as its huge four-blade propeller flew completely off the airplane and went pinwheeling out through the rest of the formation.

The mission returned with the loss of two outstanding and extremely popular pilots. A loss of two airplanes and pilots on a single fighter-bomber mission was not uncommon, but it didn't happen every day on the normal four and eight-ship missions. We had not had it occur at all in my months of commanding this squadron. It was a tough way to start out in a new theater.

While we went over the mission in detail at the debriefing and in a meeting that night, there was really nothing to highlight any reason for a change in tactics or procedures. The rest of the missions that day had been successful and without any losses at all. As a result, we pressed on with the flying as before and the missions for the next several days all had good results and no losses.

We were on a higher sortie rate here than in Italy. The first missions of the day were going off before full daylight and the last ones were returning well after sundown. To keep this rate up indefinitely was going to put a real strain on the unit. That would be true for the hard-worked ground crews, but perhaps even more so for the pilots, since we were now considerably under the normal number of pilots usually assigned. We were down close to the basic authorization of some 39 officers in a squadron instead of the 57 or so that were normally allocated in the combat theaters. However, for the moment everyone was flying a lot, and morale and spirits were quite sound with several days of highly successful combat operations.

This heavy schedule was seldom met in bright and sunny flying conditions. The weather in general could be described as not very good in Europe during the winter. Some cloud cover was coped with on most missions. Many days were dark and gloomy. There was always smoke and usually haze in the battle zones and most target areas, and in many of these the terrain was fairly rugged, too. All of this added up to some rather demanding flying conditions much of the time.

On February 28, I was leading a dive-bomb mission on a rail line east of Zweibrucken, with some broken clouds and hazy conditions in the target area. On the schedule board, this mission may have appeared as a rather innocent one. It wasn't, and it is one more that can be used in evidence of the fact there is no such thing. I came out of it with a Purple Heart (awarded for wounds in action) and as a member of the Caterpillar Club (membership limited to those who make an emergency parachute jump from an airplane).

There were some trains loaded with military equipment in the area and we were bombing to cut the tracks right in front of a train and then get it, too. Another mission was operating nearby. To stay clear of those airplanes, as well as dodge some clouds, I made a rather steep pull-up off the bomb run—probably close to vertical. I was at about 3500 to 4000 feet when there was a blinding flash and explosion on or just off the left wing. Before I could check to see what damage it and the shrapnel from it had caused, the airplane was hit direct by a second flak shell. I'm not sure if I was dazed for a second or two or if things simply happened so fast that I could not keep up with the action. Anyway, the airplane had swapped ends and was headed down, out of control—so violently so, in sharp oscillations and "snap" maneuvers, that I had no idea of what it was doing. The controls seemed damaged and ineffective, and the ground was coming up fast.

I rapidly undertook a bailout. Once the straps were off, I was no match for the airplane—it beat the hell out of me. I think I was partially out of it once, possibly hanging by one leg and foot, which were jammed somewhere in the cockpit. If so, I was immediately crashed back into the bottom of the seat and cockpit by the next gyrations of the airplane.

Then suddenly all the violent maneuvers stopped. I looked down. It was too late to get out, and I had the fateful thought that this is what the world looks like just before a pilot goes in. But the airplane was pulling up—with tremendous G-force. We missed the ground, and I was now fighting the airplane to keep it from going straight up and possibly into a tight loop. With full nose-down elevator and full right aileron (the stick positioned in the forward right-hand corner of the cockpit) the airplane flew off in a climb in the direction of our lines and almost directly on a heading for our home base. If it had been going the other direction—toward Berlin—I'm not sure what would have happened when I tried to turn around. I was not sure it could be kept under control just trying to go straight ahead.

The Germans pounded away incessantly at the airplane with flak all the way from the target until back over our side of the lines. This was probably the worst sweat on flak I had gone through in the war. I couldn't do anything except sit there and hope I could keep the airplane flying toward our lines, as well as hope the plane would not be hit direct again and blown out of the sky or out of control for a second time.

The other pilots were flying cover for me and attempting to suppress flak. However, our procedures had always called for doing that by spreading out, weaving, etc., rather than slowing up and joining in close escort—thus all becoming sitting ducks. Once on our side of the lines, the other pilots closed in to take a look at the damage to my airplane.

The first thing I heard was, "Lead, you should be out here to see this." I wished I was. The damage was described as the vertical stabilizer being puffed up something like a 55-gallon drum, along with other damage to the horizontal stabilizer and control surfaces. I could see considerable damage to the left wing and some from shrapnel in the cockpit, and a bit of the damage on the tail, but I didn't risk moving around in an attempt to see more of the tail and possibly lose what little control I had over the airplane. I took the word of the other pilots that it was a rather unusual sight, one not seen every day.

There was some damage showing to my uniform around my left knee and calf of that leg. There was also evidence of damage to that knee and leg showing on the uniform, but it did not appear to be anything of major proportions. I could certainly picture one thing right away when I started to "feel out" the airplane for a possible landing—that was a scene of me going out over the side of the cockpit in a bailout instead of trying to fly a final approach and land. My conclusion was that there was not enough control available to attempt a landing. I flew across our field to a clear area just beyond and started out over the side of the cockpit.

That was not as easy or routine as it should seem, since the second I turned the stick loose, the airplane rolled sharply left and the nose pulled under sharply, too. On the initial start over the side my left boot slipped off the seat and lodged alongside it, but I managed to force it free and then bail out. I saw a flash of the red and white stripes on the tail as my nose went right by the tail surfaces. However, I did not get much more than a quick glance of overall damage to the tail as the airplane whipped on out of sight. As it flew away, all associated sound went with it. It was actually with considerable relief that I lay there in the now-quiet sky, looking up at the clouds above. I would have liked to just have stayed that way for a while and enjoyed this peaceful setting.

I was looking up, not down. Had I been looking down, I might have had a completely different feeling. I hated heights. The one time I went up in the Leaning Tower of Pisa and stood on the low side of its slanting observation deck, I had had a feeling of the tower falling on over and me with it. Back in the States, if I stood near the lip of a canyon, there was a feeling of some unseen force pulling me on over the edge. But heights in airplanes had no such ill effects at all.

Anyway, I hadn't had a great deal of altitude when I jumped, and I didn't wait very long to reach over and pull the parachute D-ring. Amazingly, the opening shock was very smooth and light as I was whipped over in a big swinging arc, the D-ring still gripped in my right hand. I slipped it up over my left hand and onto that wrist like a bracelet. Then I grabbed the risers and started to work at reducing the oscillations under the rather flat all-white canopy, which had no ripped panels or tangled shroud lines. The ground appeared to be coming up rather fast, but I touched down softer than expected in a farmer's freshly plowed field.

However, that was only after a bit of a scare as my airplane roared by and exploded in a big ball of fire, which was much closer to being right under me than I liked—and one more airplane assigned to me with the number 39 was gone. This was the fourth one, I believe, but it was the only one I had been flying at the time of its demise.

On the landing, I was shooting for a right-leg only touchdown. That one-legged landing transformed the poise and grace of a good landing fall into a plop forward into the soft soil. There was no problem in collapsing the chute and I sat in the field rolling it up into a neat bundle while a couple of jeeps and an ambulance from my squadron raced to the scene. While sitting there, it was obvious by both sight and feel that my left leg had been the main target for harm throughout the mission—both that initially incurred over the enemy target and during the bailout in the form of some additional rasping across the rail of the cockpit and a good sprain or wrench as well.

Once in the hands of the Medics, nothing was determined as too serious—except for requiring some treatment and continued observation of the knee and leg—but just serious enough to be grounded from flying until further notice. As near as I could tell the grounding was based fully on the "Doc's" medical opinion and action, but even if there had been no wound or injury at all, I sort of felt and Group CO might have grounded me just on general principles after a mission like this.

As with all missions and any flying matters, as the pilots visited me, we freely discussed this mission and what had happened on it. Some of them were quite interested in an account of my keeping the D-ring from the parachute. There wasn't much to tell except that the thought hit me just before I pulled it to try to save it, and from then on, I made a conscious effort to keep from losing it. I have no idea how many pilots may have saved D-rings on jumps, or lost them, or even deliberately threw them away while in the air.

Some of the pilots noted that I was going up quite steeply when coming off the target on this mission, perhaps hinting that I was very close to doing an Immelmann. It wasn't exactly that, but it wasn't very far removed either, and if one wanted to take a lesson from the incident, we sure knew what had come of going almost straight up over a target. Yet in looking at all the cases of airplanes that were hit by flak, one truth stood out: While some techniques of getting in and getting out on attacks were obviously better than others, some airplanes could and would be hit by automatic weapon fire at any phase of fighter-bomber low-level operations regardless of the methods being employed.

There were certain things about this mission that neither I nor the other pilots on it could ever figure out. The pilots following me could not describe just what kind of maneuver my airplane went through over the target, except that I was up above and in front of them one second, then back behind them and down in the smoke of the bomb bursts the next. We also drew a blank as to why and how the airplane straightened out and started to pull up over the target. It could have been in a spin and something about the controls or situation caused it to recover, but there is a lot about that supposition that does not make much sense. There were no recognizable or logical answers, and, as in many situations in both life and war, why and how certain things involving life and death came to be or did not come to be were simply not known—except by God.

In about ten days, another officer from the Group and I were in the UK for an R & R. Naturally, I thought we were going to a recreation facility such as Capri or the military hotels in Rome. Instead, on our arrival at a headquarters in England, we were sent on to a large manor on a huge estate located somewhere in the vicinity of Oxford (I think). It didn't take me long to find out that certain pilots and crews were sent here if their COs thought a special rest was needed and that the place was called the "Flak House." My reaction to *that* could have been heard for some distance. If the weather had been decent (which it wasn't), I might have tried to find a tent and cot to set up in the nearby woods, since I had no desire or intention to stay in anything called a "Flak House." Instead (after contacting the higher headquarters for relief from our assignment to rest here), we picked up our B-4 bags and headed down the road to the nearest village, from which we caught a train to London, where we spent a few days in a hotel. I spent some of that time riding trains, admiring the countryside and neatness of houses and yards, getting off in various places to catch an "opening" and enjoy the hospitality in the smaller towns. However, I was somewhat amazed that there was such warm hospitality after the British Isles had been so completely overrun by U.S. troops during the war.

In London, most of the rubble had been cleaned up from the enemy bombing and V-weapon attacks, but the sight of block-sized blank areas and open spaces here and there among the otherwise closely packed buildings gave stark testimony to what had gone on here. We also heard a couple of tremendous explosions. Apparently some V-2s were still being launched against the city, as well as dud bombs being handled by disposal personnel.

The pilots in a fighter-bomber squadron might have had more overall knowledge on advancements in German weapons in the war than on our own new weapons and developments. We were aware of the German V-weapons and several new airplanes of note, including the jet-powered Me 262 and the rocket-powered Me 163. Yet we had been directly affecting much more by the improvements and advancements in the standard German fighters—the late-model Me 109s and FW 190s, which were now extremely formidable machines.

One other German development of direct impact in fighter-bomber work was flashless and smokeless gunpower. In many cases of trying to locate firing guns there were no large flashes, balls of fire, or clouds of smoke to give away the locations. As a result, many guns had to be spotted on actual view of the guns and positions, themselves, and/or a bluish haze over them, rather than by giveaway fire and smoke.

After only a few days of this so-called R & R in the UK—which was not helping my leg at all—I went back to France. I caught a ride on an airplane that stopped on a 9th AF fighter-bomber base where I knew a few people, and I decided to stay a day or two. I thought of going to Paris, but we were not supposed to go there just because we decided to; permission and orders were reported as necessary for entry into the city.

When I finally arrived back at Tantonville, I found the unit on a near-backbreaking schedule of flying, while still coping with much adverse weather in the target areas. The results on vehicles and trains had soared even higher, but much of the flying was on close support missions working with forward air controllers. The 86th had made a name for itself for hitting such targets effectively in tough conditions. All of our flight leaders and pilots were achieving excellent results. In particular, many of these missions were against tanks and other armor. Now, instead of a reputation for wrecking locomotives, flying special missions, etc., the unit had picked up

Much emphasis was placed on killing armor. (Courtesy of U.S. Air Force)

one for killing tanks.

My membership in the exclusive Caterpillar Club was received back most promptly after the unit submitted the application. There was a certificate and small lapel pin of a caterpillar, awarding membership to one whose life was spared by a parachute. The certificate indicated that it was bestowed to the end that this safety medium in the art of flying might be furthered. Membership was presented through the manufacturer of the particular parachute used. In my case, that turned out not to be a long-time or old-line maker of parachutes, but rather a manufacturer of women's underwear who had been pressed into service to make silk parachutes for the war effort.

There could be no doubt that a parachute had saved one more life and I was grateful to the ladies (I assume) who made it, as well as our personnel who packed it. I was also grateful to the other pilots on the missions, and to the "Doc" and the medics.

And, while no two pilots would necessarily have the same views on such an event in their lives, there was still the recovery of the airplane over the target to be very thankful for, too. There wasn't much doubt in my mind about Who to be grateful to for *that*.

Chapter 15

Across the Rhine

We were using a couple of new types of bomb. One type consisted of the same old GP bomb cases but with different explosive mixes. Instead of TNT, one heard mention of terms such as RDX and tritonal, the latter of which was said to be TNT and aluminum powder. Whatever was in them, they had painted bands around the bomb cases to quickly identify them— and they needed to be identified for several very good reasons.

These bombs were reported to be more powerful than the past TNT jobs and, from a pilot's view in the air, they did burst on a target with a larger, brighter explosion. That was great and should be of substantial benefit in attacks on bunkers, fortifications and the entire spectrum of bombing targets. However, it was necessary to raise the release and pullout altitudes of the airplanes on dive-bomb runs to ensure clearance of bomb fragments.

Also, these bombs were handled a bit differently than the old standbys, which everyone in a fighter-bomber unit had become closely associated with in many ways. In most units, there were always GP bombs around the area. They made excellent seats or props for a foot as pilots spent spare time on the flight line and as crew chiefs sweated out the return of their airplanes. The general officer who had made the administrative inspection of my squadron at Pisa had noted that I apparently spent more time sitting on a bomb out by the airplane than behind my GI field desk in the unit headquarters. He was right. But, at least, when sitting on a bomb, I didn't light up a cigarette nearly so often as when behind the desk.

In some units, and in dumps or elsewhere that bombs are handled, the old GP bombs (unfuzed) were often kicked off the back end of trucks to fall to the ramp or ground. Many of them had also been down-loaded or dropped from the wings of airplanes to fall to the ramp. Sometimes an empty wooden fuze or ammo box was placed under the wing for the bomb to fall on, crushing the box into splinters and perhaps cushioning the impact some. Certain people never became fully accustomed to either the sight or sound of a 500 or 1000-pounder as it hit the ramp with a tremendous thud. Some of them flinched if they were standing near the wing when it happened.

This squadron had handled munitions properly throughout, and whether some of the above practices were used in any unit or not, once these new bombs with the painted bands came along, the guidance was not to throw them around and drop them that way. There was a rumor that one of the new bombs had detonated when rolled off a truck at a handling point down in Africa or some rear area. Whether true or not, the new bombs were handled with some care — and I don't believe as many people were sitting on them, either.

Another new bomb was a fire bomb. It was an incendiary mix in a case the size and shape of a regular 500 pound GP bomb. Obviously, this allowed dive bombing with a ballistic case fire bomb, and the release and pullout altitudes could be quite low since there were no comparable blast and shrapnel effects as for a GP bomb. There was considerable discussion of just what targets these bombs would be most useful upon. Buildings and towns were certainly prime prospects.

Early in the use of these bombs, another good use for them was found. That target was tanks. Using lower altitude releases, we could put the bombs accurately enough among tanks to cover them with the burning incendiary mix.

Enemy tanks were bombed with GP bombs as well. Yet unless a tank

Some armor was actually up-ended. (Courtesy U.S. Air Force)

181

was hit direct or close enough to see major components blown off or it blown upside down or over an incline or cliff, it was hard to tell just what, if any, damage the bombs might have inflicted. Apparently GP bombs were not viewed overall as highly effective on tanks, but if the airplanes had GP bombs on board, and enemy tanks were down below, they were certainly bombed with GP bombs.

The matter of strafing tanks had long been discussed. Just area spraying of medium tanks (such as German PzKw IVs) and heavy tanks (such as Panthers and Tigers) with "fifties" might not even faze the things. First of all, our tactics called for hitting them hard with concentrated fire of all guns. Then, some specific aiming points were considered. The track and boggie wheel system was one. Of course, some enemy tanks had armor plate or mesh armor for the track system, but usually the lower part of the track and wheels could still be hit.

Another aimpoint was on the upper rear and upper rear sides, attempting to put rounds into any engine openings or louvers. And when the tanks were on hard surfaces or in open terrain, some pilots attempted to ricochet rounds up under and into the belly of the machines. Quite often, any good impact of rounds on a tank started a fire.

In our reports of attacking tanks, we were probably actually attacking more assault guns, armored artillery, and tank destroyers than tanks, but from a pilot's view they usually were all identified as tanks. As for armored cars or personnel carriers, half-tracks, and some of the Flakpanzers or antiaircraft tanks, we could usually inflict serious damage or do those in quite readily with a good concentrated burst.

We had frequent interdiction missions on the east side of the Rhine. These were much the same type of missions as flown in the Po Valley—rail cuts, and then strafe trains and trucks, which were plentiful. On one mission, up near Darmstadt, we spotted a train crossing an overpass as two trucks drove under it. We strafed and burned the two trucks first, so they could not take cover or seek a hiding spot in the small town they were leaving. The train couldn't go anywhere except to follow the tracks, and it was destroyed second in this scheme of not allowing anything to escape. At times, trains could be found lined up behind each other, all stymied by a good rail cut.

With a couple of missions under my belt, I was back in time for all hell to break loose on the ground. Up to the north of our area, American forces had found the Ludendorff Bridge at Remagen still standing and were crossing and establishing a beachhead on the east side. Among reports heard from that action were some of attempts by the Germans to bomb the bridge. In one such effort, they had a number of Ju 87s, Stukas, lined up on a road preparing to fly from there to dive-bomb the bridge—but they were spotted by U.S. fighter-bombers and those Stukas never went anywhere to bomb anything.

In our area, Saarbrucken fell and ushered in field days of fighter-bomber destruction as the German forces on the west side of the Rhine fled to and across the Rhine from the Saar-Palatinate Trap. Every route in our main area of operation, from Mainz and Frankfurt on the north, down through Mannheim and Heidelberg, and on south to Karlsruhe along the Rhine was loaded with targets. Starting with the last third of March in 1945 came one of the bigger kills yet by tactical air and fighter-bomber operations. The word "slaughter" was heard used again, as it had been on certain of the other major tactical air operations. There was one report of a U.S. Corps crediting destruction of a German Infantry Division to air attack.

We, like all other fighter-bombers, flew mission after mission, destroying about everything imaginable that could be found in, or in support of, the retreating enemy armies. Most of our effort was in the general Mannheim-Heidelburg area. Allied ground forces pushed on to and across the Rhine. The U.S. Third Army crossed at Oppenheim, near Mainz, and again farther north a few days later. The U.S. Seventh Army then went across at Worms, north of Mannheim. They were followed by the French at Speyer, south of Mannheim. This had all occurred by the first of April. In those last 11 or so days of March 1945, there may have been a wider-spread area of destruction involved than in most other big kills. At the same time, we had flown considerable direct support of the bridgeheads, such as in the Gernsheim area. And the all-out fighter-bomber effort was not over by any means. It had ended only on the west side of the Rhine. Our flying merely swung further east and south out in front of the Bomb Line on the other side of that river.

The lengthening days of spring, still with dawn-to-dusk flying, put an ever-increasing workload on the units in flying the additional sorties. In

Results of fighter-bomber attacks near Kaiserslautern. (Courtesy U.S. Air Force)

some cases the airplane gasoline was arriving in drums and had to be pumped out into trucks or planes, adding more work yet. The demanding flying schedule was met fully, but it was done by some very tired-looking troops working extremely long hours—as always, an ultimate in duty and discipline.

On top of that, one of the toughest decisions yet was faced by the unit and myself when each flying squadron was required to send some 15 men to the ground forces as critically-needed infantry replacements. This meant that Army Air Forces personnel who had been overseas for about two years working in the orderly room, kitchen, transportation, supply, etc. of a fighter squadron would now spend the final phases of the war fighting on the ground with a gun. The fact that there really were not enough people in those functions in a squadron in the first place didn't enter the picture. What hurt was having to send anyone at all, and to have to select those to go.

Some volunteers stepped forward, and the others who were named to go received and accepted the orders as true soldiers. As they assembled with field gear to depart, their spirits appeared to be higher than that of the unit personnel seeing them off. And they left with an entire unit's sincere wishes and prayers for their well-being.

We did have some critically needed personnel transferred in. These were armorers and no unit had enough armament and ordnance personnel to handle the backbreaking, long hours required to handle and load the bombs and ammo. How these fine young troops, some 15 of them, arrived here as armorers is a story in itself. They and many others were in the Aviation Cadet Program, well along on the way to becoming pilots, when much of the program had apparently been halted in place. Into the ranks went the cadets as privates, and they were sent to armament school before coming to us. That we sorely needed them was an indisputable fact, but one would assume that they could not be very happy about.

Replacement pilots were no longer coming in. We had received a few, four or five, in recent weeks. They had been invaluable and were building up missions at a rapid rate, but at the same time we could not fly them beyond reason. The total of the undermanned force of pilots, made up mostly of those I had started with back at Grosseto, Italy, had to carry the load and it was a heavy one on all of them. I was tired. Many nights I ate and fell into bed. Some others were doing the same. The "Doc" and I talked daily. We were both concerned about some of the pilots. We were both also concerned about all of them as a total, and how much longer we could keep up this pace with so few pilots and not have some problems. But the Ops Officers, flight leaders and others held steady as rocks on morale and mission performance.

Once there were no more replacements arriving, in order to eliminate questions and doubts, it had been decided that there was no longer a rotation system based on missions flown. All of the pilots here would have to stay until more pilots showed up from somewhere, or until the war ended.

The 86th FG was receiving some news attention and publicity now.

Most losses of airplanes were across the Bomb Line, but here is one on our side following a bailout.

One news item of widespread note back in the States was a photo of five pilots, whose missions flown in fighter-bomber operations collectively came to the figure of 1000. These pilots were shown standing by a P-47 that was also a veteran of many missions. Fighter-bomber airplanes that had lasted through substantial periods of combat may have warranted special note, too. It was heard that the planning factor on new replacement P-47s in Europe was 20 percent per month, and that had been increased to 30 percent in order to keep units fully equipped with airplanes.

While knowledge and use of such planning figures was not part of a squadron's daily operations, those figures probably fit pretty well with the actual experience in the combat units. Losses, and scrapping of damaged airplanes from all causes, might well average six to nine airplanes per month out of the 30 usually on hand.

In March we had used a record amount and variety of bombs, and the amount of machine gun ammo expended was over half a million rounds. Vehicles and armor destroyed were at record highs, while trains had not fallen off any. Yet many missions had been on bunkers, fortifications and artillery positions. We had destroyed a considerable number of flak guns, too. These included both vehicle-mounted guns as well as other positions. One rule on these latter flak positions was that if they were spotted and the location then known, they were probably worthwhile targets of opportunity for the risk—definitely so for heavy flak guns. On the other hand, when on armed-recce work, if the locations were unknown, particularly so for the automatic weapons, then milling around searching for them was not a good practice.

With Allied forces now across the Rhine, some of our pilots were making predictions on the end of the war in Europe. Some were offering bets on it, too. None of them I heard were talking about the next few days or a week or two. That was understandable since some major battles on the ground had developed on the other side of the Rhine. While perhaps in a hopeless military situation overall, the German forces were still fighting determinedly in many places.

The enemy was also not through in the air by any means. We had a mission jumped by 30 Me 109s and a hell of an air fight ensued. Somehow our pilots got out of it with only one airplane damaged, while shooting down two of the enemy. One report indicated another squadron didn't have a similar opportunity for a dogfight as a flight of Me 262 jets zoomed up through the squadron and shot down two of the U.S. fighter-bombers, then kept on going, using their speed for both the surprise attack and escape.

The close support missions flown for the Allied forces, now fanning out and advancing on the east side of the Rhine, were in two basic forms. First, on major ground battles (such as Karlsruhe, Heilbronn, and Aschaffenburg) the strong German opposition was pounded repeatedly by various units and missions of fighter-bombers. GP bombs, frags, fire bombs, and strafing were used on continuing strikes as some of these fierce battles lasted for a week to ten days or more. Second, missions of fighter-bombers also worked step-by-step with advancing columns, usually armored units. On many of these missions the column would advance until opposition was encountered in villages, small towns, road junctions, etc. Then the ground columns would stand clear as the overhead fighter-bombers were called in to attack the point of resistance. Once the resistance was knocked out, the ground columns would move on again.

There was yet another fire bomb or incendiary munition in the arsenal that was frequently used on villages or towns from which the enemy opened fire on advancing armored columns. We had first used these incendiaries in Italy on supply dumps and storage facilities. This munition consisted of small intense-heat "sticks," banded together in a cluster of about 500 pounds. Their use was unique among fighter-bomber munitions. Instead of delivering them as close as practical to a target, as with most other weapons and attack methods, this munition called for a fairly high-altitude release during a dive-bomb run. Such runs were started from above 10,000 feet, with releases usually above 5000 feet. After a short period of free fall the clusters popped open, spreading and showering the individual incendiary sticks over a target area. Reportedly they burned with such an intense heat that they cut their way through rooftops and storage covers, even metal or concrete, to fall on into structures and supplies to start widespread fires. Also, apparently one of the few potential ways of extinquishing or controlling the little incendiary sticks was to dump a bucket of sand on each one.

Needless to say, a munition that could be dropped high enough to stay out of the most effective range of some of the 20mm flak was a popular one. On the other hand, when using these fire bombs, many units did not just drop them and then stay up at altitude to observe and/or depart for home.

Eliminating a small village as a point of resistance at a road junction. (Courtesy USAAF, World War II).

When a tank column, for example, called for a strike on a village or town occupied by resisting enemy troops, the incendiary clusters were dropped on the target. Then, without rush or haste to expend our ammo too quickly, the target area was sprayed with rounds of "fifties" on low-level

A closer view of that action. (Courtesy USAAF, World War II)

strafing passes to keep firefighters and others on the ground from attempting to snuff out the incendiaries. In most cases in Germany, the entire village or town went up in a mass of flame, forcing the defenders out and ending the military resistance there.

Very little about burning villages and towns to the ground, while strafing the enemy, too, could be viewed as other than war at some of its worst. That would certainly be the case if the Germans had not cleared such defended villages and towns of civilians, which one would hope they had done. And these operations were not undertaken except when called for by ground controllers and confirmed as being targets of military resistance. Otherwise, we religiously never attacked villages or towns as targets in themselves, nor did we ever strafe farmers or workers in fields. These restrictions for us applied just as fully in Germany as they had in France and Italy. Also, we did not shoot livestock in fields or pens as targets of opportunity. However, there had been a case or two of missions at certain locations in the past against animals that were gathered and being used by the enemy as a major means of transportation. Those were not welcomed missions. Perhaps a few of the other missions flown were not welcomed, but overall, fighter-bombers normally operated against only military targets and direct military support targets such as transportation and supplies.

Obviously, with actions such as curtailment of the Aviation Cadet Program and shutdown of the replacement pilot flow to Europe, the higher levels of our service were viewing the war as headed for an end. From a planning standpoint, those are major changes in the conduct of the war. Yet, from the view of a pilot flying missions, not one thing had changed yet. We

Smoke screens the vehicle targets on the road in this village, but without military targets therein, such villages were not attacked. (Courtesy USAAF, World War II)

Traveling into Germany brought forth extensive and widespread scenes of destruction of equipment. (Courtesy U.S. Air Force)

were still on an all-out effort and still facing the same flak and other defenses. And whether there was recognition of the war winding down or not, and whether it would last more weeks or more months yet, did not erase the knowledge that it took only a fraction of a second in that period for an individual serviceman to lose out forever on seeing the end when it did come. That part certainly hadn't changed.

Our ground parties left on the 13th of April to set up facilities on a new home airfield. Of all the moves we had made during the war, this one probably generated the most interest and excitement. Our new base was called Braunschardt Airfield. It was located on the edge of the small town of Gross Gerau, on the east side of the Rhine River near Darmstadt, in Germany itself.

If the flying from Tantonville had been a hard grind of combat operations, there had been the satisfaction of flying the missions into Germany, the enemy homeland. Now we would fight the rest of the war flying from within that homeland itself.

Chapter 16

Final Days

Our new airfield consisted of a German-constructed, long, wide concrete runway and surrounding grain fields and nearby forests of tall pine trees. An extensive set of PSP taxiways and parking areas had been added by our engineers. This was the first paved-surface runway I had flown from in combat during the entire war. This field was unique in one other way for the war zone: There were small deer and big rabbits running through the squadron area, and the cooks and others had immediate plans for some of these in the mess system.

The runway extended almost into the town of Gross Gerau. While the enlisted men were camped in a forest bordering the airfield, the officers were quartered in houses in that town, among German neighbors. However, we were following rather close on the trail of advancing American ground forces, and the buildings and houses in town remained boarded up with white flags flying. Parts of the small town were being used by our ground forces as a tank repair and service point. The presence of tanks in the streets did not hurt at all in considerations of security, and one Armored Division we had worked with in combat since arrival in the ETO left a present for our Group in the form of two truckloads of the finest white wine one was likely to find anywhere.

The airfield and quarters were guarded as always, but there were no fences, barricades, wire, etc., around either. The main extra precautions taken were in blackout and light-trap entrances to keep from exposing personnel at night to possible sniper fire by die-hards such as the Werewolves or other Hitler Youth fanatics. Boobytraps had been discussed but no evidence of major problems with them around the airfield or town had been found. And the entire unit was armed as it always was to protect itself when necessary.

Our airfield in Germany.

Except for some damage in the center of Gross Gerau and to outlying commercial facilities, it was intact, and a most attractive and clean little village. There were definite signs of war around. The hulks of burned-out trucks and vehicles could be seen on roads in the area, including two on the edge of town near a railroad, on which sat a train with a destroyed locomotive. This was a loco that had been strafed by fighter-bombers, and if there had ever been any question as to just what strafing did to a loco, it could be answered here. The engine was completely riddled throughout and totally destroyed. The stranded train contained mostly Luftwaffe supplies of uniforms, flying equipment, parachutes, etc., and an initial and very handy source of souvenirs.

If Gross Gerau showed only limited signs of war, one had only to go the few miles off the other end of the runway to Darmstadt to see what war can be. More accurately, one would be going to what *used* to be Darmstadt, since it was among the most completely destroyed of the many German cities that met such a fate in the war. Darmstadt was an all-flattened sea of rubble, with a few paths cleared in it as passageways for vehicles to move on through.

There was other evidence of war in the area, too. In a compound at Gross Gerau were some 2000 displaced persons (DPs). These were Russians, probably there as slave labor. Some of them got out and launched their own now one-sided war of revenge on the local Germans. We were almost in a position of having to fight on the wrong side to stop it while the DPs were put back into the compound. At about the same time, there was a report of an American bomber crew who bailed out over a town some 15 miles away, and all had been killed by the local Germans rather than held and turned over to the military. On hearing that, some pilots were in favor of

Many German cities and towns looked like this from poundings by both air and ground weapons. (Courtesy U.S. Air Force)

turning the Russians loose again.

Despite the grim nature of our surroundings, the move into Germany seemed to have an invigorating effect on most personnel. I no longer felt tired at all, even though my leg still bothered me now and then. No one else

Industrial and transportation facilities had received similar treatment. (Courtesy U.S. Air Force)

seemed to be tired now, either. It was just as well we weren't, because we immediately launched into a maximum flying effort of destroying enemy airplanes on the ground. The targets were mainly airfields in Bavaria, in the general Augsburg and Munich areas; there were many of them there, containing a wide variety of aircraft, but with fighters as the key targets in most cases.

German airfields always remained consistent in two characteristics. One, the airplanes were not conveniently parked for easy killing from the air. They were dispersed, sometimes miles away from the flying fields, and were camouflaged and/or protected by revetments. Two, automatic-weapon flak could be counted on to be intense, and would often include flak towers as well as other positions. The flak on some fields had been described as "intense to unbearable." Attacking airfields was certainly nothing new to us. We had done it off and on for a long time, and had a number of such missions in the past two weeks. However, starting with the 15th of April, almost every mission on the schedule board from daylight to dark was an airfield attack. Frag bombs were carried on some missions, but most went with just the guns. If the war was coming to an end, one might reflect on "how lucky can you get" at this point to draw a steady diet of strafing airfields—which was recognized by some as the most deadly of fighter-bomber operations.

Yet we were proud of being assigned the task. Even with a steady daily diet of strafing airfields, and with results of enemy airplanes destroyed soaring, nothing about the operation became a routine. Each airfield was looked at quite closely and each mission specifically planned for that attack. Missions on airfields never did become "just another one," as some pilots might have said about rail cuts.

Then too, all of the German airplanes on the ground were not found on airfields. Stretches of the autobahns, or super highways, were used as flying fields, the airplanes dispersed and hidden in forests alongside that nationwide network of four-lane concrete roadways. Many of the Me262 jets, prized as strafing targets, were found in the woods near airfields and autobahns.

In places the medians of the autobahns had been paved over to make a broad and excellent runway. That giveaway median strip of pavement might be painted green, brown, etc., to camouflage its existence, but a more effective method was used as well. The median strip had holes into which freshly cut trees from the forests could be set to show from the air as a growing stand of trees in the median. It was assumed that with the trees removed, the holes could be plugged and/or either side of the concrete highway used as runways.

In most cases, stretches of autobahn that were used as runways were located by flying low enough along them to spot either a paved median strip or some of the airplanes under camouflage nets of tree limbs in the forest. In our case, this was done from the area of Stuttgart on down to and past Munich. One of our missions lucked out by spotting a damaged German fighter sitting out on the autobahn, which may have wrecked on landing and had not been removed before our mission came on the scene. We racked up a good score of enemy airplanes in the woods in that area. Also, airplanes might be found well down the highway from a suspected stretch of runway. Apparently they taxied or were towed considerable distances at times.

Strafing airplanes nestled among the tall trees (which someone said were fir trees in the Black Forest area, but which most pilots usually called pines) demanded some good shooting for effective results. The airplanes were normally spread out enough to require the pilots to find and select one or two planes as specific targets on a pass, rather than just shooting up the area. Often a pilot would see a plane, then have to turn back to make a strafing pass on it. Such targets were hard to keep in sight and some last-second maneuvering might be needed to put the guns on the target. As a result, some P-47s flew into the tall trees. In most units it was not uncommon for fighter-bombers to nip the tops of trees in various parts of Germany, and many units probably had far more serious encounters than that.

We had a classic in which one of our finest young leaders mushed down into the trees on a strafing pass of a Me 262. I saw it happen, and so help me, the airplane seemed to just stay down there ever so long under the treetops. Finally it came back up, leaving a swath of falling tree tops almost the width of the wingspan of a P-47. The swath was not quite that wide because some of the wings were left in the trees, and what remained of them on the airplane didn't look too good, either. The cowling and skin on the nose were smashed to bits. After sweating to first see if he could get high enough to

Many target airplanes were among trees. (Courtesy U.S. Air Force)

bail out and then to see if the airplane could stay in the air, there was probably more marveling at, rather than sweating over, the plane as it flew on home, where the pilot made a normal landing.

Our effort on enemy airplanes peaked on April 20, when five missions by my squadron obtained such outstanding results that they were a key contribution to the award of a second Presidential Unit Citation to our group. I didn't fly on any of these missions. They were led by flight leaders and assistants—Captains G.S. Brown, J.P. Botten, J.E. Brink, W.M. Bieber, and Lt. G.C. Moore. Major G.C. Covington, Captains C. Grantham Jr., R.B. Moyle, W.P. Curtin, and all the other leaders had accomplished the same kind of results on missions throughout. Yet none of it would ever have been done in this unit or any other without the dedicated duty and combat performance of each pilot on each mission.

Among many others, they include: Jordan, Green, Mauk, Bannister, Jenkins, Mapp, Delanty, Senneff, Worley, Mitchell, Mart, Westfall, McEmber, Baranek, Burkey, Stewart, Lock, and Mozniak.

The combat missions flown, besides those against airfields, were in direct support of the armies, on armed recce, and against certain supply dumps. The advancing Allied columns had fighter-bombers available throughout each day. Support was provided in more major battles, such as at Crailsheim and Nuremberg. When Nuremberg fell on the 20th or so, an Armored division there sent our Group a huge Nazi flag, which reportedly had flown over the site of the national assemblies of the Nazi party in that city. There were also some missions in support of the French as they advanced to Stuttgart and the Black Forest, as well as some missions in support of both French and Americans as they reached Ulm and went on across the Danube River. Earlier, we had flown a few scenic missions along that famous river, shooting barges and boats of any and all kinds.

On armed recce missions, a leader could almost be selective. The roads were choked in many areas, and in southern Bavaria there were still plenty of trains. Perhaps the only appropriate word for these operations was slaughter. Yet we (and I'm sure other outfits as well), were selecting targets that appeared to be organized military units and transportation systems and/or those sending up flak. One report indicated a German unit, trapped in a field with some 200 to 300 vehicles, put up white flags and surrendered to an air unit of fighter-bombers overhead.

We had some spectacular missions on various supply dumps and depots, leaving some massive fires and clouds of smoke in the skies. However, our maps now contained some red-hatched markings identifying prohibited areas around certain supply dumps. No attacks of any kind were to be made on or near these areas. They were storage sites of poison gas, reportedly including the extremely deadly colorless and odorless nerve gas. We stayed well clear.

Strafing ammo dumps could always provide some real fireworks. We had a classic in that regard, one that was much more thrilling than just a good display. I was not on this mission, and didn't think I would ever regret the fact I wasn't. Not more than a few rounds of strafing fire had hit the target area when there was a blinding flash across the countryside of Bavaria. Then, with ungodly speed, an enormous mass of fireball, dust, smoke, earth, trees, and ammo rushed skyward. As the monstrous explosion sped towards the attacking airplanes, many rounds of the ammo being carried aloft were set off, sending them out like skyrockets in advance of the main body of the oncoming disaster. The airplanes were engulfed as the deadly cloud and debris carried on up to 15,000 feet or more.

These pilots were called upon for one more demanding task as fighter-bomber pilots—flying instruments in an explosion. They all got out of the explosion, but with an upright attitude of the airplanes not having too much to do with it. And they all made it back to home base, even though each airplane had some damage. The planes of the leader and his wingmen, who were closest and took the brunt of the blast, were stripped clean of paint and other markings. Their windscreens were also so pitted and marred that they had to fly home with the canopies open in order to see out.

Gun camera film recorded the explosion as seen by the pilots. It was rather terrifying to watch the footage due to the speed with which the explosion rose to engulf the airplanes and camera.

Missions on airfields did not stop. We flew some on April 29 and lost a pilot when his plane was hit with flak at low level and crashed into a hangar on the airfield. While this was our first loss since the initial bad beginning in the ETO, it was a hard-felt one because the war obviously was now coming to an end. Reportedly the heavy bombers of the massive strategic bombing effort had already been pulled off strategic targets, no doubt with an eye on the war with Japan. U.S. ground forces had linked up with the Russians. Munich was in U.S. hands by the end of the month and apparently the war was already over in Italy. In Italy, it was reported that the Germans withdrawing north across the Po River had no usable bridges, and fighter-bombers destroyed ferries and waiting equipment—resulting in the Germans north of the river being basically an unequipped force who could not continue an effective fight.

Po River ferry. (Courtesy U.S. Air Force)

Enemy vehicle park, Italy. (Courtesy U.S. Air Force)

The U.S. fighter-bomber units operating in Italy during the final phase were the 57th, 79th, and 350th Fighter Groups. The 57th and 79th were real veterans of a full and continuous war of fighter-bomber combat throughout—from Egypt on to the end. From what I had seen, the 57th, followed closely by the 79th, had to rate as the longevity champions of

We and other pilots had left destroyed enemy airplanes and worlds of other wreckage all over Germany and Europe. (Courtesy U.S. Air Force)

sustained U.S. fighter-bomber operations against the Axis.

The fighter-bombers in Germany were still in action, and there were some real veterans involved here, too. April 29 had marked the second overseas anniversary of the 86th FG. The 27th, 86th, and 324th Fighter Groups (all now in the ETO, but all originally from the MTO) were not too far behind the 57th and 79th in continuous fighter-bomber combat. And there had been many others involved from the days of Northwest Africa and on this point.

The entire Ninth Air Force fighter-bomber force could hardly be viewed as anything but real veterans, too, with many Groups going back in combat to long before Normandy.

During April the weather had been quite good, and so were combat results. The squadron had destroyed over 230 trucks and vehicles, and damaged over 350. Locomotive claims were nearly 40 destroyed and over 50 damaged. Results on gun positions were about 50 destroyed and the same number damaged, and of barracks and buildings there were over 400 destroyed and 300 damaged. We had almost completely gone out of the tank-killer business with very few attacked. However, results on enemy airplanes had soared, with over 60 destroyed and over 70 damaged. A number of Me 262s were included in the kills.

Some of our activities on the ground in Germany were rather interesting. Sightseeing was one, but it was not the normal type of sightseeing. A main attraction was the forests along the autobahn south of Darmstadt. They were full of German airplanes, some destroyed and damaged, but many were untouched, brand-new late-model Me 109s and FW 190s. They were beautiful machines, with many new spare engines and other parts on hand. Moving a few of them to our field was investigated.

Souvenirs were the basis of a booming business. Some people were out seeking a few on their own, but the ground forces would send a truckload in now and then to deal off items such as P-38 and Luger pistols, Mausers, Schmeisser machine pistols, ceremonial swords, helmets, etc. There were a few cameras, binoculars, and some valuables involved, too.

While air units could not match the ground forces in acquiring front-line type souvenirs, we could do quite well in some other areas. Requisitioning automobiles was one. We had a growing fleet of them, properly documented and marked as staff and other essential vehicles. In these matters, we were following regulations. German military equipment and official vehicles were fair game, or spoils of war. Provisions also existed to acquire other vehicles in the best interest and/or needs of the service. I might have stretched the intent a bit in the interpretation and scope of our needs for vehicles, but otherwise we went strictly "by the book." For example, we did not stretch the meaning of vehicles to include bicycles, and I strictly prohibited acquiring or possessing bicycles. And, of course, "the book" held just as firm and inviolate regarding crimes of any kind against the German people and their property as anywhere else in the world.

However, that did not mean all things in Germany were the same as

Even squadrons had staff cars now, this one an ex-German commander's car.

elsewhere. For the time being, we were still at war and the Germans were still the enemy. Then the Allied forces faced the official "nonfraternization policy" for occupation of Germany, which prohibited all "mingling with Germans upon terms of friendliness, familiarity or intimacy, individually or in groups, in official or unofficial dealings." For the moment, there was no mingling to be prevented or squashed, but we had already held a few serious discussions about some of the problems this policy might create after the shooting stopped. Some individual forecasts were that up to half the Allied troops in Germany might end up behind bars in efforts to enforce a policy that prohibited servicemen from associating with members of the opposite sex, even if those opposites were on the other side in a war.

Right now the opposites were not out in numbers and we could press on as usual with the war, but they were around somewhere and would be out soon. I didn't look forward to it. One officer, who to the best of my knowledge had never been interested in local females, seemed incensed when *told* he couldn't be interested in them. Another proposed a plan that would consider a pretty girl to be a DP instead of a German, therefore exempt from the policy. I almost liked the idea when someone said maybe the war would last a few more weeks and put off having to face the peacetime occupation. Yet it wasn't a joking matter; the policy had to be enforced.

There had been some non-mingling contacts with the Germans, who were now seen more each day going about their business in town. Some little girls, not much more than toddlers, would get out of their houses or yards now and then, and come straight to our quarters to sit on a bench out front. Their mothers would bravely retrieve them. An older lady, owner of one of the houses we used, came over worried about certain of her belongings and beautiful flower garden. We packed and stored the items of concern for safekeeping and already had a couple of pilots as volunteers to be gardeners. I had the task of having a bar built for the club. That took a few of us to the military government and mayor's office to find and arrange a contact with a craftsman. A few young ladies were working there, and if these very attractive and shapely fraulein (or, in GI terminology, "fraulines") were representative of what the troops were being told not to mingle with, the "Non-Frat" policy could become extremely unpopular in the future.

The first few days of May we flew as usual, but now with a welcomed reduction in sortie rate. Targets, when we had any, were in pockets of resistance here or there. We had quit general armed-recce work, and hit only targets that were specified on ordered missions or requested by the ground forces. Berlin fell to the Russians and most major enemy combat commands surrendered to counterpart Allied commanders in the West. Then there were no more ground targets for us as the forces we normally supported moved on into Austria, to Innsbruck, and linked up with Allied forces from Italy. The air-to-ground war was over in Europe for our unit.

In the 86th Group many pilots had chosen to fly combat in flying suits rather than uniforms, which choice was left to them. We also received a shipment of anti-G suits as the war was winding down, and the pilots had a choice of using them. I never wore one—we had pulled some tremendous G forces all during the war without the suits. We never used—and, in fact, never possessed—any flak jackets or vests.

Most of our airplanes were now late-model, high dash-number versions of the P-47D—"Dash 30s" and up, with a dorsal fin added. I had flown an old veteran "Dash 25" regularly since returning to flying. It was one of our few airplanes equipped with a hydromatic propeller instead of the electric props prevalent on the late-models. The only artwork displayed on this gallant old airplane was the crew chief's self-chosen and hand-painted name of "Red Head." Together, this airplane and I had not been hit by flak on any mission, and had undergone no real hairy experiences otherwise. Also, it kept a string going for me of never aborting a mission in combat. Overall, we had very few aborts, a credit to the ground personnel and the pilots.

Even though the ground targets were no longer there, our flying operations were not over yet. We switched to flying air patrols, mostly over southern Bavaria and along the Austrian border. There was considerable German air activity. Last-ditch attacks on the U.S. forces certainly could happen as the Luftwaffe had somehow stayed active in some areas. Yet the main traffic was probably individual efforts by German pilots who could get an airplane into the air from one of the last remaining pockets of enemy vestige such as parts of Czechoslovakia, in an attempt to fly back to the vicinity of their homes, or to end the war in an area of their now-defeated nation that was held by Americans, British, or French forces instead of in areas in the hands of the Russians.

Most of the traffic was of support-type airplanes; instead of being shot down, these were escorted as "captives" in the air until on the ground in Allied hands in the western part of Germany. One of our squadron missions encountered a small twin-engine enemy transport and literally captured it when they brought it home with them and had it land on our field. That slick little machine was quickly tucked away in our squadron area, with plans for using it to travel around Europe after the war. A sister squadron brought in a couple of single-engine trainers, which should be excellent for towing gliders or sailplanes.

Incidently, my squadron now had about 40 new replacement pilots, yet none of them were flying missions. They were glider pilots, here to be checked out in the P-47. They would man the unit during the occupation so the combat veterans could go home. My initial estimates on the results of checking out that many glider pilots in single-cockpit P-47s, and making fighter pilots out of them, were that if things did not go *too* badly I should have only about 15 letters to write to the next of kin of those killed in the process.

Those letters to the next of kin of casualties were in addition to the War Department telegrams of notification. They were written by the immediate commanding officer, expressing official condolences of the unit and outlining the circumstances. While replies were received from grieving mothers, fathers, and wives on most of them, at the time it could not be known that there would be subsequent lifelong exchanges of correspondence and friendship between some of those next of kin and myself and my family—such as with the family of 1st Lt. John V. Conner, Jr., killed in action in the Po Valley of Italy.

At one point rumors floated around over Germany about as thick as the flak had once been. Key attention-getters among them were some that indicated we were going direct from here to the CBI for combat against the

We had a few non-GI airplanes on our airfield.

Japs. These particular rumors were not very popular. However, such rumors were "shot down" when we were in time notified that the 86th Group would remain in operation in Germany as part of the occupation force. The combat personnel would rotate home on the "point" system. While the Group CO, myself, and other veteran pilots had the most points (based on months of service, overseas time, combat decorations, battle stars, etc.), which would give us priority for shipment home, in the 86th the COs were not going home until all of the other pilots and the men who had served so long and well had gone home. As a result, I wasn't going home anytime soon. It had taken years to get all of the several million troops to the ETO and MTO; it would probably be at least months in getting them back.

As the war clouds drifted away, so did a promotion to lieutenant colonel for me. I needed only a little over a week more time in grade as a major to receive that promotion to the authorized rank for a squadron CO. Every indication was that the war would end while leaving me just a few days short of being an "L/C."

All through the war, as we moved up behind our advancing ground forces, we sent teams out to check the sites where pilots from our squadron had been shot down or crashed. For those checked in Germany, the findings had all been bad. All three of those pilots had been killed in the crashes of their airplanes. One had apparently made it to the ground okay for a crash landing, but then hit a dike in an otherwise flat field. On the other hand, there was some good news as the U.S. POWs were freed. A few pilots we had not known to be POWs came out with those we did know to be POWs. And one pilot who went down in the Po Valley near Bologna in late 1944 had avoided capture the entire time since.

That pilot had last been seen on the ground running into the reeds or bulrushes along a canal. The Germans did not find him but friendly Italians

These visiting Jugs made an interesting collection of unit markings.

A last mission on May 8, 1945.

did. They smuggled him into Bologna and he was hidden by a family in the basement of their house. The owner of the house ran a bicycle shop above the basement and as our pilot rode out the rest of the war below ground as a member of the family, he repaired bicycles and became fluent in the Italian language. One day, when the shop owner was ill, the pilot went upstairs and ran the business. After that, he frequently worked in the shop, serving the public—and many of the customers were German soldiers.

With the Russian DPs indoctrinated on the fact that any fighting that remained to be done in the war was to be done somewhere other than in Gross Gerau, we now had some of them voluntarily working in the squadron. The women who cleaned our quarters, apparently all from rural farming areas, would not use GI mops and brushes. They kept the buildings spic-and-span but did it on hands and knees. If they finished everything before the trucks came to pick them up, they would clean again. Apparently they were as anxious to get home as we were, and there was a little sendoff ceremony when they did depart for home.

The general surrender was signed at Rheims on the 7th, and as we understood, it would be officially effective late on the 8th of May. Reportedly there was fighting going on up through the 7th by the U.S. Third Army and apparently fighter-bomber missions were still being flown by some units. We continued to fly patrols, but attention was turned to making baseball and softball diamonds out of soccer fields, and the weather was warming enough to allow full use of the olympic-type swimming pool out behind our quarters.

Our last mission was flown late in the day on May 8, 1945, or V-E Day for the troops in Europe. I led an eight-ship patrol along the German-Austria border. In two hours and 45 minutes in the air on a beautiful spring day, we did not hear a sound on the radio nor did we see a thing in the sky. There was also little or nothing moving on the ground. As we landed it was well into the evening, even though the sun was just setting in the long daylight days of Europe as summer neared. If not the last mission in the war, it was one of the very last because the official end came not too long after we landed. The fighter-bombers stationed in Germany flew up to the very end, long after many other type units had stopped combat operations.

If the war and the combat were over, some war-related flying might still go on. Some units flew victory demonstration flights, or fly-bys, over various cities in Europe. They were reports that airplanes of various types, from fighters to heavy bombers, were making their own victory salutes—such as flying through the open spaces at the base of the Eiffel Tower in Paris. Since we had missed out on such flying to date, some of our pilots proposed that we take a four-ship flight in close formation under the tower tomorrow morning.

There were celebrations in the ETO that night and I guess the lights came on again in some cities, but I didn't see any come on in Germany. We stayed blacked out. At the club, commanders and pilots engaged in a few toasts. One toast was to our national leadership and command and the people at home; one was to those in the Pacific and Asia, who were still at war; one was to the ground personnel of our units; and one was to fighter-bomber pilots and the road of war we had traveled together. There may have been others, too, but the one regarding the road of war traveled together held my mind momentarily.

A fighter-bomber pilots's war was not one of individual statistics and records on combat results. Those were tallied by mission, unit, and on up the line, growing into massive scores of varied targets destroyed and damaged by fighter-bombers on a theater-wide basis. Even so, many reports on fighter-bomber operations stressed only results in terms of the contribution made to the support of ground forces. For example, one report on the all-out effort we participated in on enemy airfields in April emphasized that the Seventh Army operated almost completely free of enemy air attacks in its push through Germany. Such examples regarding interdiction and direct support results were almost unlimited in number back through the war.

Other than inclusion of the comparatively few enemy airplanes shot down, the individual records of fighter-bomber pilots on combat results were pretty much limited to missions flown, medals, awards, and battle stars. However, if one looked closely at certain aspects of a pilot's missions, and the results of his unit, the basis for some perhaps revealing, if unpublicized, figures could pop into mind.

For our Group CO, Col. George T. Lee, the road of war had run from Egypt to the end here in Germany. He had flown over 250 missions. From my start in southern Italy and continuing on to the end, I had 208 missions. A good friend of ours, Lt. Col. John F. Martin, in our old Group, the 79th, had 200 missions in his combat flying from Egypt to the end in Italy. We knew of various others in the MTO who had flown over 150 missions. In the 86th FG there was a substantial number in that category. In my squadron, for example, at the war's end in Europe, 17 pilots (more than half of my combat pilots) had over 100 missions; some of them were closer to 200 than 100.

Considering these pilots known to me who flew fighter bomber operations throughout all of their tours and were in units that did a lot of strafing—they had made many hundreds of strafing passes—certain of them possibly reaching or exceeding 1000.

At times, pilots talked about such figures. Sometimes that was in terms of how many targets of various kinds might have been destroyed by individual pilots, but we didn't usually work on targets that way. We destroyed things in elements, flights, and missions. A few pilots had posed an even grimmer—though probably more applicable—thought of how many enemy personnel would have been killed. If one chose to consider that subject, it was pretty obvious that many of the targets attacked when bombing, and practically all of them when strafing, did include enemy crews and operators of armor, guns, trains, vehicles, barges, ships, etc. Also, one would remember targets of troop trains, trucks loaded with people, combat positions, troop concentrations, and airfield personnel.

While debriefing reports carried some estimates of enemy personnel killed on various missions, in most cases they didn't. For example, 20 trucks could be reported as destroyed and 20 more damaged on a mission with no mention at all of enemy personnel. The same was true for locomotives, barges, and some small scores such as two trucks and a train in a village. Many gun positions went into the records as destroyed, with only a note on occasion that some personnel were probably casualties. Fire-bomb missions, such as the one of napalm across the street from friendly troops, reported the bombs delivered on the target of enemy positions, but without any figure of personnel killed—yet the enemy front-line combat troops in that particular town were later reported to have been annihilated for all practical purposes.

In looking at missions flown and the targets involved, it might be concluded that in addition to fighter-bombers putting a severe crimp in the enemy's ability to supply and support their combat units, the fighter-bombers also put a substantial drain on enemy personnel, both combat troops and those supporting them, through the scope of casualties in killed and wounded that were inflicted. Figures on those might be shockingly high for both units and some individual pilots.

I thought about that. I also thought about what it had cost in lives of fine young men to do that, while flying combat in fighter-bomber squadrons. Without regard to loss rates by sorties or other high-level statistical data, or to comparisons with any other kind of combat flying or fighting, that cost in lives was apparent through the same means as it had been seen and felt by pilots in squadrons. You could count how many pilots came in against how many went home. For the several squadrons I was familiar with (and by figures in the unit histories of four of those squadrons), comparing the total number of pilots assigned throughout the units period of time in combat vs. the total loss of pilots killed in action and Missing In Action (still unaccounted for after V-E Day) showed an average loss for the squadrons of just over 23 percent of their pilot force. That did not count pilots shot down who evaded capture or became POWs. These squadrons were in combat a long time—approximately two years or more. They also had a substantial number of pilots flying more than one tour of 80 or 100 missions. Had all pilots rotated home at 70 missions, as I understood one theater used as a tour, the figures might have been different.

And whether standing there in Germany on the night of V-E Day, or at scheduled memorial services and ceremonies tomorrow and in the future, as well as on through the days of life that might ensue, foremost and above all to be remembered about being a fighter-bomber pilot, and remembered ever-so-well, would be those fellow pilots who so gallantly and unselfishly gave their lives in the service of their country in World War II.

Since this book concludes with V-E Day in 1945 (and, apparently, as per various references, one can take a choice of May 8 or May 9 for that day), I might clear up a few loose ends in the story by mentioning that we did *not* fly a formation under the Eiffel Tower. We prohibited such victory antics—at least on a planned or official basis. Also, the glider pilots did become fighter pilots and not one of them in our unit was killed in the process. We flew the little German transport airplane several times, but higher headquarters took it away from us before we traveled Europe extensively in it. Nonfraternization did cause widespread problems during the occupation, with some tragedy involved, too. It was abandoned rather quickly. I did not get home until the end of summer in 1945, after the use of atomic bombs on Japan and end of the war with that nation, having served as CO of the squadron for one year.

My wife still had the car. We drove it for several years while starting a family and continuing a career in the military. Now retired from that, I celebrated our 40th wedding anniversary with her in 1983, with our son and daughter and their families, including a grandson in college of about the same age we were when we decided to start a life together in the middle of World War II. At the time of that celebration, we were hard at work on this book, as I had been for a long time in preparing to write it.

In my home today is a cherished little model of a German Me 262 fighter airplane of World War II. It is a gift from a good friend in England, who served with high distinction and valor in combat as a fighter pilot of the Royal Air Force in that war, and whose son handcrafted the superb likeness and remembrance of a potent machine of war from so many years ago. With the model was sent a letter of best wishes on this undertaking and a small plaque containing these words:

"Lest We Forget"

Epilogue
To This Third Edition

The epilogue of the preceding edition noted my career after World War II. That included continued fighter flying (F-51s and F-84s) and command of an F-84 fighter-bomber squadron in combat in the Korean War. Then I was honored to be selected by the Air Force Operational Test Center, Air Proving Ground Command, Eglin AFB, FL, to head the operational suitability testing of atomic bomb capability on fighter aircraft and development of low-altitude delivery tactics for use in combat. On completion of that major project, I stayed with that Command for some five years in positions as pilot/group commander/chief of test operations. Among aircraft we tested were the F-100, F/RF-101, F-104, and F-105 with all munitions and support equipment. My professional postgraduate level education included Command and Staff, Air University, and Industrial College of the Armed Forces. I spent close to six years in the field of operational requirements, part as Director of Requirements, Tactical Air Command, stating needs for both improved and new aircraft and other tools of war for tactical air forces – specifying capability and performance requirements – also participating in development and overseeing using command testing. This covered the F-4E, F-111, A-7, F-15, and F-16 weapon systems. Specific needs of the Vietnam War were included too, from small immediate improvements to new major capabilities such as the gunships and laser-guided bombs. This involved duty in Vietnam and limited combat missions. My final assignment was Commander, 326th Air Division, Pacific Air Forces.

The point was made of my close ties to fighter-bomber history in that career – and that while airplanes and weapons received much coverage in histories/articles, news and TV/movies over those years – fighter-bomber flying and fighting itself, and experiences of pilots and ground crews, did not. That epilogue ended: "May many more of them (their stories) come forth – before they are lost forever."

Quite rewarding to me is that several WW II and Korean War pilots have reported that this book played a part in their undertaking manuscripts. A review in the *U.S.I. Journal, India's Oldest Journal on Defense Affairs* cited this book "a model" for warriors to follow in preserving combat history. Numerous pilots and ground crews have said they were encouraged to at least write or record some material in effort to save experiences; so were their families.

In the past 20 years a number of newer programs have come into being to encourage and help warriors save individual accounts and records -- such as oral history and archival programs at universities (Florida State, Oregon, and Tennessee are three that fellow members of WW II associations and I have participated in). Libraries have undertaken similar programs, including a major one by the Library of Congress.

My son, Bill Colgan, Jr. intrigued with one mission in this book (Montelimar, France, Chapter 9) asked me numerous questions on it, and also located and interviewed pilot Bagian. He then wrote an article what was featured in *World War II* magazine, November 2002, and republished as the key air war coverage in *World War II's* special issue, *1944 A Year in Review*. That article covered Bagian's story both in the air and during his amazing crash survival and evasion -- additional history saved and made known to more of the public.

The French organization, Association Rhodanienne Pour Le Souvenir Aerien, ARSA, used this book plus further questioning of Bagian, his son, and me to finish and publish their report, *UNE MISSION DE GUERRE, 28 Aout 1944, 79th Fighter Group* on that mission. They relate the air action; plus pin down locations, give additional accounts from local records and witnesses on the ground, and show photos of crash sites. In effect, their report provides a mission report for Red Flight (which wasn't made in 1944 because Red Flight did not return for a debriefing), and it brings forth the honor given by French townspeople in placing monuments to Bagian and Jennings.

Thus, evidence seems to support that this book has played a part in additional fighter-bomber history and heritage being saved. However, perhaps a single incident in 2000 reflects that best. A woman at a hotel one night just passing by picked up a copy of this book left on the registration table of a WW II unit reunion. She scanned it, then sat in the lobby and read it. Seeing that the reunion was a unit covered in the book, she waited in the lobby next morning to catch some of the members checking out. She wanted to get a few books for her family, school and town library; and asked if they were available here and would some of the old veterans autograph them? A "yes" to both was replied and gladly accomplished. Then she expressed this sentiment: "I'm glad I picked up this book (and read it), it would have been a shame never to know what you brave fighter-bomber guys did -- and to be thankful for it."

With those words long held in mind, I'll end this epilogue on the same theme as the previous -- may many more warrior experiences come forth -- before they are lost forever.

Index

A

Allen, Anita Lamae, 5

B

Bagian, Philip, 107-112, 115-116
Bates, Earl E., 32
Battle of the Bulge, 167
Beck, John L., 85, 118
Boone, John T., 107, 119
Botten, John P., 153
Braunscharat Airfield, 189-190

C

Cannon, John K., 165
Capadichino Airdrome, 62
Chidlaw, Benjamin W., 146
Conner, John V. Jr., 201
Curtiss P-36, 17
Curtiss P-37, 9-10
Curtiss P-40F, 30
Curtiss P-40K, 21

D

Dale Mabry Field, 18, 20

E

Eagle Pass Field, 16
Eaker, Ira C., 79
Ermis, Raymond A., 78-79, 90

F

Falaise Gap, 167
Firmo LG, 47
First Tactical Air Force, 166-167, 171
Foggia #3, 47, 51

G

Goodfellow Field, 13

H

Hiers, Wayland, 6-9

I

Isola LG, 47

J

Jennings, Russell K., 107-112, 116

K

Keesler Field, 8
Kelly Field, 11
Kennedy, David, 6-9
Kennedy, William, 6-9

L

Lackland Field, 11
Lee, George T., 56, 85, 118, 163, 164, 204
Link trainer, 14
Lowry Field, 8-9

M

Madna LG, 54
Martin, John F., 204
Montelimar, road to, 109
Morrison, Bruce L., 56
Moyle, Richard B., 146

N

North American AT-6, 15-17

O

Oldham, Richard G., 131
Operation Strangle, 76

P

Pascara Airfield, 49
Penny Post, 47
Phillips, W.W., 3
Pisa airport, 133-134
Pisticci LG, 47
Pomigliano, 90

R

Randolph Field, 11
Republic P-47, 24, 73-74
Rogers, William B., 42

S

Sele Airfield, 121
Selective Service System, 5
Serragia Airfield, 88
"Short Snorters", 28

U

Uhrich, Benjamin, F., 33
USAAF Fighter Groups:
  1st FG, 29, 88-89
  14th FG, 88-89
  27th FG, 70, 88, 120, 164, 171, 198
  31st FG, 70, 88-89
  33rd FG, 70
  36th FG, 171
  48th FG, 171
  50th FG, 171
  52nd FG, 70, 89
  57th FG, 32, 52, 70, 88, 120, 149, 197-198
  79th FG, xii, 29, 32, 63, 68, 70, 73, 80, 88, 120, 164, 197-198
  81st FG, 70
  82nd FG, 88-89
  86th FG, xii-xiii, 70, 88, 120-122, 132, 139, 143, 164-165, 171, 178, 184-185, 198, 202, 205
  324th FG, 31, 70, 88, 120, 171, 198
  325th FG, 70, 89
  332nd FG, 70, 89-90
  337th FG, 20
  350th FG, 70, 88, 197
  354th FG, 171
  358th FG, 171
  362nd FG, 171
  363rd FG, 171
  365th FG, 171
  366th FG, 171
  367th FG, 171
  368th FG, 171
  370th FG, 171
  371st FG, 171
  373rd FG, 171
  404th FG, 171
  405th FG, 171
  406th FG, 171
  474th FG, 171
USAAF Fighter Squadrons:
  85th FS, 37, 95
  86th FS, 37, 52
  87th FS, 33, 73, 95
  98th FS, 20
  99th FS, 54, 73, 90
  316th FS, 31
  525th FS, 121, 124, 131-132, 133, 138, 143, 157
  526th FS, 163
USAAF Numbered Air Forces:
  Eighth AF, 52, 96, 171
  Fifteenth AF, 52, 70, 88
  Ninth AF, 29, 52, 166-167, 171
  Twelfth AF, 52, 62, 70, 76, 88, 96, 146, 165

V

Valence Airfield, 94, 115-116
Vultee BT-13, 14
VanEtten, Chester, 20, 26

ABOUT THE AUTHOR

Col. William B. Colgan, USAF (Ret.)

Colonel Bill Colgan, a native of Waycross, Georgia, had an exceptional military career as a fighter pilot doing multi-mission flying and fighting—a "fighter-bomber pilot." In World War II he was in action almost two years, 1943-45; ten months as Flight Leader (79th Ftr Gp) and a year as Commander of the 525th Fighter Squadron (86th Ftr Gp). He served in Sicily, Italy, and Southern France of the MTO; then in Northern France and Germany of the ETO with the rank of major. He flew 208 missions (normal tours are 70-100) in P-40s and P-47s. He was in the news back home for action in air dogfights over Anzio; but his, and his squadron's, main work was deadly air-ground fighting (bomb and strafe) where they inflicted heavy destruction and casualties on enemy ground, air, and even sea forces. Colgan was especially noted for strafing kills, also for flying battle-damaged aircraft home. He was wounded once, crash landed twice, and was forced to bailout once. His combat spanned the entire American ground war on the European continent and he flew all types of missions—a firm basis for a prime and definitive story of World War II fighter-bomber pilots. In the Korean War, he commanded the 111th Fighter-Bomber Squadron flying seventy-two missions in F-84s. With the Air Force Operational Test Center, Eglin AFB, Florida, he ran the test of atomic weapons on fighters and was commander of the fighter test group and chief of test operations during test of the "Century Series" fighters. He graduated from the Industrial College of the Armed Forces in addition to prior Air University courses. As Director of Operational Requirements, Tactical Air Command, he played a key role in the birth of the F-15 and other weapon systems. He also covered needs in Vietnam with duty there and participated in twelve combat missions. He retired in 1972 from his position as Commander, 326th Air Division, Pacific Air Forces. His decorations include the Silver Star, Legion of Merit (1 OLC), Distinguished Flying Cross (3 OLC), Air Medal (14 OLC), Purple Heart, Presidential Unit Citation (2 OLC), French Croix de Guerre (w silver star), and some thirty-five campaign/battle/service medals. Colonel Colgan was inducted into The Georgia Aviation Hall of Fame in 1996, "Top Fighter-Bomber Pilot;" and is a nominee for the National Aviation Hall of Fame. He and Anita Allen, hometown sweethearts, were married in July 1943 and now reside in Florida—family life foremost as always.

www.ingramcontent.com/pod-product-compliance
Lightning Source LLC
Chambersburg PA
CBHW071436150426
43191CB00008B/1142